The

Music Industry Directory 2024

The

Music Industry Directory 2024

EDITOR

J. PAUL DYSON

Published in 2023 by JP&A Dyson
27 Old Gloucester Street, London WC1N 3AX, United Kingdom

https://www.jpandadyson.com
https://www.musicsocket.com

ISBN 978-1-909935-49-5

Foreword

This directory includes hundreds of listings of **record labels** and **managers**, updated in **MusicSocket**'s online databases between 2021 and 2023.

It also provides free access to the entire current databases, including over 1,200 record labels, and over 500 managers, with dozens of new and updated listings every month.

For details on how to claim your free access please see the back of this book.

Included in the subscription

A subscription to the full website is not only free with this book, but comes packed with all the following features:

Advanced search features

- Save searches and save time – set up to 15 search parameters specific to your work, save them, and then access the search results with a single click whenever you log in. You can even save multiple different searches if you have different types of work you are looking to place.
- Add personal notes to listings, visible only to you and fully searchable – helping you to organise your actions.
- Set reminders on listings to notify you when to submit your work, when to follow up, when to expect a reply, or any other custom action.
- Track which listings you've viewed and when, to help you organise your search – any listings which have changed since you last viewed them will be highlighted for your attention!

Daily email updates

As a subscriber you will be able to take advantage of our email alert service, meaning you can specify your particular interests and we'll send you automatic email updates when we change or add a listing that matches them. So if you're interested in labels dealing in hard rock in the United States you can have us send you emails with the latest updates about them – keeping you up to date without even having to log in.

User feedback

Our databases include a user feedback feature that allows our subscribers to leave feedback on each listing – giving you not only the chance to have your say about the markets you contact, but giving a unique artist's perspective on the listings.

Save on copyright protection fees

If you're sending your work away to record labels and managers you should first consider protecting your copyright. As a subscriber to **MusicSocket** you can do this through our site and save 10% on the copyright registration fees normally payable for protecting your work internationally through the Intellectual Property Rights Office (https://www.CopyrightRegistrationService.com).

For details on how to claim your free access please see the back of this book.

Contents

Foreword v

Contents vii

Protecting Your Copyright 1

Record Labels

US Record Labels 3

UK Record Labels 37

Canadian Record Labels 71

Record Labels Index 73

Managers

US Managers 93

UK Managers 131

Canadian Managers 173

Managers Index 175

Free Access

Get Free Access to the MusicSocket Website 193

Protecting Your Copyright

Protecting your copyright is by no means a requirement before submitting your work, but you may feel that it is a prudent step that you would like to take before allowing strangers to hear your material.

These days, you can register your work for copyright protection quickly and easily online. The Intellectual Property Rights Office operates a website called the "Copyright Registration Service" which allows you to do this:

- *https://www.CopyrightRegistrationService.com*

This website can be used for material created in any nation signed up to the Berne Convention. This includes the United States, United Kingdom, Canada, Australia, Ireland, New Zealand, and most other countries. There are around 180 countries in the world, and over 160 of them are part of the Berne Convention.

Provided you created your work in one of the Berne Convention nations, your work should be protected by copyright in all other Berne Convention nations. You can therefore protect your copyright around most of the world with a single registration, and because the process is entirely online you can have your work protected in a matter of minutes.

US Record Labels

For the most up-to-date listings of these and hundreds of other record labels, visit https://www.musicsocket.com/recordlabels

*To claim your **free** access to the site, please see the back of this book.*

4AD

Email: demos@4ad.com
Email: 4ad@4ad.com
Website: https://www.4ad.com
Website: https://www.facebook.com/fourad

Genres: Indie; Rock

Record label with offices in New York, Los Angeles, and London. Send demos by email.

76Label Music

Email: 76labelmusic@gmail.com
Website: http://www.76label.com
Website: https://myspace.com/76label

Genres: Electronic; Dance; Pop

Contact: Tommy McGinnis

Founded in 1999 as an independent record label and artist marketing company, now also deals in writer management and marketing.

88 Rising

PO Box 45903
Los Angeles, CA 90045
Email: info@88rising.com
Website: https://88rising.com

Genres: All types of music

Record label based in Los Angeles, California.

A&M Records

2220 Colorado Avenue, 5th Floor
Santa Monica, CA 90404
Website: https://www.interscope.com
Website: https://www.facebook.com/interscope

Genres: Indie; Pop; Rock; Singer-Songwriter; Alternative; R&B

Part of a record label based in Santa Monica, California.

A-F Records

1215 N Canal St
Pittsburgh, PA
Website: http://www.a-frecords.com
Website: https://www.facebook.com/AFrecordsPGH/

Genres: Punk Rock

Independent punk rock record label based in Pittsburgh, Pennsylvania.

A389 Recordings

Website: http://www.a389records.com
Website: https://a389recordings.bandcamp.com

Genres: Hard Rock; Metal

DIY hard rock and metal label.

Abet Publishing

Website: https://www.abetpublishing.com
Website: https://twitter.com/AbetPublishing

Genres: Pop; Rock; World; Electronic; Acoustic; Ambient; Chill; Alternative; Classical

A multimedia publishing company offering eclectic variety of genres. From world music, classical to cutting-edge electronica, acoustic, ambient, chill mood, rock, and alternative.

ABKCO Music & Records Inc.

Fax: +1 (212) 582-5090
Email: info@abkco.com
Website: https://www.abkco.com
Website: https://www.facebook.com/abkco/

Genres: Pop; R&B; Rock

Handles pop, R&B, and rock. Does not accept unsolicited mss. Submission policy on website states that by submitting any material you automatically transfer all rights to them over that work.

Acoustic Disc

PO Box 992
Port Townsend, WA 98368
Email: customerservice@acousticdisc.com
Email: business@acousticdisc.com
Website: https://acousticdisc.com

Genres: Acoustic Jazz; Acoustic Latin; Acoustic Folk; Classical; Acoustic Blues; Roots; World

Handles acoustic music only.

Aeronaut Records

PO Box 26621
Los Angeles, CA 90026
Website: http://www.aeronautrecords.com
Website: https://www.facebook.com/AeronautRecords

Genres: Pop; Rock

Pop/rock label based in Los Angeles, California. An independent label that "attempts to release music that doesn't suck".

Affluent Records

New York, NY
Email: oscarsanchez@affluentrecords.com
Website: https://affluentrecords.com
Website: https://www.facebook.com/theaffluentrecords

Genres: Urban

Contact: Oscar Sanchez

A full service New York City entertainment company specializing in label and artist services consisting of artist development, music production, brand management, media, executive production, promotions and content creation.

Alias Records

838 EAST HIGH STREET # 290
Lexington, KY 40502
Email: accounts@aliasrecords.com
Website: http://www.aliasrecords.com
Website: https://www.facebook.com/Alias-Records-186847657059/

Genres: Indie Rock; Electronic; Singer-Songwriter

Record label based in Lexington, Kentucky.

All Star Music Corporation

9663 Santa Monica Boulevard
Beverly Hills, CA 90210-4303
Email: rnathanfriedman@gmail.com

Genres: All types of music

Contact: Jodi White

Record label based in Beverly Hills.

Alligator Records

P.O. Box 60234
Chicago, IL 60660
Email: info@allig.com
Website: https://www.alligator.com
Website: https://www.facebook.com/AlligatorRecords

Genres: Blues; Americana; Roots

Handles blues and blues-based music only. Send a maximum of four songs by post. Response by post only, so ensure legible postal address included. No email submissions or requests to visit artist's website. Response time of three months or more.

Alpha Pup Records

Email: hello@alphapuprecords.com
Website: http://www.alphapuprecords.com
Website: https://twitter.com/ALPHAPUP

Genres: Indie; Electronic; Hip-Hop; Pop

Spotify-preferred Distributor and Record Label. 100% family-owned. Celebrating diversity and brilliant artistry since 2004.

Alternative Tentacles Records

PO Box 419092
San Francisco, CA 94141
attn. Jello Biafra
Fax: +1 (510) 596-8982
Email: jb@alternativetentacles.com
Website: http://www.alternativetentacles.com

Genres: Country; Hardcore; Indie; Metal; Pop; Punk; R&B; Rock

Contact: Jello Biafra

Accepts demos on CD, tape, or vinyl. No MP3s. Will not listen to music online. Most demos get listened to, but response not guaranteed. No way to "check status" of your submission so don't ask for updates after you've submitted.

Amathus Music

Website: https://amathusmusic.com
Website: https://soundcloud.com/amathusmusic

Genres: Electronic Dance; Underground House; Trance; Commercial

Send query through demo submission form on website, with SoundCloud links. No MP3 attachments, or hard copy submissions. Response not guaranteed.

American Eagle Recordings

12 Lake Forest Court West
St. Charles, MO 63301-4540
Fax: +1 (636) 724-1325
Email: info@americaneaglerecordings.com
Email: americaneaglerecordings@earthlink.net
Website: http://www.americaneaglerecordings.com

Genres: All types of music

Contact: Dr. Charles Max E. Million

Record label based in St Charles, Missouri. Send demos by CD only, accompanied by completed Questionnaire (available for download from website). Extensive submission guidelines on website. Any submissions not adhering to the submission guidelines will be ignored. No MP3s or links by email.

American Laundromat Records

P.O. Box 85
Mystic, CT 06355-0085
Email: americanlaundromat@hotmail.com
Website: https://www.alr-music.com
Website: https://www.facebook.com/americanlaundromatrecords

Genres: Alternative; Folk; Indie; Pop; Rock; Singer-Songwriter

Record label based in Mystic, Connecticut. Not accepting new submissions as at January 2023.

American Recordings

Website: https://www.universalmusic.com/label/republic-records/#american-recordings

Genres: All types of music

An independent record label headed by the record producer and co-founder of Def Jam Recordings. The label was formed in 1988 and then changed its name in 1993.

Amherst Record Sales, Inc.

Email: info@amherstrecords.com
Website: https://www.amherstrecords.com

Genres: R&B; Jazz; Rock; Pop

Label handling R&B, Jazz, Pop, and Rock.

Anti

Website: https://www.anti.com
Website: https://www.facebook.com/antirecords

Genres: Indie Rock

Record label based in Los Angeles, California.

Aphagia Recordings

San Francisco
Website: https://www.aphagiarecordings.com
Website: https://aphagiarecordings.bandcamp.com/

Genres: Experimental Electronic Industrial Progressive Glitch Instrumental Rock Soundtracks

A San Francisco based Independent Record Label focusing on odd forms of electronic and rock music.

API Records

PO Box 7041
Watchung, NJ 07069
Email: apirecords@verizon.net
Website: http://www.apirecords.com

Genres: Classical; Pop Rock

Record label based in Watchung, New Jersey. Accepts solicited demo submissions only. Unsolicited submissions will be discarded without being listened to.

Appleseed Recordings

1416 Larch Lane
West Chester, PA 19380
Website: https://appleseedmusic.com

Genres: Contemporary; Folk; Roots

An independent, idealistic and internationally distributed record label devoted to releasing socially conscious contemporary, folk and roots music by both established and lesser-known musicians. Send demo on CD or CD/R (no MP3s or cassettes) with bio and other relevant info. Listens to everything but response not guaranteed if not interested. See website for full guidelines.

Arabesque Recordings

1600 Harrison Avenue, Suite 307 A
Mamaroneck, NY 10543
Email: info@arabesquerecords.com
Website: https://www.arabesquerecords.com

Genres: Classical; Jazz

Record label based in Mamaroneck, New York, specialising in elegant classical and jazz music. Send query via form on website with info about you and your project and links to the music online.

Arctic Siren Records

4105 E Turnagain Blvd, Suite L
Anchorage, AK 99517
Email: artcsirn@acsalaska.net
Website: https://www.arcticsiren.com/arctic-siren-label.html
Website: https://www.facebook.com/arcticsiren

Genres: Acoustic

Dedicated to the production and distribution of quality recordings of independent artist and is committed to the financial independence of songwriters and performers.

Arkadia Entertainment Corp

PO Box 77
Saugerties, NY 12477
Email: info@arkadiarecords.com
Website: https://arkadiarecords.com
Website: https://www.facebook.com/arkadiarecords

Genres: Jazz; World

Record label based in Saugerties, New York.

Artists' Addiction Records

Fax: +1 (818) 230-9800
Email: info@artistsaddiction.com
Email: services@artistsaddiction.com
Website: http://www.artistsaddiction.com

Genres: Soundtracks

Contact: Jonathan Scott Miller

Record label based in Encino, California, focusing on film and TV soundtracks.

Aspenbeat LLC
Website: https://aspenbeat.com
Website: https://www.facebook.com/aspenbeat

Genres: All types of music

Radio show, record label, and playlist curation.

Asthmatic Kitty Records
830 Glenwood Ave, Suite 510-414
Atlanta, GA 30316
Website: http://asthmatickitty.com
Website: https://www.facebook.com/asthmatickitty

Genres: Alternative Pop

Record label based in Atlanta. Not accepting submissions as at May 2023. Check website for current status.

Astralwerks Records
1750 Vine Street
Hollywood, CA
Email: astralwerks.astralwerks@gmail.com
Website: https://www.astralwerks.com
Website: https://www.facebook.com/astralwerks

Genres: Alternative; Electronic; Dance; Techno

Record label based in New York.

Asylum Records
Website: https://www.asylumrecords.com
Website: https://www.facebook.com/asylumrecordsus

Genres: Hip-Hop; Rap

Rap and hip hop label.

Atlan-Dec/Grooveline Records
2529 Green Forest Ct./P.O.Box 1676
Snellville, GA 30078-4183
Fax: +1 (770) 985-1686
Email: Atlandec@Prodigy.net
Website: http://www.atlan-dec.com

Genres: Country; Hip-Hop; Jazz; Pop; R&B; Rap; Rock; Urban; Rhythm and Blues

Record label based in Snellville, Georgia.

Atlantic Records
75 Rockefeller Plz Ste 3
New York, NY 10019
Website: https://www.atlanticrecords.com
Website: https://www.facebook.com/atlanticrecords

Genres: All types of music

Record label based in New York.

ATO Records
New York, NY 10016
Email: info@atorecords.com
Website: https://atorecords.com
Website: https://www.facebook.com/atorecords/

Genres: Alternative; Rock; Acoustic; Indie; Pop

Independent record label committed to artists and building their careers.

AvatarDigi
2029 Hyperion Avenue
Los Angeles, CA 90027
Email: info@avatardigi.com
Website: http://www.avatardigi.com

Genres: All types of music

Digital music distributor allowing you to place your music on iTunes, etc. directly. $50 set-up cost, then royalty on sales.

Average Joes Entertainment
3728 Keystone Avenue
Nashville, TN 37211
Email: info@averagejoesent.com
Website: https://averagejoesent.com

Genres: Country

Independent record label specialising in film, television, technology and country music.

Ba Da Bing Records & Management

181 Clermont Avenue, Suite 403
Brooklyn, NY 11205
Email: hello@badabingrecords.com
Website: http://www.badabingrecords.com
Website: http://soundcloud.com/badabingrecords

Genres: All types of music

Record label based in New York, operated by film and TV comedian.

Babygrande Records, Inc.

101 West 23rd Street Suite 296
New York, New York 10011
Email: inquiries@babygrande.com
Website: https://babygrande.com
Website: https://soundcloud.com/babygrande

Genres: Hip-Hop; Rock; Indie Rock; Electronic; Instrumental

Record label based in New York. Describes itself as "one of the premier independent record labels operating today". Send query by email with relevant info and streaming links only.

BackWords Recordings

334 Tonti St.
South Bend, IN 46617-1149
Email: tim@backwordsrecordings.com
Website: https://www.backwordsrecordings.com

Genres: Avant-Garde; Alternative; Electronic; Melodic; Psychedelic; Traditional; Spoken Word; Singer-Songwriter; Rock; Mystical; Instrumental; Indie;; Guitar based; Classical

Contact: Tim Backer

An Independent Culture Production House.

Bar/None Records

PO Box 1704
Hoboken, NJ 07030
Email: glenn@bar-none.com
Website: http://www.bar-none.com
Website: https://soundcloud.com/barnonepop

Genres: Alternative; Indie; Rock

Record label based in Hoboken, New Jersey. Those looking to approach are asked to check out the website and artists currently worked with, then if you still think it's appropriate send a query by email with a link to music online. No large music file attachments by email.

Barbarian Productions

Email: talent@barbarianproductions.com
Website: http://www.barbarianproductions.com

Genres: Pop; R&B; Hip-Hop; Singer-Songwriter; Soundtracks

Send submissions by email.

Barsuk Records

PO Box 22546
Seattle, WA 98122
Email: questions@barsuk.com
Website: https://www.barsuk.com
Website: https://www.facebook.com/barsukrecords

Genres: Indie; Rock

Record label based in Seattle. Send links to demos or electronic press kits online via form on website. Do not send audio files or physical CDs. Response not guaranteed.

Basin Street Records

5500 Prytania Street, #110
New Orleans, LA 70115
Fax: +1 (504) 483-7877
Email: info@basinstreetrecords.com
Website: http://www.basinstreetrecords.com
Website: https://www.facebook.com/BasinStreetRecords

Genres: Blues; Jazz; Latin; Pop; R&B; Rock

Record label based in New Orleans.

Beggars Group (US)

Email: banquet@beggars.com
Website: https://beggars.com

Genres: Alternative; Dance; Electronic; Indie; Punk; Rock; Singer-Songwriter; World

International group with offices in the UK, US, and Canada. The group is not accepting demos itself, but individual labels are – see website for links.

Berman Brothers

Email: info@bermanbrothers.com
Email: carloc@bermanbrothers.com
Website: https://bermanbrothers.com
Website: http://www.facebook.com/bermanbrothers

Genres: Dance; Pop; R&B

Contact: Christian Berman; Frank Berman

A two-brother team. Recipients of more than 90 gold and platinum awards, two BMI awards, a Golden Globe nomination, a Grammy nomination and a Grammy Award.

Better Looking Records

Website: https://betterlookingrecords.com
Website: https://www.facebook.com/betterlookingrecords

Genres: Alternative; Modern Rock

Contact: David Brown; Paul Fischer

An independent record label founded in 2000. Offices are headquartered in the founder's bedrooms in Los Angeles and New York.

Bifocal Media

Email: charles@bifocalmedia.com
Website: https://bifocalmedia.com

Genres: Electronic; Hardcore; Punk; Rap; Hip-Hop

Contact: Charles Cardello; Brad Scott

Media company founded in 1997.

Big3 Records, Inc.

6090 Central Avenue
St. Petersburg, FL 33707
Email: jb@big3entertainment.com
Website: http://www.big3records.com
Website: https://www.facebook.com/Big3Records/

Genres: All types of music

Record label based in St Petersburg, Florida. Embraces the philosophy that whether reinventing an established artist or developing and introducing new talent to the world, the artist and music comes first.

Black Dahlia Music

P.O. Box 631928
Highlands Ranch, CO 80163
Email: blackd@blackdahlia.com
Website: https://blackdahlia.com

Genres: All types of music

Record label based in Highlands Ranch, Colorado.

Blue Canoe Records

Email: contactbcr@bluecanoerecords.com
Website: https://www.bluecanoerecords.com
Website: https://www.facebook.com/bluecanoerecords

Genres: All types of music

Only accepts recommendations from their staff producers. Unsolicited material will not be listened to.

Blue Elan Records

10880 Wilshire Boulevard, Suite 2000
Los Angeles, CA 90024
Email: info@blueelan.com
Website: https://blueelan.com
Website: https://www.facebook.com/blueelan/

Genres: All types of music

A few years ago, we started out with a simple idea to become the most artist-friendly record label in the world. From the studio to release day and everything in between, we are passionate about our artists making the music they love, and support their growth at every step of the way.

Blue Jackel Entertainment

PO Box 87
Huntington, NY 11743-0087
Email: info@bluejackel.com
Website: http://www.bluejackel.com

Genres: Electronic; Folk; Jazz; Latin; Roots; World

Record label based in Huntington, New York.

Blue Wave Records

3221 Perryville Road
Baldwinsville, NY 13027
Email: info@bluewaverecords.com
Website: https://www.bluewaverecords.com
Website: https://www.facebook.com/Blue-Wave-Records-2387752671363478

Genres: Blues; Non-Commercial;

Describes itself as an "ARTIST ORIENTED, NON-COMMERCIAL, INDEPENDENT MUSIC LABEL". Handles blues and blues-related music.

Boosweet Records

Website: https://boosweet.com

Genres: Jazz; Alternative; Country; Dance; Classical; Rock; Metal; Latin; R&B; Hip-Hop; Rap; Blues; Folk; Acoustic; Pop

Describes itself as "a full-service indie music label with industry critical global connections along with worldwide presence and reach."

Broken Arrow Records

Email: info@brokenarrowmusic.com
Website: https://www.brokenarrowmusic.com
Website: https://www.facebook.com/BrokenArrowMusicMkt

Genres: Rock; Singer-Songwriter

Independent label and artist marketing management featuring melodic singer/songwriters from America, Germany, Switzerland, Iceland and elsewhere.

Broken Bow Records

Email: contactus@bbrmusicgroup.com
Website: https://www.bbrmusicgroup.com
Website: https://www.facebook.com/BBRMusicGroup/

Genres: Country

Founded in 1997, quickly grew from a fledgling independent label into one of the largest independent Country label groups in the US.

Casablanca Records

Website: https://www.casablancarecords.com
Website: https://www.facebook.com/casablancarecs

Genres: Electronic; Dance

Record label with a focus on dance and electronic music.

Cexton Records

Email: johncexton@aol.com
Website: https://www.cexton.com

Genres: Jazz; Swing

An Audiophile Jazz, Big Band and Italian Music Record Label started in 1984, featuring live recordings and top quality audio CDs

Closed Sessions

Email: alex@closedsessions.com
Website: https://www.closedsessions.com
Website: https://www.facebook.com/ClosedSessionsChicago/

Genres: Hip-Hop

A record label with deep roots in Chicago's Hip Hop scene, and the national Hip Hop community. Started as a content partnership during the wild west like environment of the blog era. Beginning in late 2008, it hosted first market plays from the era's most innovative and emergent artists. In addition, it took fans into the studio with these artists to provide an examination of their art as well as original recordings.

Columbia Nashville

Website: https://www.sonymusicnashville.com/label/columbia-nashville/

Genres: Country

Country music focused subdivision of major international label. Based in Nashville, Tennessee.

Columbia Records

25 Madison Avenue
New York, NY 10010
Website: https://www.columbiarecords.com
Website: https://www.facebook.com/columbiarecords

Genres: All types of music

Record label based in New York.

Craniality Sounds

Email: cranialitysounds@gmail.com
Website: http://www.cranialitysounds.com
Website: https://www.facebook.com/CranialitySounds/

Genres: Underground House; Underground Dance; Funky House

An underground house music label dedicated to bringing out the essence and eclectic of underground dance music while having fun at it. Focus is funky house music, but have been known to drop other styles of house music.

Daemon Records

PO Box 1207
Decatur, GA 30031
Website: https://www.daemonrecords.com
Website: https://www.facebook.com/DaemonRecords/

Genres: All types of music

An independent record label that was founded in 1990 as a vehicle for recording artists to express their artistic vision without the confines and restrictions of a corporate major record label. The label is operated from the artist's perspective, with an emphasis on community development on all fronts including the arts, the environment, and human rights. The label aims to help break down barriers within the music community, while providing an opportunity for musicians to create and control their own recordings within a free and nurturing environment.

Dancing Cat Records

Email: jennifer@dancingcat.com
Website: https://www.dancingcat.com
Website: https://www.facebook.com/DancingCatRecords/

Genres: Instrumental; World

This label's dual mission for the past 20 years has been to produce and promote the music of George Winston, as well as Hawaiian slack key guitar. The production wing of the company is the in-house management and concert production company for George Winston and also assists in the coordination of slack key guitar concerts.

Def Jam Recordings

Website: https://www.defjam.com
Website: https://www.facebook.com/DefJam/

Genres: Hip-Hop; R&B; Rap; Urban

Record label based in New York.

Delicious Vinyl LLC

6607 Sunset Blvd.
Los Angeles, CA 90028
Email: contact@deliciousvinyl.com
Website: https://www.facebook.com/deliciousvinyl
Website: https://twitter.com/DeliciousVinyl

Genres: Hip-Hop; Pop; Rap; Reggae; Rock

Record label based in Los Angeles.

Dim Mak Records

Los Angeles
Email: syncs@dimmak.com
Email: sponsorships@dimmak.com
Website: https://www.dimmak.com
Website: https://www.facebook.com/dimmak

Genres: Pop; Punk; Rap; Hip-Hop; Rock; Dance; Electronic; Indie

Send links to music online via online demo submission form.

Dischord Records

3819 Beecher St. NW
Washington, DC 20007-1802
Email: orders@dischord.com
Website: http://www.dischord.com

Genres: Punk; Rock

Only releases music by bands in the DC area, through an organic process of getting to know bands active in the area. No formal contracts.

Downtown Music

155 6th Avenue, Floor 15
New York, NY 10013
Website: https://www.downtownmusic.com
Website: https://twitter.com/downtownmusic

Genres: Indie; Pop; Rock; Singer-Songwriter; Urban

Record label based in New York.

Easy Star Records

PO Box 1069, Cooper Station
New York, NY 10276
Fax: +1 (646) 602-9655
Email: easystar@easystar.com
Website: http://www.easystar.com
Website: https://www.facebook.com/EasyStarRecords/

Genres: Reggae

Reggae label based in New York, not currently accepting submissions as at April 2021. Any demos submitted will not be listened to, or returned.

Ecko Records

485 North Hollywood Street
Memphis, TN 38112
Fax: +1 (901) 320-9251
Website: http://www.eckorecords.com

Genres: Contemporary Blues; R&B; Soul; Gospel

Contact: John Ward; Larry Chambers

Label founded in 1995 in Memphis, Tennessee, describing itself as "home of great contemporary Soul, Blues and Gospel Music".

eenie meenie records

PO Box 691397
Los Angeles, CA 90069
Email: reiko@eeniemeenie.com
Website: https://www.eeniemeenie.com
Website: https://www.facebook.com/eeniemeenierecords

Genres: Electronic; Indie; Pop; Rock; Singer-Songwriter; Dance

Aims to help artists develop and market their music by providing ongoing and extensive press and radio campaigns, tour promotion, festival exposure, street marketing, film and TV licensing, retail marketing and merchandising.

Emperor Jones Records

PO Box 4730
Austin, TX 78765
Email: brutus@emperorjones.com
Website: http://www.emperorjones.com

Genres: Alternative; Folk; Indie

Record label based in Austin, Texas.

ESP-Disk' Ltd

365 West End Ave. #203
New York, NY 10024
Email: shipping@espdisk.com
Website: http://espdisk.com

Genres: All types of music

Record label based in New York.

Estrus Records

PO Box 2125
Bellingham, WA 98227
Email: website@estrus.com
Website: http://estrus.com

Genres: All types of music

Record label based in Bellingham, Washington. No unsolicited demos.

Fantasy Records

Email: support@fantasyrecordings.com
Website: https://fantasyrecordings.com
Website: https://www.facebook.com/FantasyRecords

Genres: All types of music

Established in San Francisco in 1949. A home for innovative, authentic artists whose music impacts the world.

Fat Wreck Chords

2196 Palou Ave.
San Francisco, CA 94124
Email: mailbag@fatwreck.com
Website: https://fatwreck.com
Website: https://www.facebook.com/fatwrecksf/

Genres: Alternative; Punk; Rock

Contact: Mike

Independent record label based in San Francisco. Send demos by email.

Favored Nations Entertainment

17328 Ventura Boulevard, Suite 165
Encino, CA 91316
Email: info@favorednations.com
Website: https://www.favorednations.com
Website: https://www.facebook.com/Favorednationsentertainment

Genres: Contemporary; Blues; Classical; Jazz; Metal; New Age; Rock; Acoustic

Contact: Steve Vai

Record label based in Encino, California. Approach by email if you'd like to submit music for consideration.

Fedora

106 West 71st Street
New York, NY 10023
Fax: +1 (212) 877-0407
Email: jazzdepo@ix.netcom.com
Website: http://www.jazzdepot.com

Genres: Blues

Blues record label based in New York, dealing with artists whose lineage reaches back to the roots of blues.

Fever Records

PO Box 219
Yonkers, NY 10710
Email: fevermusic@aol.com
Website: https://feverrecords.com
Website: https://www.facebook.com/FeverRecords

Genres: All types of music

Record label based in Yonkers, New York.

Fire Tower Entertainment

Los Angeles, CA
Email: artists@firetowerent.com
Website: https://firetowerent.com
Website: https://www.facebook.com/firetowerent

Genres: Indie; Pop

Record label based in Los Angeles, California. New artists can apply via system on website.

First Access Entertainment (FAE)

Email: contact@faegrp.com
Website: https://www.faegrp.com
Website: https://www.facebook.com/faegrp

Genres: All types of music

Record label with offices in London, New York, and Los Angeles.

5 Points Records

12 West 37th Street, 4th Floor
New York, NY 10018
Fax: +1 (212) 629-0017
Email: demos@5pointsrecords.com
Website: http://www.5pointsrecords.com

Genres: Contemporary; Electronic; Dance; Pop

Aims to release a wide range of music, including electronica, dance and pop. Accepts unsolicited demos, but no items returned and no phone calls regarding submissions. Accepts MySpace links by email, but no MP3s.

Freddie Records

5979 S Staples St
Corpus Christi, TX 78413
Fax: +1 (361) 992-8428

Email: martzcommusic@gmail.com
Website: https://www.freddiestore.com
Website: https://www.facebook.com/FreddieRecords/

Genres: Hip-Hop; Latin; Rap; Urban

Record label based in Corpus Christi, Texas.

Gearhead Records

PO Box 2375
Elk Grove, CA 95759
Email: info@gearheadhq.com
Email: michelle@gearheadhq.com
Website: https://www.gearheadhq.com

Genres: Punk; Rock; Rock and Roll; New Wave Power Pop; Melodic Punk

Record label based in Elk Grove, California. Do not send demos. Instead, get involved with the community, and – if you are good enough – you will get noticed.

Grim Reality Entertainment, LLC

1209 Northwest Hwy, #143
Garland, TX 75041
Email: grimrealityent@gmail.com
Website: https://grimrealityentertainment.net
Website: https://www.facebook.com/Grimrealityent

Genres: Underground Hip-Hop; Rap

Aan independent hip-hop label based out of California, USA, with regional, national, and international acts.

Harmonized Records

Asheville:

107 McFalls Road
Asheville, NC 28806

Mebane:

6520 Oak Grove Church Rd.
Mebane, NC 27302
Website: https://www.harmonizedrecords.com

Genres: Blues; Electronic; Jazz; Rock

Contact: Brian Asplin; Lee Crumpton

Record label with offices in Asheville and Mebane.

Heads Up International

Website: https://concord.com/labels/heads-up-international/

Genres: Contemporary Instrumental; Contemporary Jazz; Traditional Jazz; World; Contemporary Latin Jazz

Founded in 1990 to release contemporary instrumental music.

Heartland Recordings

337 Dearstone Private Drive
Bristol, TN 37620
Email: heartlandrecordings@btes.tv
Website: http://www.heartlandrecordings.com

Genres: Americana; Acoustic; Christian; Folk; Gospel; Roots; Singer-Songwriter; Country

Founded in 1987. We are dedicated to preserving and promoting Bluegrass, Folk, Americana and other forms of acoustic music.

We are located in the heart of the Appalachian Mountains. In the middle of the richest Bluegrass music scenes in the country.

Heaven's Disciples, LLC

Email: info@heavensdisciples.com
Email: rodney.burutsa@heavensdisciples.com
Website: https://www.heavensdisciples.com
Website: https://twitter.com/HeavensDisciple

Genres: Christian Rap; Christian R&B; Christian Reggae; Christian Reggaeton; Christian Rhythm and Blues; Instrumental

Contact: Rodney Burutsa

A multimedia entertainment company featuring music, books, comics, films, games, merchandise, and clothing.

Hydra Head Records

Website: http://www.hydrahead.com
Website: https://www.facebook.com/hydrahead

Genres: Hard Rock; Metal; Experimental; Hardcore

Independent record label specialising in heavy and experimental music.

iHipHop Distribution

8033 West Sunset Boulevard
Suite 1038
Los Angeles, CA 90046
Email: pr@ihiphopdistribution.com
Website: https://distribution.ihiphop.com
Website: https://www.facebook.com/ihiphop

Genres: Hip-Hop

Founded in 2009 in an attempt to provide artists with a new paradigm for distributing their music and building their brand. Has worked successfully with many artists (check out our list of Top Sellers) and continues its partnership with the A3C Hip-Hop Festival for the release of its annual hip-hop compilation.

Also maintains its own innovative worldwide digital distribution platform, providing superior distribution and marketing services to artists worldwide.

Integrity Music

1646 Westgate Circle, Suite 106
Brentwood, TN 37027
Email: CustomerCare@IntegrityMusic.com
Website: https://www.integritymusic.com

Genres: Christian; Gospel

Christian gospel label based in Colorado Springs. Not accepting submissions as at August 2021.

Invisible Records

Chicago
Website: http://www.invisiblerecords.com
Website: https://www.facebook.com/InvisibleRecords

Genres: Gothic; Metal; Rock

Contact: Katie/Jarin

Record label based in Chicago, specialising in goth, metal and rock.

Island Records (US)

1755 Broadway
New york, NY 10018
Website: http://www.islandrecords.com
Website: https://www.facebook.com/IslandRecords

Genres: Contemporary; Indie; Metal; Pop; Punk; R&B; Rap; Hip-Hop; Rock; Urban

Record label based in New York.

Jade Tree

2310 Kennwynn Road
Wilmington, DE 19810
Email: jadetree@jadetree.com
Website: https://jadetree.com
Website: https://soundcloud.com/jadetree/

Genres: Hardcore; Pop; Punk; Rock

Contact: Tim Owen; Darren Walters

Independent record company based in Wilmington, DE.

K2B2 Records

Email: webmaster@k2b2.com
Website: https://www.k2b2.com
Website: https://www.facebook.com/k2b2records/

Genres: Blues; Classical; Jazz; Avant-Garde Jazz

Record label founded in 1979 as an outlet for the distribution of unorthodox yet locally popular avant-garde jazz that the major jazz labels weren't interested in.

!K7 Records

55 Washington Street
Suite 734, Brooklyn, NY 11201
Website: https://k7.com
Website: https://www.instagram.com/k7.music

Genres: All types of music

Record label based in Berlin, Germany, with offices in Brooklyn, New York, and London.

Knitting Factory Records

Email: info@knittingfactoryrecords.com
Website: https://store.partisanrecords.com/knitting-factory-records
Website: https://www.knittingfactory.com

Genres: Contemporary; Blues; Country; Electronic; Folk; Jazz; Metal; Punk; Rock; World

Company including labels, music venue and concert tour promotion.

Kung Fu Records

P.O. Box 3061
Seal Beach CA, 90740
Email: info@kungfurecords.com
Website: http://www.kungfurecords.com
Website: https://www.facebook.com/KungFuRecords/

Genres: Hardcore; Pop; Punk; Rock

Record label based in Seal Beach, California. Send links to music online by email. No CDs.

La Corporación Muzic

Email: info@lacorpamuzic.com
Website: http://www.lacorpamuzic.com
Website: https://www.facebook.com/LACORPAMUZIC
Website: https://myspace.com/lacorpamuzic

Genres: Electronic; Latin; Reggae; Pop; Rock; Alternative; Rap; Latin Urban

Record label based in City of Industry, California.

Light In The Attic

P.O. Box 31970
Seattle, WA 98103
Fax: +1 (206) 706-1008
Email: info@lightintheattic.net
Website: https://lightintheattic.net

Genres: All types of music

Contact: Matt Sullivan; Josh Wright

Record label based in Seattle.

Loveslap! Recordings

Website: http://www.loveslap.com
Website: https://www.facebook.com/LoveslapRecordings

Genres: Dance; House

Independent record label and publisher founded in San Francisco in 1997.

Luaka Bop

New York
Email: iwasthinking@luakabop.com
Website: https://www.luakabop.com
Website: https://www.facebook.com/luakabop1989

Genres: World

Contact: David Byrne

Record label based in New York.

Mack Avenue

Website: https://mackavenue.com
Website: https://www.facebook.com/mackavenue

Genres: Jazz

Jazz record label founded in Detroit in the nineties.

Mailboat Records

15250 Ventura Blvd. Suite #400
Sherman Oaks, CA 91403
Fax: +1 (818) 501-1568
Email: info@mailboatrecords.com
Website: https://www.mailboatrecords.com

Genres: Country; Folk; Pop; Rock

Label established in 1999, based in Sherman Oaks, California.

Malaco Music Group

PO Box 9287
Jackson, MS 39286-9287
Fax: +1 (601) 982-4528
Email: demo@malaco.com
Email: malaco@malaco.com
Website: https://www.malaco.com
Website: https://www.facebook.com/malacomusic

Genres: Blues; Gospel; R&B; Soul; Jazz

Record label based in Jackson, Mississippi. Send demos by email.

Manifesto Records, Inc.

1180 South Beverly Drive, Suite 510
Los Angeles, CA 90035-1157
Fax: +1 (310) 556-9801
Email: esc@manifesto.com
Website: https://manifesto.com

Genres: Alternative; Pop; Rock; Punk; Indie

Contact: Evan S. Cohen

Record label based in Los Angeles.

Mega Truth Records

Website: http://www.jonbare.net/jonbaremegatruth.htm

Genres: Blues; Rock

Contact: Jon Bare

Independent record label devoted to "capturing the world's best musicians playing music that makes you feel good".

Megawave Records

Email: info@megawavemusic.com
Website: http://www.megawaverecords.com

Genres: Blues; Electronic; Jazz; Reggae; Rock; World; Gospel

Small label, big sound – based in Michigan but has a global ear. With roots in graphic arts, audio and video production, it is now an independent full-service media company that is home for both developing and legacy artists alike.

Meloden Nashville

Email: MelodenMusic@gmail.com
Website: https://meloden.com

Genres: Alternative Acoustic Christian Commercial Contemporary Funky Mainstream Melodic Modern New Wave Americana Blues Country Folk Gospel Guitar based Indie MOR Pop Rock Rock and Roll Rockabilly Singer-Songwriter

An independent record label which also owns and operates an in-house music publishing unit (ASCAP affiliate.) We have partnerships with music distributors worldwide. At this time, we are not accepting unsolicited material from artists and songwriters.

Memphis International Records

Email: jeff@memphisinternational.com
Website: https://memphisinternational.com
Website: https://www.facebook.com/MemphisInternationalRecords/

Genres: Roots; Blues; Rockabilly; Swing; Americana; Country; Folk; Jazz; R&B

Record label based in Memphis, Tennessee. Aims, simply, to produce music that the founders like, focusing on the "music" part of the "music business". Check website to see the kind of music produced, and if you think yours fits in send CD by post.

Mercury Nashville

Website: https://www.umgnashville.com
Website: https://www.facebook.com/UMGNashville

Genres: Country

Country label based in Nashville, Tennessee.

Mosley Music Group

Email: gm@mosleymusicgroup.com
Email: Thomas.Leijgraaff@monomusicgroup.com
Website: http://www.mosleymusicgroup.com

Genres: All types of music

Contact: Gary Marella; Thomas Leijgraaff Sr

Music group with over 25 million albums and over 40 million singles sold.

Mountain Apple Company

P.O. Box 22569
Honolulu, HI 96823
Email: info@mountainapplecompany.com
Website: https://www.mountainapplecompany.com

Website: https://www.facebook.com/mountainapplecompany

Genres: Regional; Traditional; Contemporary

Record label releasing traditional and contemporary Hawaiian music.

MRG Recordings

Email: submissions@mrgrecordings.com
Email: info@mrgrecordings.com
Website: https://mrgrecordings.com
Website: https://www.facebook.com/mrgrecordings

Genres: All types of music

Digital-focussed record label. Approach by email with links to music online. No audio file attachments (these will be deleted).

New Pants Publishing

119 N. Wahsatch Ave
Colorado Springs, CO 80903
Fax: +1 (719) 634-2274
Email: rac@crlr.net
Website: http://www.newpants.com

Genres: Country; Folk; R&B; Rap; Pop; Rock

Contact: Robert A. Case

Company based in Colorado Springs, Colorado.

NexGen Music Group, LLC

Email: demos@nexgenmusicgroup.com
Email: info@nexgenmusicgroup.com
Website: https://www.nexgenmusicgroup.com
Website: https://soundcloud.com/nexgenrecs

Genres: Underground; Downtempo; Chill; Drum and Bass; Dubstep; Garage; House; Electronic; Hip-Hop; Soul; Funk; Experimental; Dance; Pop

Contact: Daniel Clarke

An established worldwide independent record label with more than a decade of history behind its innovative approach to the fusion of live, vocal and electronic music. The label is dedicated to the creation of groundbreaking musical compositions, as well as introducing new audiences to the depth and diversity within the dance and electronic music genres. The label showcases multiple musical styles including; Downtempo, Drum & Bass, Dubstep, Chill-Out, Nu-Jazz, Future Jazz, Experimental, Deep House, and Electronica.

Represents 30+ pioneering artists and musicians from across the globe, and supplies music for the television, motion picture and interactive entertainment industries. Has completed music projects for organizations like: BBC, Lionsgate, and OTC Films, securing placements in musical compilations and highly-rated major film and television shows in the UK & US.

Includes industry/scene pioneers and legends such as Chris Paul & Mia V (aka Stolen Identity), Earth Leakage Trip, and D.A alongside established and up-and-coming artists: Rob Sparx, Kyro, Qumulus, Undersound, Physical & Crimea, Faible among many others.

An artist-centric brand committed to creating a forward-looking, inclusive and multi-faceted musical community. Its personalized service includes worldwide distribution, promotion and marketing, alongside top-quality production services and one-on-one industry consultations. The label fosters a philosophy of artistic growth, collaboration and experimentation, uniting promising new talent with established industry musical magicians.

Nitro Records

Website: https://nitrorecords.com
Website: https://www.facebook.com/nitrorecords/

Genres: Punk; Rock

Record label synonymous with the Southern California punk scene.

NoFace Records

Email: demos@nofacerecords.com
Website: https://www.nofacerecords.com

Website: https://soundcloud.com/nofacerecordsofficial

Genres: Electronic; Dubstep; House; Techno; Trance

Contact: Max Vangeli

Electronic music record label. Send demos by email. Promises to respond to every demo within two weeks.

Noisy Poet Records

276 5th Avenue, Suite 704
New York NY 10001
Email: admin@noisypoet.com
Email: booking@noisypoet.com
Website: https://www.noisypoet.com
Website: https://www.facebook.com/noisypoet/

Genres: All types of music, except: Doom Black Metal; Doom

Music arm of a multi-media company with worldwide music distribution. We deliver the sounds of tomorrow through ear-picked, unique, and authentic artists poised to breathe new life into the music industry. Doesn't aspire to reach the pinnacle of today's music landscape; we are driven to transform it.

NYC Records

Email: info@nycrecords.com
Website: http://www.nycrecords.com

Genres: Folk; Jazz

Contact: Michael Mainieri

Independent label created in 1992 by an award-winning jazz vibraphonist who has also worked as producer, arranger, and composer.

Oh Boy Records

PO Box 150222
Nashville, TN 37215
Email: info@ohboy.com
Website: https://ohboy.com
Website: https://www.facebook.com/OhBoyRecords/

Genres: Folk; Roots

Folk / roots label based in Nashville, Tennessee.

Om Records

1890 Bryant Street. #305
San Francisco, CA 94110
Email: connect@om-records.com
Email: info@om-records.com
Website: https://www.om-records.com
Website: https://www.facebook.com/omrecords

Genres: Contemporary; Dance; Electronic; Hip-Hop; Rap; Rock; Singer-Songwriter; Urban

Contact: Gunnar Hissam

San Francisco based music and lifestyle company.

1-2-3-4 Go! Records

420 40th Street #5
Oakland, CA 94609
Email: store@1234gorecords.com
Website: https://1234gorecords.com
Website: https://www.facebook.com/1234gorecords

Genres: Rock; Punk; Indie; Hardcore; Garage; Classic Rock; R&B; Soul; Jazz; Hip-Hop; Reggae; Ska; Funk; Country

An Independent record store and label based in Oakland, California.

The Orchard

Website: https://www.theorchard.com
Website: https://www.facebook.com/theorchard/

Genres: All types of music

Describes itself as the industry's leading distributor and artist and label services company.

Pendulum Records

96 Linwood Plaza, #354
Fort Lee, NJ 07024
Email: ruben@rubenrodriguezentertainment.net
Website: http://www.pendulumrecords.biz

Website: http://www.facebook.com/PendulumRecords

Genres: Christian; Gospel; Latin; Pop; R&B; Hip-Hop; Rap; Urban

Record label based in Fort Lee, New Jersey.

Phunk Junk Records Inc

Email: phunkjunkinfo@gmail.com
Website: https://www.phunkjunk.com
Website: https://www.facebook.com/phunkjunkmusicgroup

Genres: Electronic Club Dance House IDM Trance

Contact: Lary Saladin

We are all about EDM Music. House, Progressive House, Electro House, Tech House, some Deep House..

No DNB, No Dubstep, No Trap, etc etc.

Submit demos through online form.

Pi Recordings

Brooklyn, NY
Email: info@pirecordings.com
Website: https://pirecordings.com
Website: https://www.facebook.com/PiRecordings/

Genres: Electronic; Jazz

Contact: Seth Rosner

Record label based in Brooklyn, New York.

Posi-Tone

PO Box 2848
Los Angeles, CA 90294
Email: info@posi-tone.com
Website: https://www.posi-tone.com
Website: https://soundcloud.com/posi-tone-records

Genres: Jazz

Jazz label based in Los Angeles, California, releasing both contemporary interpretations of classic material and fresh new ideas by innovative players.

Pravda Records

4245 N Knox, Suite 7
Chicago, IL 60641
Email: kenn@pravdamusic.com
Website: https://www.pravdamusic.com
Website: https://www.facebook.com/PravdaRecordsUSA/

Genres: Alternative Rock; Alternative Country; Rockabilly; Pop; R&B; Soul; Rock

Contact: Kenn Goodman

Independent record label based in Chicago. Full-service music licensing company with two in-house publishing companies.

Primarily A Cappella

Website: https://www.singers.com
Website: https://twitter.com/newsacappella

Genres: Contemporary; Jazz; Christian; World

Record label based in San Anselmo, California, specialising in a cappella. Releases include Christmas, Contemporary, Barbershop, Choral, Vocal Jazz, Christian, World, Vintage Harmony, Collegiate, Doo Wop, and Children's Choirs.

Psychopathic Records

Website: https://www.psychopathicrecords.com

Genres: Hardcore; Hip-Hop; Rap

Record label founded by rap duo from Detroit.

Ramp Records

Email: info@ramprecords.com
Website: http://www.ramprecords.com

Genres: All types of music

Contact: Michael McDonald; Jeff Bridges; Chris Pelonis

Co-founded by a well-known Hollywood actor. Not accepting submissions as at February 2022.

Rampage Records

197 Illinois St
Battle Creek, MI 49014
Email: contact@rampagerecords.net
Email: demos@rampagerecords.net
Website: https://rampagerecords.net
Website: https://www.facebook.com/RampageRecordsWorldwide/

Genres: All types of music

Contact: Chandler Culler

An independent record. Demos accepted by post or by email.

Razor Sharp Records South, Inc.

3772 Pleasantdale Road, Suite 200
Atlanta, GA 30340
Email: admin@razorsharprecordssouth.com
Website: https://www.razorsharprecordssouth.com
Website: https://www.facebook.com/razorsharprecordssouth

Genres: All types of music

Contact: Herbert Goodwin Jr

Independent record label. Company specialises in Artist Management and Development services for all genres of music. Send links to your music online via email or contact form on website.

Reach Out International Records (ROIR)

Website: https://roir-usa.com
Website: https://www.facebook.com/roirusa

Genres: Reggae; Rock; Punk; Indie

New York label begun in 1979 as a cassette-only label. Send demo via song and talent filtering service.

Rebel Records

PO Box 7405
Charlottesville, VA 22906
Email: questions@rebelrecords.com
Website: http://www.rebelrecords.com
Website: https://www.facebook.com/RebelRecordsBluegrass

Genres: Country; Folk; Roots

Record label based in Charlottesville, Virginia. Handles bluegrass, country, folk, and roots.

Relapse Records

Email: mailorder@relapse.com
Website: http://www.relapse.com
Website: https://www.facebook.com/RelapseRecords

Genres: Indie; Metal; Rock

Independent metal label.

Renaissance Records

20860 N. Tatum Blvd, Suite 300 Unit 304
Phoenix, AZ 85050
Email: john@renaissancerecordsus.com
Email: devon@renaissancerecordsus.com
Website: https://renaissancerecordsus.com/

Genres: All types of music, except: Ambient Black Metal Black Origin Break Beat C-DUB Blue Beat Blues Classical Club Cuban Dance Dancehall Deep Funk Disco Doom Drum and Bass Dub Dubstep Ethnic Emo Fusion Funk Glitch Gospel Gothic Grind Grime Hardcore Hi-NRG Hip-Hop House IDM Jazz Jungle Latin MOR Mystical New Age Noise Core R&B Psychebilly Punk Nostalgia Ragga Rap Reggaeton Reggae Remix Relaxation Rockabilly Rhythm and Blues Roots Shoegaze Ska Skool Soul Spoken Word Surf Swing Techno Trance Trip Hop World

Contact: John Edwards

While we have primarily found ourselves working with classic artists, we are always searching for new artists. We are looking for those new, modern
artists to bring new life to the company as well as bring new life to Vinyl releases. We are moving into the next phase of our history with some great new talent and a worldwide focus on music from around the planet. We are currently looking for rock-centric artists, but have plans in the near-future to broaden our label and become more inclusive of more modern artists. Feel free to reach out to any of the below emails with any interest or any

further questions and we will be happy to help!

Republic Records

Website: https://www.republicrecords.com
Website: https://www.facebook.com/RepublicRecordsOfficial

Genres: All types of music

Record label based in New York.

Reunion Records

Website: https://www.providentlabelgroup.com
Website: https://www.facebook.com/ProvidentLabelGroup/

Genres: Christian; Pop; Rock

Record label specialising in Christian music.

Revelation Records

PO Box 5232
Huntington Beach, CA 92615-5232
Email: webmaster@revhq.com
Website: http://www.revelationrecords.com
Website: https://www.facebook.com/revelationrecords/

Genres: Hardcore; Punk; Rock; Emo

Record label based in Huntington Beach, California.

Rhombus Records

PO Box 7938
Van Nuys, CA 91409
Fax: +1 (818) 709-8480
Email: rhombusrecords@gmail.com
Website: https://rhombus-records.com

Genres: Blues; Jazz; Latin; Reggae; World; Americana; Jazz Fusion; Traditional Jazz; Funky Jazz; Rock; Pop; Progressive Rock; Latin Rock; New Age; Contemporary Folk; Latin Jazz; Avant-Garde Jazz; Ambient Jazz

Label founded in 1986 to release the owner's music, now has an extensive list of clients.

Rhymesayers Entertainment

Minneapolis, MN
Website: https://rhymesayers.com
Website: https://www.facebook.com/Rhymesayers/

Genres: Hip-Hop

Independent hip hop record label based in Minneapolis, Minnesota, founded in 1995.

Robbins Entertainment

A&R Dept.
35 Worth St., 4th Floor
New York, NY 10013
Email: info@robbinsent.com
Website: https://www.robbinsent.com
Website: https://www.facebook.com/robbinsentertainment

Genres: Country; Dance; Electronic; Pop

Record label based in New York. Send demos as download links by email (e.g. YouSendIt / Soundcloud, etc.) or by post. No MP3 email attachments. See website for full details.

Rockzion Records

673 Valley Drive
Hermosa Beach, CA 90254
Fax: +1 (310) 379-6477
Email: rockzionrecords@rockzion.com
Website: https://rockzion.com

Genres: Christian; Rock

Record label based in Hermosa Beach, California, specialising in Christian and crossover rock.

Ropeadope Records

203 W. Atlantic Ave
Haddon Heights, NJ 08035
Email: orders@ropeadope.com
Email: publicity@ropeadope.com
Website: https://ropeadope.com
Website: https://www.facebook.com/ropeadope99/

Genres: Electronic; Folk; Indie; Jazz; Rock; Singer-Songwriter; World

Record label based in Haddon Heights, New Jersey.

Rotten Records

Website: https://www.rottenrecords.com
Website: https://soundcloud.com/rottenrecords

Genres: Extreme Metal; Hardcore; Punk

For the last 20 years, we have held an unyielding fist to the mainstream music industry. We've crushed all walls of conventional industry standards, carved our own niche and have always fought hard for our bands. With a staff of industry veterans and the power of major label distribution, we have always been on the cutting edge of extreme music, taking chances that other labels would never think about.

Round Hill Music

818 18th Ave. S, Suite 940
Nashville, TN 37203
Fax: +1 (615) 695-7706
Website: https://roundhillmusic.com

Genres: Roots

Record label with offices in New York, Los Angeles, Nashville, and London.

Rounder Records

Website: https://rounder.com
Website: https://www.facebook.com/RounderRecords/

Genres: Blues; Folk; Jazz; Rock; Roots; Americana

Describes itself as one of the world's most historic Americana and bluegrass record labels.

The Royalty Network, Inc.

Email: creative@roynet.com
Email: admin@roynet.com
Website: https://www.roynet.com
Website: https://www.facebook.com/RoyNetMusic

Genres: All types of music

Describes itself as one of the country's most esteemed independent music publishing companies, representing over 700,000 compositions. The company has been increasing its client roster dramatically from year to year, boasting a perpetually growing catalog of some of the most prolific songwriters, producers and artists across a multitude of genres.

Saddle Creek

Email: info@saddle-creek.com
Website: https://saddle-creek.com
Website: https://www.facebook.com/SaddleCreekRecords/

Genres: Indie Rock; Rock; Country Rock; Electronic

An independent record label founded in Omaha in 1993 with staff in Omaha, NE, Los Angeles, CA, New York, NY, Seattle, WA and Glasgow, Scotland (UK).

Schoolboy Records

Email: info@scooterbraun.com
Website: http://scooterbraun.com
Website: https://www.facebook.com/SBProjects

Genres: Pop

Part of a diversified entertainment and media company based in New York, with ventures integrating music, film, television, technology, and anthropology.

SCI Fidelity Records

Email: kevin@scifidelity.com
Email: allie@scifidelity.com
Website: https://scifidelity.com
Website: https://www.facebook.com/scifidelity

Genres: Blues; Electronic; Rock; Singer-Songwriter

Contact: Kevin Morris

Record label based in Boulder, Colorado.

Secret Formula Records, Inc.

Email: gary1@secretformularecords.com
Website: http://secretformularecords.com
Website: https://www.facebook.com/secretformularecords

Genres: Classical; Jazz; New Age; Acid Classic Commercial Contemporary

Electronic Non-Commercial Post Classical Dance Fusion Funk Hip-Hop Instrumental Jazz Lounge New Age Rock Relaxation Rock and Roll Soundtracks Techno Trance Trip Hop

Contact: Gary Farr

A bi-coastal record label with the corporate office in the State of Florida and the recording studio in Los Angeles California.

Secretly Canadian

213 S. Rogers
Bloomington, IN 47404
Email: info@secretlycanadian.com
Website: https://secretlycanadian.com
Website: https://www.facebook.com/SecretlyCanadian

Genres: Country; Folk; Hardcore; Indie; Pop; Punk; Rock; Roots

Record label based in Bloomington, Indiana.

Segue Records

Email: wayne@peacefulwaters.com
Website: https://www.peacefulwaters.com/segue-records

Genres: All types of music

Contact: Wayne Warnecke

An independent music company concentrating on quality new music releases of all genres.

Shady Records

Website: https://www.shadyrecords.com
Website: https://www.facebook.com/ShadyRecords

Genres: Hip-Hop; Rap; Urban

Record label specializing in hip hop music.

Shanachie Entertainment

37 East Clinton Street
Newton, NJ 07860
Email: facebook@shanachie.com
Website: http://www.shanachie.com
Website: https://www.facebook.com/shanachie.entertainment

Genres: Blues; Country; Electronic; Folk; Gospel; Jazz; R&B; Reggae; Singer-Songwriter; World

Record label based in New Jersey.

Shangri-La Projects, Inc.

PO Box 40106
Memphis, Tennessee 38174
Email: sherman@shangrilaprojects.com
Website: http://www.shangrilaprojects.com

Genres: Alternative Rock

Record label based in Memphis, Tennessee, with publishing and music tour arms to the business.

Shrapnel Records

Navato, CA
Email: shrapnel1@aol.com
Website: https://www.shrapnelrecords.com
Website: https://twitter.com/shrapnelrecords

Genres: Heavy Metal; Hard Rock; Blues; Progressive Metal; Blues Rock; Country; Guitar based; Jazz

Record label based in Navato, California.

Sick House Entertainment

Website: https://www.facebook.com/SickHouseEntertainment

Genres: All types of music

Contact: Nathan Sappington; Chandler Culler

Independent record label.

Side One Dummy Records

Email: info@sideonedummy.com
Website: https://sideonedummy.com
Website: https://www.facebook.com/SideOneDummy

Genres: Punk; Reggae; Hardcore; Ska; Alternative

Contact: Bill Armstrong; Joe Sib

Record label based in Los Angeles, California.

Signature Sound Recordings

32 Masonic Street
Northampton, MA 01060
Fax: +1 (509) 691-0457
Email: info@signaturesounds.com
Website: http://www.signaturesounds.com
Website: https://www.facebook.com/SignatureSoundsRecordings

Genres: Pop; Rock; Roots; Singer-Songwriter; Americana; Modern Folk; Indie

Record label based in Northampton, Massachusetts.

Silver Blue Productions / Joel Diamond Entertainment

3940 Laurel Canyon Boulevard, Suite 441
Studio City, CA 91604
Email: JDiamond20@aol.com
Website: https://www.joeldiamond.com

Genres: All types of music

Record label and publishing company based in Studio City, California. Handles a wide range of music, including classical.

Silver Wave Records

Boulder, CO
Email: jamesm@silverwave.com
Website: https://www.silverwave.com
Website: https://www.facebook.com/silverwaverecords/

Genres: Contemporary; World; Regional; New Age

Independent music label, specialising in World, New Age, and contemporary North American Indian music.

Six Degrees Records

PO Box 411347
San Francisco, CA 94141
Email: info@sixdegreesrecords.com
Website: http://sixdegreesrecords.com
Website: https://www.facebook.com/sixdegreesrecords

Genres: Electronic; Latin; Pop; Rock; World; Ambient; Folk; Contemporary; Classical; Dance

Record label based in San Francisco. Produces and markets accessible, genre-bending records that explore world music traditions, modern dance grooves, electronic music, and overlooked pop gems. Not generally accepting unsolicited demos, unless “you are determined”, in which case send a private link to your music. No attachments.

Skaggs Family Records

PO Box 2478
Hendersonville, TN 37077
Fax: +1 (615) 264-8899
Email: info@skaggsfamilyrecords.com
Website: https://skaggsfamilyrecords.com
Website: https://www.facebook.com/rickyskaggsofficial

Genres: Blues; Country; Roots; Christian

Record label based in Hendersonville, Tennessee.

Skate Mountain Records

Email: info@skatemountain.com
Website: https://www.skatemountainrecords.com
Website: https://www.facebook.com/skatemountainrecords/

Genres: Alternative; Americana; Blues; Country; Hip-Hop; Pop; R&B; Rap; Rock; Rock and Roll; Roots Rock; Singer-Songwriter; Soul; Soundtracks; Classic; Commercial; Mainstream; Soulful Rock; Alternative Soul; Alternative Country; Garage; Punk

Bringing Alabama to the forefront of the music industry. With a history of success in film production, we are uniting Alabama's rich music scene with the global film business while concurrently developing and nurturing local and national talent.

This label is a family. With an ear to the street and an eye on quality, we are a close-knit group of artists, musicians, filmmakers and producers collaborating to create a truly unique one-stop shop for music and film production.

Currently creating a catalog of original music that's specifically for the filmmaker.

Music from a variety of genres is available for licensing. With our vast resources in the entertainment industry from music and film experience, we uniquely provide the ability to connect artist with artist, filmmaker with musician. We produce custom music for film allowing the filmmaker to have a creative say as well as providing our traditional catalog of bad ass music.

Founded by music lovers with the artist in mind. The structure is not designed to just sell records; but to create damn good records. The rest will speak for itself.

Slip-N-Slide Records

Email: demos@slipnsliderecords.net
Email: ryan@slipnsliderecords.net
Website: https://www.slipnsliderecords.com
Website: https://soundcloud.com/officialslipnsliderecords

Genres: Hip-Hop; Pop; Rap; Reggae; Urban; R&B

Record label hailing from South Florida. Responsible for selling over 30 million records. Send demos by email.

Slumberland Records

PO Box 19029
Oakland CA, 94619
Email: demos@slumberlandrecords.com
Email: slr@slumberlandrecords.com
Website: http://www.slumberlandrecords.com
Website: https://www.facebook.com/SlumberlandRecords

Genres: Post Punk; Indie; Pop; Punk; Lo-fi; Shoegaze

Record label based in Oakland, California. Send query by email with links to music online. No MP3 attachments.

Slush Fund Recordings

Email: david@slushfund.co
Website: https://www.slushfund.co

Genres: Rock

Rock record label established in 2007.

Smog Veil Records

1521 Alton Rd #625
Miami Beach, FL 33139
Fax: +1 (904) 212-0401
Email: franklisa@aol.com
Website: https://www.smogveil.com
Website: https://www.facebook.com/Smog-Veil-Records-66696836527/

Genres: Underground Rock and Roll

Handles bombastic underground rock n' roll.

Sonic Safari Music

Jonkey Enterprises
663 West California Avenue
Glendale, CA 91203-1505
Email: chuck@sonicsafarimusic.com
Website: http://www.sonicsafarimusic.com
Website: https://www.facebook.com/SonicSafariMusic/

Genres: Ethnic; World; Traditional

Contact: Chuck Jonkey

Record label based in Glendale, California.

Sony Music Entertainment – Legacy Recordings

Website: https://www.legacyrecordings.com/
Website: https://www.facebook.com/LegacyRecordings/

Genres: Blues; Country; Folk; Jazz; Pop; R&B; Reggae; Rock; Hip-Hop; Gospel; Soundtracks; Ethnic; World

Re-releases and compilations / box-sets from the parent company's back catalogue. No submissions.

Sony Music Entertainment

25 Madison Avenue
New York, NY 10010
Website: https://www.sonymusic.com
Website: https://www.facebook.com/sonymusic/

Genres: All types of music

International music group with offices around the world. Only accepts demos submitted through an established music industry professional, such as a manager, lawyer, agent, producer, artist, programmer, or tastemaker.

Sony Music Nashville

Website: https://www.sonymusicnashville.com
Website: https://www.facebook.com/SonyMusicNashville/

Genres: Country

Country label based in Nashville, Tennessee.

Sound Feelings

18375 Ventura Blvd. #8000
Tarzana, CA 91356
Email: information@soundfeelings.com
Website: http://www.soundfeelings.com
Website: https://www.facebook.com/soundfeelingspublishing

Genres: New Age; Pop; Relaxation

Contact: Howard Richman

Music therapy for transformation offers drug-free audio products for specific illnesses and conditions. Our recordings provide a music therapy alternative to traditional expressive arts therapy.

Southern Lord Recordings

Email: info@southernlord.com
Website: https://southernlord.com
Website: https://www.facebook.com/SLadmin

Genres: Metal; Hard Rock

Heavy metal label based in Los Angeles, California. Send demos as bandcamp stream or similar. No zip files, MP3, or WAV. Do not submit via social media.

Southland Records

PO Box 15086
Odessa, TX 79762
Email: realcountry@southlandrecords.com
Website: https://www.southlandrecords.com

Genres: Traditional Country; Swing; Gospel; Pop; Rock

Record label based in Odessa, Texas, specialising in Western Swing, traditional Country, gospel, pop, and rock.

Spinefarm Records

1755 Broadway
New York, NY 10019

UK OFFICE
Beaumont House,
Kensington Village,
Avonmore Rd.,
London W14 8TS

FINLAND OFFICE
Merimiehenkatu 36 D
00150 Helsinki
Finland
Email: info@spinefarmrecords.com
Email: contact@spinefarm.fi
Website: https://www.spinefarmrecords.com
Website: https://www.facebook.com/spinefarm

Genres: Hard Rock; Metal

Record label with offices in New York, London, and Helsinki.

Spiral Galaxy Entertainment

Los Angeles, CA 91343
Email: spiralgalaxyent@gmail.com
Website: https://spiralgalaxyent.com
Website: https://www.facebook.com/Spiral-Galaxy-Entertainment-237987439580429/

Genres: Dance; Jazz; Hip-Hop; Gospel; Pop; R&B

Contact: Reggie Calloway

Record label based in Los Angeles, California.

Stackhouse & BluEsoterica

3516 Holmes Street
Kansas City, MO 64109
Email: jim@bluesoterica.com
Email: Stackhouse232@aol.com
Website: http://www.bluesoterica.com

Genres: Blues; World

Contact: Jim O'Neal

Record label based in Kansas City, Missouri.

Star Time Intl

Website: https://www.startimeintl.com
Website: https://www.facebook.com/StarTimeInternational

Genres: All types of music

Record label based in New York.

Stef Angel Music

Email: musicsubmission@stefangelmusic.com
Email: info@stefangelmusic.com
Website: https://stefangelmusic.com

Genres: All types of music

Send query by email with link to your music online, or for instructions on where to send physical submissions.

Stones Throw Records

2658 Griffith Park Boulevard #504
Los Angeles, CA 90039
Website: https://www.stonesthrow.com
Website: https://soundcloud.com/stonesthrow

Genres: All types of music

Record label based in Los Angeles, California.

Strange Music Inc.

Peppergreen Media
2248 Broadway #1127
New York, NY 10024
Website: http://www.strangemusic.com

Genres: Alternative

Record label based in New York.

Strictly Rhythm

New York
Email: demos@strictly.com
Website: http://strictly.com
Website: https://www.facebook.com/strictlyrhythm/

Genres: House

House record label. Send query by email.

Sub Pop Records

2013 Fourth Avenue, Third Floor
Seattle, WA 98121
Fax: +1 (206) 441-8245
Email: info@subpop.com
Website: https://www.subpop.com
Website: https://soundcloud.com/subpop/

Genres: Americana; Electronic; Folk; Indie; Metal; Pop; Rock; Punk; Singer-Songwriter

Record label based in Seattle, the original home of Nirvana, Soundgarden and Mudhoney. Send demos via Soundcloud. See Facebook page for details.

Subliminal Records

Email: tracks@subliminalrecords.com
Website: http://www.subliminalrecords.com
Website: https://www.facebook.com/subliminalrecords

Genres: Electronic; Dance; House; Techno

New York house and techno imprint. Send demos by email.

Suburban Noize Records

Burbank, CA
Website: https://suburbannoizerecords.com
Website: https://www.facebook.com/suburbannoizerecords

Genres: Hard Rock; Hip-Hop; Punk; Underground

Record label based in Burbank, California.

Sugar Hill Records

Website: https://www.sugarhillrecords.com
Website: https://www.facebook.com/sugarhillrecords

Genres: Blues; Roots; Americana

Label handling bluegrass, Americana and roots.

Sumerian Records

Email: info@sumerianrecords.com
Website: http://www.sumerianrecords.com
Website: https://www.facebook.com/SumerianRecords

Genres: All types of music

Record label based in Los Angeles, California.

Summit Records, Inc
PO Box 13692
Tempe, AZ 85284-3692
Email: sales@summitrecords.com
Website: https://www.summitrecords.com

Genres: Classical; Blues; Jazz

Record label founded in the late 1980s, based in Tempe, Arizona.

Sunnyside Records
Email: francois@sunnysiderecords.com
Website: http://www.sunnysiderecords.com
Website: https://www.facebook.com/SunnysideRecords

Genres: Jazz; Blues; World

Describes itself as a relaxed, independent label, with an acceptance of any jazz style.

Suretone Records
1411 5th Street, #200
Santa Monica, CA 91401
Website: http://www.suretone.com

Genres: Rock

Record label based in Santa Monica, California.

Surfdog Records
Attn: A&R
1126 South Coast Highway 101
Encinitas, CA 92024
Fax: +1 (760) 944-7808
Email: demo@surfdog.com
Website: https://surfdog.com

Genres: Contemporary; Folk; Indie; Pop; Punk; R&B; Hip-Hop; Rap; Reggae; Rock; Singer-Songwriter; Urban

Record label based in Encinitas, California. Send demo by email as links to music online (no MP3 attachments).

Surfview Records
Website: http://www.surfviewrecords.com

Genres: All types of music

Record label based in Phoenix, Arizona.

Symbiotic Records
Los Angeles, CA
Website: http://www.symbioticrecords.com
Website: https://www.facebook.com/symbioticrecords

Genres: All types of music

Contact: Eric Knight; Jerjan Alim

Full service record label based in Los Angeles, California. Send demo using form on website.

Team Love Records
New Paltz, NY
Email: info@team-love.com
Website: https://test.team-love.com
Website: https://twitter.com/teamloverecords

Genres: All types of music

Record label based in New Paltz, New York. Send submissions by email as Soundcloud or Bandcamp track / playlist. No Microsoft attachments or Google Drive links.

Tee Pee Records
Website: https://teepeerecords.com
Website: https://www.facebook.com/teepeerecords

Genres: Indie; Metal; Punk; Rock

New York-based label dealing in indie, metal, punk and rock.

Terminus Records
Atlanta, GA
Email: admin@terminusrecords.com
Website: https://terminusrecords.com
Website: https://www.facebook.com/TerminusRecords/

Genres: Rock; Modern Rock; Blues

Record label based in Atlanta, Georgia.

Thin Man Entertainment

Email: Submissions@ThinManEntertainment.com
Email: AR@ThinManEntertainment.com
Website: http://thinmanentertainment.com
Website: https://www.facebook.com/profile.php?id=100070572305110

Genres: Alternative Rock; Gothic; Industrial; Jazz; Punk; Psychebilly; Underground

Record label focused on underground music of all genres. Send submissions by email.

Third Man Records

623 7th Avenue South
Nashville, TN 37203
Email: nashvillestore@thirdmanrecords.com
Website: https://thirdmanrecords.com
Website: https://www.facebook.com/ThirdManRecords/

Genres: All types of music

Record label based in Nashville, Tennessee. Considers itself "an innovator in the world of vinyl records and a boundary pusher in the world of recorded music".

37 Records & Management

3617 East Broadway Avenue #19PH
Long Beach, CA 90803
Email: Steven@37records.com
Email: Info37records@aol.com
Website: http://www.37records.com
Website: https://www.facebook.com/37records/

Genres: All types of music

Contact: Steven McClintock

Record label and management company based in Long Beach, California.

300 Entertainment

New York, NY
Email: info@threehundred.biz
Website: https://300ent.com

Genres: All types of music

Music company based in New York.

ThrillerTracks

Email: contact@thrillertracks.com
Website: https://www.thrillertracks.com

Genres: Electronic Ambient Instrumental Soundtracks

Contact: Shane Cormier

An indie music label, specializing in background production music for film and video. Our music has been featured in BMW and Lexus commercials in the Netherlands, Germany and Italy.

Thrive Records

Email: demos@thrivemusic.com
Email: info@thrivemusic.com
Website: https://www.thrivemusic.com

Genres: Alternative; Dance; Electronic; Indie; Rock

Send demo by email.

Throne of Blood Records

New York, NY
Email: james@throneofbloodmusic.com
Website: http://www.throneofbloodmusic.com
Website: https://www.facebook.com/tobrecnyc/

Genres: Electronic; Club; Disco; House

Record label based in New York, specialising in House, Electro, Disco, and Club music.

Thump Records

Email: customersupport@thumprecords.com
Website: https://thumprecords.com
Website: https://www.facebook.com/thumprecords

Genres: Dance; Electronic; Latin; Pop; R&B; Rap; Hip-Hop; Urban

Home of the World's Favorite Party Music! We specialize in music from the streets representing decades of great sounds.

Tommy Boy

Website: https://www.tommyboy.com
Website: https://twitter.com/TommyBoyRecords

Genres: Electronic; Hip-Hop; Latin Hip-Hop; Dance; Alternative; Pop

Hip Hop and Electronic label founded in New York City in 1981.

TommyBoy Entertainment LLC

New York, NY
Website: https://www.tommyboy.com
Website: https://twitter.com/TommyBoyRecords

Genres: Hip-Hop; Dance; Electronic; Alternative; Pop

Legendary Hip Hop and Electronic label founded in NYC in 1981.

Tooth & Nail Records

P.O. Box 12698
Seattle, WA 98111
Email: resume@toothandnail.com
Website: https://www.toothandnail.com
Website: https://www.facebook.com/toothandnail

Genres: Alternative; Rock

Record label based in Seattle, tracing its origins back to the early '90s punk and hardcore music scene. Send your best three tracks on CD by post.

Topshelf Records

540 NE Tillamook Street
Portland, OR 97212
Email: info@topshelfrecords.com
Website: https://www.topshelfrecords.com
Website: https://soundcloud.com/topshelfrecords

Genres: All types of music

Record label based in Portland, Oregon. Not accepting demos as at August 2022.

Toucan Cove Entertainment

800 Fifth Avenue #101-292
Seattle, WA 98104-3191
Website: https://toucancove.com
Website: https://twitter.com/toucancove

Genres: All types of music

Full service entertainment company.

Touch and Go Records

Po Box 25520
Chicago, IL 60625
Website: http://www.touchandgorecords.com

Genres: Alternative; Hardcore; Indie; Punk; Rock; Singer-Songwriter

Not currently accepting demos.

Triple Crown Records

PO Box 222132
Great Neck, NY 11022
Email: info@triplecrownrecords.com
Website: http://www.triplecrownrecords.com
Website: https://www.facebook.com/triplecrownrecords

Genres: Alternative; Rock

Record label based in Great Neck, New York.

Tuff City Music Group

Website: https://tuffcity.com
Website: https://www.facebook.com/TuffCityRecords/

Genres: Blues; R&B; Jazz; Funk; Soul; Hip-Hop

Originally rooted in hip-hop, has transitioned its focus toward rescuing thousands of blues, jazz, funk, soul and R&B treasures from obscurity.

Ultra Music

Email: info@ultrarecords.com
Website: https://www.ultrarecords.com
Website: https://www.facebook.com/UltraRecordsOfficial/

Genres: Electronic; Pop; Rap; Hip-Hop; Reggae; World; Dance

Describes itself as "one step ahead in the world of dance music" and "the leading independent electronic label".

Unfun Records

PO Box 40307
Berkeley, CA 94704
Email: johnny@unfunrecords.com
Email: unfunrecords@hotmail.com
Website: http://unfunrecords.com

Genres: All types of music

Record label based in California. Send demo on CD by post.

Union Entertainment Group (UEG), Inc.

Email: info@ueginc.com
Website: http://www.ueginc.com

Genres: All types of music

Record label based in the Los Angeles area since 1987, with offices in California, Texas, Florida, Washington, Canada, and Amsterdam.

Universal Music Group Nashville

Website: https://www.umgnashville.com
Website: https://www.facebook.com/UMGNashville

Genres: Country; Rock; Americana

Record label based in Nashville, Tennessee.

Urband & Lazar

Los Angeles, CA
Email: help@urbandlazar.com
Website: https://www.urbandlazar.com

Genres: Indie Rock; Alternative; Singer-Songwriter

A premier, Grammy-Award winning music publishing company.

Vagrant Records

Website: https://vagrant.com
Website: https://www.facebook.com/vagrantrecords

Genres: All types of music

Record label based in California. Focuses on rock, but features artists in a variety of other genres including folk, soul, electronic, and pop.

Valley Entertainment

Email: jon@valley-entertainment.com
Email: erika@valley-entertainment.com
Website: https://www.valley-entertainment.com
Website: https://www.facebook.com/valleyent

Genres: Jazz; New Age; Rock; World; Blues; Country; Celtic; Instrumental

A privately owned record label that was founded in the mid-nineties. The label includes an eclectic repertoire from pop to alternative, with focus on singer-songwriters, modern Irish musicians and World music.

Van Richter

Email: manager@vanrichter.net
Email: vanrichterrec@gmail.com
Website: https://www.vanrichter.net
Website: https://www.facebook.com/vanrichter.net/

Genres: Industrial; Gothic; Ambient; Synthpop

Our Artists cover the entire spectrum of the Industrial sub genres including Aggro, Electro, Darkwave, Noise, and Ambient.

Verve Label Group

Universal Music Group
2220 Colorado Ave
Santa Monica, CA 90404
Website: https://www.vervelabelgroup.com
Website: https://www.facebook.com/ververecords/

Genres: Jazz; Contemporary; Pop; R&B

Record label based in Santa Monica, California.

Victory Records

Fax: +1 (312) 666-8665
Email: info@victoryrecords.com

Website: https://victoryrecords.com
Website: https://www.facebook.com/VictoryRecords

Genres: Metal; Rock; Indie; Hardcore; Punk

Formed in 1989, it separated itself from the pack as the definitive independent label for punk, hardcore, emo, metal and alternative. Supplying 30 years of formative music to diehard audiences everywhere, the Chicago-bred and -based label cranked up the voices of three generations of iconoclasts and built a culture without compromise.

Vineyard Worship

Email: info@vineyardworship.com
Website: https://www.vineyardworship.com
Website: https://www.facebook.com/VineyardWorship

Genres: Christian

Record label releasing Christian music.

Viper Records

Website: https://www.viperrecords.com
Website: https://www.facebook.com/viperrecords/

Genres: Hip-Hop; Rap

A boutique indie label created to level an uneven playing field between artists and labels. Approach via online contact form. Tries to respond, but not always possible due to volume of submissions.

Visionary Music Group

Website: http://www.teamvisionary.com
Website: https://www.facebook.com/VisionaryMusicGroup

Genres: Urban

Not accepting enquiries as at October 2022.

VP Records

89-05 138th Street,
Jamaica, NY 11435

FLORIDA:
6022 S.W. 21st Street
Miramar, FL 33023

LONDON:
Room 302, Edinburgh House
170 Kennington Lane
London
SE11 5DP
UK

JAMAICA, WI:
1 Upper Sandringham Ave,
Kingston 10, Jamaica
Fax: +1 (718) 658-3573
Email: information@vprecords.com
Website: https://www.vprecords.com
Website: https://soundcloud.com/vp_records

Genres: Reggae

Record label based in Jamaica, New York, with offices in Florida, London, and Jamaica.

VSR Music Group

3520 E Brown Rd
Mesa, AZ 85213
Email: vsrmusicgroup@gmail.com
Website: http://vsrmusic.com
Website: https://www.facebook.com/VSRMusicGroup

Genres: Christian Rock

Looking for Christ-centered artists who are willing to share the Word of God through music.

Warner Music Group (WMG)

1633 Broadway
New York, NY 10019
Website: https://www.wmg.com
Website: https://www.facebook.com/warnermusicgroup

Genres: All types of music

No direct submissions. Demos should be submitted to specific label via an established industry professional, such as a manager, agent, lawyer, journalist, or existing artist, etc.

Warner Music Nashville

Website: https://www.warnermusicnashville.com
Website: https://www.facebook.com/WarnerMusicNashville

Genres: Country

Country label based in Nashville Tennessee.

Warner Records

1633 Broadway
New York, NY 10019
Website: https://www.warnerrecords.com

Genres: All types of music

Record label based in New York.

Warrior Records

7095 Hollywood Blvd., #826
Hollywood, CA 90028
Email: info@warriorrecords.com
Website: https://www.warriorrecords.com
Website: https://www.facebook.com/OfficialWarriorRecords/

Genres: All types of music

Contact: Jim Ervin

Accepts unsolicited submissions but does not review websites. Send three or four tracks and type all correspondence. Include SASE or email address for response, and picture/bio if available. Expect response to take at least 6-8 weeks.

Watertower Music

Email: wtmsupport@Warnerbros.com
Website: http://www.watertower-music.com
Website: https://soundcloud.com/watertowermusic

Genres: Soundtracks

Record label based in Los Angeles, California, specialising in movie soundtracks.

Waveform Records

Email: webguest@waveformhq.com
Website: https://www.waveformrecords.com
Website: https://www.facebook.com/waveformrecords

Genres: Downtempo Electronic; Chill; Ambient

Handles mid to downtempo chill and ambient music they call "exotic electronica".

Send query by email with links to music online.

Wax Records Inc.

Email: info@waxrecords.com
Website: https://www.waxrecords.com

Genres: Pop; Rock

Always looking to expand their roster with new and exciting talent. Send query by email with links to music online. No large file attachments.

Waxploitation Records

Los Angeles
Email: artists@waxploitation.com
Website: https://waxploitation.com
Website: https://soundcloud.com/waxploitation

Genres: Hip-Hop

Record label based in Los Angeles, California.

West Clark Records

Email: westclarkrecords@gmail.com
Website: https://www.facebook.com/westclarkrecords
Website: https://westclarkrecords.bandcamp.com

Genres: Electronic Hard Heavy Non-Commercial Mainstream Underground Acoustic Alternative Club Dance Drum and Bass Dubstep Emo Garage Guitar based Hardcore Indie Lo-fi Metal Punk Remix Rock Rock and Roll Rockabilly Ska Surf Techno

A little label created in a basement in the suburbs of St. Louis with nothing more than a dream.

Wicked Cool Records

New York
Website: http://wickedcoolrecords.com
Website: https://www.facebook.com/WickedCoolRecords/

Genres: Garage Rock; Rock and Roll

Label based in New York, created in 2005 to support new Rock and Roll.

Wild Records

Los Angeles, CA
Website: https://wildrecordsusa.com
Website: https://twitter.com/wildrecords

Genres: Blues; Garage; Rockabilly; Soul; Surf

Contact: Reb Kennedy

Record label based in Los Angeles, California.

Word Records

Website: https://www.curb.com/WordRecords/
Website: https://www.facebook.com/curbrecords

Genres: Contemporary; Christian; Country; Hip-Hop; Rap; Rock

Faith-based record label.

Yep Roc Records

Email: info@yeproc.com
Website: https://www.yeproc.com
Website: https://www.facebook.com/yeproc

Genres: Blues; Country; Folk; Pop; Rock; Roots

We believe in the vision of each of our Artists. We strive to serve each project based on its unique characteristics. Through strong promotional and marketing efforts, our goal is to reach as large an audience as possible with each new release.

UK Record Labels

For the most up-to-date listings of these and hundreds of other record labels, visit https://www.musicsocket.com/recordlabels

To claim your ***free*** *access to the site, please see the back of this book.*

Aardvark Records Ltd

75 Alderwood Parc
Penryn
Cornwall
TR10 8RL
Email: sophsweet@gmail.com
Email: mail@aardvarkrecords.co.uk
Website: http://www.aardvarkrecords.co.uk

Genres: Dance; Rock; Pop; Acoustic; Folk; New Age; World; Chill; Downtempo; Break Beat; Drum and Bass; Traditional Soul; Traditional R&B; Ambient Chill; Commercial Dance; House; Techno; Techno Trance; Alternative Rock; Progressive Rock; Blues; Celtic; Indie; Reggae; Soul

Contact: Andy Reeve; Sophie Sweatman

Record label based in Cornwall. Describes itself as a Fair Trade record label and music publisher; staunchly independent; and green. See website for demo submission guidelines.

Acid Jazz Records

146 Bethnal Green Road
London
E2 6DG
Website: https://www.acidjazz.co.uk

Genres: All types of music, except: Black Metal; Metal; Rap

Record label based in London, founded in 1987 at the start of the "acieed" explosion.

Actual Size Music

Website: https://www.actualsizemusic.org.uk

Genres: Experimental

Artist run record label based in London, UK and releasing experimental material. Run as a means for the artists operating the label to release their own music, so does not sign other artists.

AD Music

5 Albion Road
Bungay
Suffolk
NR35 1LQ
Email: contact@admusicshop.com
Website: https://www.admusicshop.com
Website: https://www.facebook.com/ADmusiconline

Genres: Instrumental Electronic; Chill

Record label based in Bungay, Suffolk. Releases electronica, chill out and instrumental synth electronic music (not dance) only. No submissions.

Adasam Limited

Website: http://www.adasam.co.uk/

Genres: All types of music

Home to a number of independent record labels, covering a wide range of genres. See individual websites of labels for specific details.

Alcopop! Records

Email: jack@ilovealcopop.co.uk
Email: LukeAnR@hotmail.com
Website: https://ilovealcopop.co.uk
Website: https://www.facebook.com/ilovealcopop

Genres: Alternative; Indie

Record label founded in Oxford in 2006, home to independent music.

Alex Tronic Records

Email: info@alextronicrecords.co.uk
Website: http://www.alextronicrecords.co.uk
Website: https://www.facebook.com/Alex-Tronic-Records-Recording-Studios-281100465296557

Genres: Dance; Electronic; Downtempo; Ambient; House; Drum and Bass; Break Beat; Hip-Hop

Contact: Becki Bardot (A&R)

Record label based in Edinburgh, Scotland. Prefers to receive CDs in the post, but will accept links to music online by email. Will not download large files, however.

Almighty Records Limited

PO Box 414
Stroud
GL6 1HR
Email: info@almightyrecords.com
Website: https://www.almightyrecords.com
Website: https://www.facebook.com/AlmightyRecordLabel/

Genres: Dance; Pop

Record label based in Stroud, Gloucestershire.

Alter Ego Records

Email: home@alteregorecords.com
Website: http://www.alteregorecords.com
Website: http://www.label-worx.com/demo/alteregomusic

Genres: Trance; Progressive; House

Record label based in Cardiff. Send demos by uploading to DemoBox online only.

Amazon Records

Email: frank@amazonrecords.co.uk
Website: http://www.amazonrecords.co.uk
Website: https://www.facebook.com/amazonrecords/

Genres: Indie; Pop; Rock; Punk; Folk; Country

Once again taking up the challenge of signing new and interesting artists. Contact by email.

Amber Artists

Email: records@amberartists.com
Website: http://www.amberartists.com

Genres: Commercial; Contemporary; Pop

Independent artist management company and independent record company.

Ambiel

15 Hatch Lane
Chigford
London
E4 6LP
Email: pr@ambiel.co.uk
Website: https://ambielmusic.com
Website: https://www.facebook.com/ambielmusic

Genres: All types of music

Make contact through Facebook. Do not send submissions or artist/promo packs through contact form on website. Aims to listen to everything sent to them, but cannot respond to everyone.

The Animal Farm

4th Floor, Block A
Tower Bridge Business Complex
100 Clements Road
London
SE16 4DG
Email: info@theanimalfarm.co.uk
Website: http://www.theanimalfarm.co.uk
Website: https://www.facebook.com/theanimalfarmmusic

Genres: Indie; Pop; Rock; Acoustic; Alternative; Metal

An independently owned music company offering a wide range of creative and business services to artists and songwriters: produces and mixes records and writes songs in their two recording studios in London; manages artists and songwriters; run an independent record label and a publishing company and a booking agency. Send query with link to music online by email or via online contact form.

ARC Music Productions International

A & R Department
PO Box 111
East Grinstead
West Sussex
RH19 4FZ
Email: anr@arcmusic.co.uk
Email: info@arcmusic.co.uk
Website: https://www.arcmusic.co.uk
Website: https://www.facebook.com/arcmusicprod/

Genres: World; Folk; Celtic; Latin

Record label based in East Grinstead, West Sussex. Send demo as attachment by email (if less than 10MB), or by download site e.g. yousendit if larger. Alternatively send CD and info by post.

Ariwa Sounds Ltd

34 Whitehorse Lane
London
SE25 6RE
Email: info@ariwa.com
Email: ariwastudios@gmail.com
Website: https://www.ariwa.com
Website: https://www.facebook.com/Ariwasounds

Genres: Dub; Roots; Reggae; Electronic

Produces Dub, Lovers Rock, and Roots & Culture reggae music.

Armellodie

Glasgow
Scotland
Email: info@armellodie.com
Website: http://www.armellodie.com
Website: https://twitter.com/Armellotweet

Genres: Leftfield Rock; Indie; Avant-Garde

Record label based in Glasgow, Scotland, describing itself as "a tiny wee independent label, stable, collective, R.O.C.K consortium,".

Audiobulb Records

Sheffield
Email: contact@audiobulb.com
Website: https://www.audiobulb.com
Website: https://www.facebook.com/audiobulb/

Genres: Dance; Electronic Experimental Downtempo Avant-Garde Alternative Leftfield; Ambient

An exploratory music label designed to promote creativity in all its forms. Releases artist works on CD and download formats as well as multimedia works, VST, audio hardware and other creative tools. Works supported by this label often explore the interface between the electronic and natural world. We embrace the complexity of unique electronics, intricate acoustics and detailed microsounds.

Backwater Records

Website: https://backwaterrecords.com
Website: https://soundcloud.com/backwater-records

Genres: Alternative Country; Acid Folk; Psychedelic Pop Rock; Singer-Songwriter

Suffolk-based label releasing Suffolk-based bands/artists.

Banquet Records

52 Eden Street
Kingston
Surrey
KT1 1EE
Email: shop@banquetrecords.com
Website: https://www.banquetrecords.com/banquet-label
Website: https://www.facebook.com/banquetrecords/

Genres: Hardcore; Indie; Punk

Record shop in Kingston, Surrey, with its own record label.

Barely Breaking Even Records

Arch 376
10 Helmsley Place
London
E8 3SB
Email: staff@bbemusic.com
Website: https://www.bbemusic.com
Website: https://www.facebook.com/bbemusic/

Genres: Dance; Jazz; Funk; Techno; Garage; Hip-Hop; Disco

Record label based in London.

Basick Records

Email: info@basickrecords.com
Website: https://www.basickrecords.com
Website: https://soundcloud.com/basickrecords

Genres: Metal; Progressive

A fiercely heavy and progressive record label from London, UK.

Beggars Group

17-19 Alma Road
London
SW18 1AA
Email: banquet@beggars.com
Website: https://beggars.com

Genres: Indie

Record label with offices around the world.

Big Dada Recordings

PO Box 4296
London
SE11 4WW
Email: demos@ninjatune.net
Website: https://www.bigdada.com
Website: https://soundcloud.com/bigdadasound

Genres: Hip-Hop; Alternative Hip-Hop; Grime

Record label based in London. Started as an underground hip hop label, but now releases a full range of Black Music. Send query by email only with links to MP3 files, soundcloud, pages, or websites. No MP3 attachments. Response if interested. Do not chase for response.

Big Scary Monsters Recording Company

Email: connor@bsmrocks.com
Email: dave@bsmrocks.com
Website: https://bsmrocks.com/
Website: https://www.facebook.com/bigscarymonsters

Genres: Post Rock; Punk; Alternative; Hardcore; Acoustic

Record label based in Oxford. Send query by email describing your act and providing links to your music online.

Black Acre Records

Bristol
Email: hello@blackacrerecords.co.uk
Website: http://theblackacre.co.uk

Genres: Electronic

Electronic record label based in Bristol. Send query by email with links to music online.

Black Butter Records

London
Email: info@black-butter.co.uk
Email: demos@black-butter.co.uk
Website: https://www.black-butter.com
Website: https://soundcloud.com/black-butter-records

Genres: Dance; Hip-Hop; Urban

Record label based in London. Send query by email with "Demo" in the subject line, including Soundcloud links.

Blindsight Records

Email: info@blindsightrecords.co.uk
Website: http://www.blindsightrecords.co.uk
Website: https://soundcloud.com/blindsight-records

Genres: Rock; Electronic; Ambient; Post Rock; Hardcore; Metal

Record label based in the United Kingdom. For demo submissions make contact by email, or use Soundcloud.

Bohemian Jukebox

Email: recordings@bohemianjukebox.com
Website: https://www.bohemianjukebox.com
Website: https://soundcloud.com/bencalvert

Genres: Post Folk; Singer-Songwriter; Psychedelic; Alternative Acoustic; Leftfield Acoustic; Experimental

Contact: Ben Calvert

Record label with offices in Birmingham. Works with Post-Folk, Alternative and Psychedelic lyric-centric songwriters who have a way with poetics.

Bomber Music Ltd

125-135 Preston Road
London
BN1 6AF
Email: postbox@bombermusic.com
Website: https://www.bombermusic.com
Website: https://www.facebook.com/bombermusic

Genres: Punk; Rock and Roll; Rockabilly; Reggae; Ska; Underground;

Label set up in 2010 by an independent music company, describing itself as the UK's leading alternative music publisher.

Border Community

Website: http://www.bordercommunity.com
Website: https://soundcloud.com/border-community

Genres: Electronic

Record label based in London. Send streaming links via online contact form.

Boslevan Records

Email: boslevanrecords@gmail.com
Email: vinosangre@gmail.com
Website: https://boslevanrecords.co.uk
Website: https://www.facebook.com/BoslevanRecords

Genres: Hardcore; Indie; Punk; Punk Rock

DIY record label based in Cornwall.

Botchit & Scarper Records

Website: https://www.botchitandscarper.com
Website: https://www.facebook.com/botchit

Genres: Break Beat

Record label founded in 1995. Describes itself as unique in present times, in that it concentrates on artist development; and "has reinvented the way breakbeats impact the dance world".

Brain Bomb Productions (BBP)

Website: https://www.brainbomb.com/
Website: https://soundcloud.com/brainbomb

Genres: Ambient; Chill; Downtempo; Break Beat; House; Techno; Tribal; Trance; Drum and Bass

Contact: Luke Harrison

Small indie label that has grown organically over many years into a high impact producer of music audio and video productions.

Burning Shed Limited

Unit B, Yarefield Park
Old Hall Road
Norwich
NR4 6FF
Email: support@burningshed.com
Website: https://burningshed.com

Genres: Ambient; Electronic; Singer-Songwriter; Progressive; Rock

Contact: Tim Bowness; Peter Chilvers; Pete Morgan

Online label and record store. Send demos by post or as emails with download links. No attachments. Response not guaranteed unless interested.

Buzz Records

Email: studio@thebuzzgroup.co.uk
Website: https://thebuzzgroup.co.uk
Website: https://www.facebook.com/buzzpublicity

Genres: Alternative Roots; Blues; Country; Folk; Alternative Blues

A small independent alternative bluses label focusing on "music that has an insurgent twist and an original angle, dragging old-time sounds kicking and screaming into the 21st century." Focussing now on a single artist, so not taking on any new acts.

Buzzin' Fly Records

Website: http://www.buzzinfly.com
Website: https://www.facebook.com/buzzinflyrecords/

Genres: Electronic; House; Techno

Contact: Ben Watt

Record label based in London. On hiatus since 2013.

Candlelight Records

Beaumont House
Kensington Village
Avonmore Rd
London
W14 8TS
Email: info@spinefarmrecords.com
Website: https://www.candlelightrecords.co.uk
Website: https://www.facebook.com/candlelightrecords/

Genres: Metal

Metal record label based in London, with offices in New York and Helsinki.

Caritas Records

Achmore
Moss Road
Ullapool
Ross-shire
IV26 2TF
Email: caritas-records@caritas-music.co.uk
Email: info@caritas-music.co.uk
Website: https://www.caritas-music.co.uk

Genres: Classical

Contact: Katharine Douglas

Record label handling Classical and Choral music.

Champion Records

181 High Street
Harlesden
London
NW10 4TE
Email: rob@championrecords.co.uk
Email: raj@championrecords.co.uk
Website: https://www.championrecords.co.uk
Website: https://www.facebook.com/championrecords/

Genres: Garage; House; Singer-Songwriter

Record label based in Harlesden, London.

Chandos Records Ltd

Chandos House
1 Commerce Park
Commerce Way
Colchester
Essex
CO2 8HX
Fax: +44 (0) 1206 225201
Website: https://www.chandos.net

Genres: Classical

Classical record label, based in Colchester, Essex.

Chemikal Underground Records

Glasgow
Email: info@chemikal.co.uk
Website: https://chemikal.co.uk
Website: https://soundcloud.com/chemikal-underground

Genres: Alternative

Record label based in Glasgow, Scotland.

Cherry Red Records

Power Road Studios
114 Power Road
London

W4 5PY
Fax: +44 (0) 20 8747 4030
Email: infonet@cherryred.co.uk
Email: ideas@cherryred.co.uk
Website: https://www.cherryred.co.uk
Website: https://www.facebook.com/CherryRedRecords

Genres: All types of music

A proudly independent record label making noise in West London for more than 40 years.

Chocolate Fireguard Music Ltd

PO Box 461
Huddersfield
West Yorkshire
HD5 8WL
Email: info@chocolatefireguard.co.uk
Website: http://www.chocolatefireguard.co.uk
Website: https://www.facebook.com/ChocolateFireguardMusic
Website: http://www.myspace.com/chocolatefireguardmusic

Genres: Dance; Electronic; Hip-Hop; Rock

Record label based in Huddersfield, West Yorkshire. Always looking for new music, so submit your tracks if you think they are right for this label after consulting the website.

Circuit Records

c/o Higher Rhythm Ltd
53-57 Nether Hall Road
Doncaster
South Yorkshire
DN1 2PG
Email: mail@circuitrecords.co.uk
Website: https://www.circuitrecords.co.uk
Website: https://www.facebook.com/circuitrecordsuk

Genres: All types of music

Record label from a Yorkshire based music and media company, also running a radio station, a recording studio, artist development programmes, live events, and lots of other things. Accepts approaches from artists from Yorkshire.

Circus Records

17 Chocolate Studios
7 Shepherdess Place
Shoreditch
London
N1 7LJ
Email: info@circus-records.co.uk
Website: https://circus-records.co.uk
Website: https://soundcloud.com/circusrecords

Genres: Electronic

Electronic record label based in Shoreditch, London. Send query by email with soundcloud links for up to two tracks.

Cityscape Records

Website: https://cityscaperecords.bandcamp.com

Genres: Electronic; Indie; Pop

A long established kitchen table label which has been championing DIY pop from a Bolton terrace since '96. Recording in glamorous locations such as the 'back room'.

Clue Records

Leeds
Email: info@cluerecords.com
Website: https://cluerecords.bandcamp.com
Website: https://www.facebook.com/ClueRecords

Genres: Alternative; Indie; Rock

An independent record label based in Leeds, UK. "We work with artists we adore and release music we love."

Commercially Inviable Records

41 Gristhorpe Road
Birmingham
B29
Email: info@cominrecords.com
Website: http://www.cominrecords.com
Website: https://www.facebook.com/cominrecords

Genres: Acoustic; Country; Folk

Record label based in Brimingham. No A&R policy as such, but anyone having some music they think might be suitable may get in touch using the contact form on the website.

Concrete Recordings

Website: http://www.concreterecordings.co.uk

Genres: Acoustic; Guitar based; Indie; Post Punk

Record label based in Manchester.

Confidential Records (UK) Ltd

Cadman Lane
SNAITH
EAST YORKSHIRE
DN14 9JR
Website: https://www.confidentialrecords.co.uk
Website: https://www.facebook.com/confidentialrecordsuk

Genres: All types of music

Record label based in Snaith, East Yorkshire. Maximum roster of 40. Check website to see if they currently have scope for taking on a new act.

Cooking Vinyl

12 & 13 Swainson Road
London
W3 7XB
Email: info@cookingvinyl.com
Website: https://www.cookingvinyl.com
Website: https://www.facebook.com/cookingvinylrecords/

Genres: All types of music

Record label based in London. Home to an eclectic mix of acclaimed artists.

Cr2 Records

Email: demos@cr2records.com
Email: info@cr2records.co.uk
Website: http://www.cr2records.co.uk
Website: https://soundcloud.com/cr2records

Genres: Dance; House; Techno; Electronic

Contact: Mark Brown

Send demos by email as private Soundcloud links, or via online submission system. No MP3 email attachments.

CRD Records Limited

TRURO
TR2 5YJ
Email: info@crdrecords.com
Website: https://www.crdrecords.com
Website: https://www.facebook.com/CRDrecords

Genres: Classical

Classical record label based in Truro, Cornwall.

Criminal Records

Email: pr@criminalrecords.cc
Website: http://www.criminalrecords.cc
Website: https://soundcloud.com/criminal-records

Genres: Indie; Rock; Electronic

Always on the lookout for good bands. Send email with links to your music online.

Critical Music

Email: badger@criticalmusic.com
Website: https://criticalmusic.com
Website: https://www.facebook.com/criticalmusicdnb

Genres: Drum and Bass; Electronic; Dance

Electronic dance music label committed to shining a light on the new generation of Drum & Bass artists. Submit demos via online form on website.

Cruise International Records

Alerton Grange Vale
Leeds
LS17 6LS
Email: info@cruisedigital.co.uk
Website: https://www.cruisedigital.co.uk
Website: https://www.facebook.com/cruisedigitalmusic/

Genres: All types of music

Record label based in Leeds, West Yorkshire. Send query through form on website.

D.O.R.

Website: https://dor.co.uk/contact/
Website: https://www.facebook.com/DORlabel/

Genres: Experimental

Experimental music for the future.

Dancing Turtle Records

London
Website: https://www.dancingturtle.com
Website: https://www.soundcloud.com/dancingturtle

Genres: Electronic; Experimental; Folk; Indie; World

Company based in London, incorporating a record label, film production company, creative agency and global news hub.

Dead by Mono Records

Email: info@deadbymono.com
Website: https://www.deadbymono.com
Website: https://www.facebook.com/DeadbyMonoRecords

Genres: Garage Rock Rhythm and Blues Rock and Roll Surf Rockabilly Psychebilly Punk Instrumental Blues Horror Alternative New Wave Psychedelic

Independent record label and mail order based in the UK. Dedicated to garage rock, surf music and rock'n' roll since 2005.

Dead Happy Records

3B Castledown Avenue
Hastings
East Sussex
TN34 3RJ
Email: dave@deadhappyrecords.co.uk
Website: http://www.deadhappyrecords.co.uk

Genres: Dance; Indie; Trance

Label based in Hastings, East Sussex.

Defected

Email: demos@defected.com
Website: https://defected.com
Website: https://www.facebook.com/DefectedRecords

Genres: Dance; House

Record label based in London. Dedicated to the finest in house, from its label and numerous associated imprints, to its events and festivals.

Dirtee Stank

14 Havelock Walk
London
SE23 3HG
Website: https://soundcloud.com/dirteestankrecordingsltd
Website: https://find-and-update.company-information.service.gov.uk/company/05579928

Genres: Hip-Hop; Garage; Rap; Grime; Urban

Record label based in London, intended to bridge the gap between indies, majors and the street.

Dirty Hit

Email: info@dirtyhit.co.uk
Website: https://dirtyhit.co.uk
Website: https://www.facebook.com/DirtyHit/

Genres: Alternative

Independent record label formed in 2009, with a desire to develop and nurture homegrown artists. Frustration with outdated record company models means a commitment to long-term career building principals. Send query by email with links to music online.

Dirty Water Records

47 Moresby Road
Flat 2, top floor
London
E5 9LE
Email: label@dirtywaterclub.com
Website: https://www.dirtywaterrecords.co.uk

Website: https://www.facebook.com/dirtywaterrecords

Genres: Garage; Power Pop; Punk Rock; Rock and Roll; Rhythm and Blues

Record label based in London. Send query by email with links to music online. Also recommends sending a CD-R by post.

Dissention Records

Website: https://www.dissentionrecords.com
Website: https://twitter.com/dissentionmgmt

Genres: Punk; Alternative

Independent record label started in Boston but now based in the UK. Heavily influenced by punk rock music, specifically the DC hardcore scene.

Divine Art Record Company

176-178 Pontefract Road
Cudworth
Barnsley
S72 8BE
Email: info@divineartrecords.com
Website: https://divineartrecords.com

Genres: Classical

Classical music label with offices in the UK and US. See website for brochure on recording with the label, and the new project proposal form. No forms of current popular music. Offers both recording service arrangement and traditional royalty arrangement, covering up-front costs. See website for full details.

Dog Knights Productions

Email: info@dogknightsproductions.com
Email: dogknightsproductions@hotmail.co.uk
Website: https://dogknightsproductions.com/
Website: https://www.facebook.com/dogknights

Genres: Hardcore; Punk

UK-based independent record label.

Dome Records Ltd

Email: info@domerecords.co.uk
Website: http://www.domerecords.co.uk
Website: https://www.facebook.com/domerecords/

Genres: R&B; Soul

Describes itself as the UK home of Soul and R&B.

Domino Recording Company

Website: https://www.dominomusic.com
Website: https://soundcloud.com/dominorecordco

Genres: Alternative

Founded in Putney, South West London, in 1993. Send demos via Soundcloud.

Dorado Music

19A Douglas Street, Unit B
London
SW1P 4PA

US OFFICE:
4770 Biscayne Blvd. Suite 900
Miami, FL 33137
United States
Email: contact@dorado.net
Email: ollie@dorado.net
Website: https://dorado.net
Website: https://www.facebook.com/doradorecords/

Genres: Acid Jazz; Drum and Bass; Jazz; Electronic; Hip-Hop; Soul

Record label with offices in London and Florida.

Dramatico Entertainment Ltd

Box 214
Farnham
Surrey
GU10 5XZ
Email: mail@dramatico.com
Website: http://www.dramatico.com
Website: http://www.facebook.com/Dramatico

Genres: Alternative; Pop

Record label based in London. Unusual among record labels, it controls marketing and sales throughout much of the world by means of direct control from London, rather than licensing to other labels in other territories.

Drum With Our Hands

Email: info@drumwithourhands.com
Email: steve@drumwithourhands.com
Website: http://www.drumwithourhands.com
Website: https://www.facebook.com/DWOHrecords

Genres: Electronic; Alternative Folk; Classic Pop; Ambient

Contact: Andy; Steve

Indie/DIY record label from North Wales.

Earache London

Email: tim@earache.com
Email: dan.hardingham@earache.com
Website: https://www.earache.com

Genres: Metal

Send submissions via Artist Submission Form on website.

East Central One

Creeting House
All Saints Road
Creeting St Mary
Suffolk
IP6 8PR
Fax: +44 (0) 1449 726067
Email: enquiries@eastcentralone.com
Website: https://www.eastcentralone.com

Genres: All types of music, except: Dance

Contact: Steve Fernie; Helen Milner

Record label based in Ipswich, founded in 1998 by a former employee of EMI and BMG.

Engineer Records

Email: label@engineerrecords.com
Email: info@engineerrecords.com
Website: https://www.engineerrecords.com
Website: https://www.facebook.com/engineerrecords

Genres: Hardcore Punk; Emo; Alternative; Indie

Independent, alternative record label from England since 1999 sending over 300 releases out to the world. Send query by email with bio, band pic, and any record artwork, with mp3s or links to music online. No large files.

Enhanced Music

20-24 Old Street
London
EC1V 9AB
Email: info@enhancedmusic.com
Email: shop@enhancedmusic.com
Website: https://www.enhancedmusic.com
Website: https://www.labelradar.com/labels/enhancedmusic/portal

Genres: Ambient; Chill; Electronic; Trance

Record label based in London. Send demos via online upload system. See website for link.

Esoteric Recordings

Email: esotericrecordings@aol.com
Website: http://www.esotericrecordings.com
Website: https://www.facebook.com/EsotericRecordings/

Genres: Progressive Rock; Psychedelic Rock; Classic Rock; Electronic; Alternative Pop

Contact: Vicky Powell

The home of quality reissues in the Progressive, Classic Rock and Psychedelic genres.

Fantastic Plastic

Unit 6 Trident House
London
SE1 8QW
Email: info@fpmusic.org
Website: https://www.fpmusic.org
Website: https://www.facebook.com/fpmusicco

Genres: Alternative Guitar based

Independent record label also offering artist management and music publishing.

Far Out Recordings

Email: info@faroutrecordings.com
Website: https://www.faroutrecordings.com
Website: https://soundcloud.com/faroutrecs

Genres: Regional; Electronic

London-based record label dealing in Brazilian and electronic music.

Farmyard Records

Nottingham
Email: info@farmyardrecords.com
Website: http://www.farmyardrecords.com
Website: https://www.facebook.com/farmyardrecords

Genres: Indie; Pop; Soul; Alternative

Label, management, and promoters based in Nottingham.

Fast Static

Website: https://faststatic.co.uk
Website: https://www.facebook.com/FastStatic

Genres: Alternative

Independent record label and events collective.

Fat Hippy Records

c/o Captain Tom Music
11 – 15 Ann Street
Aberdeen
AB25 3LH
Email: info@fathippyrecords.co.uk
Website: http://www.fathippyrecords.co.uk
Website: https://www.facebook.com/fathippyrecords

Genres: All types of music

Independent record label based in Aberdeen, Scotland. Founded in 2002 to help raise the profile of the burgeoning North East Scotland music scene, and with the hope of overthrowing the "evil tyranny of the $ driven corporate music industry" and replacing it with their own "slightly nicer one".

FatCat Records UK

PO Box 3400
Brighton
BN1 4WG
Email: info@fat-cat.co.uk
Website: https://www.fat-cat.co.uk
Website: https://soundcloud.com/fatcatrecords

Genres: All types of music

Record label based in Brighton. Send demos by email as links to music online, or by post.

FatCat Records UK

PO Box 3400
Brighton
BN1 4WG
Email: info@fat-cat.co.uk
Website: http://www.fat-cat.co.uk
Website: https://soundcloud.com/fatcatrecords

Genres: All types of music

Record label with offices in the US and UK. Send email with links to music online. Also accepts physical demos by post.

Fellside Recordings

Website: https://www.fellside.com
Website: https://www.facebook.com/fellsiderecordings

Genres: Folk; Traditional; Roots

Record label specialising in Folk, Traditional and Roots music. A wide range of styles and presentation and an equally wide range of artists, from those well-established to those making their debut albums.

Fence Records

Website: http://www.fencerecords.com

Genres: Acoustic; Singer-Songwriter

Record label based in Anstruther, Fife.

Fiction Records

Website: https://fictionrecords.co.uk
Website: https://soundcloud.com/fictionrecords

Genres: All types of music

London-based record label originally founded in 1978 and then, after a period of inactivity, re-started in 2004.

Fierce Panda Records

Email: simon@fiercepanda.co.uk
Email: chris@fiercepanda.co.uk
Website: http://www.fiercepanda.co.uk
Website: https://www.facebook.com/fiercepanda

Genres: Indie; Rock

Indie rock label based in London. Approach by email with links to music on Soundcloud or Bandcamp or Facebook.

Fika Recordings

Email: demos@fikarecordings.com
Email: info@fikarecordings.com
Website: http://fikarecordings.com
Website: https://www.facebook.com/fikarecordings

Genres: Folk; Guitar based; Indie

Send query by email with bio, details of artists you like, bands you've played shows with, links to press or radio coverage, and links to streaming music online (e.g. Soundcloud or Bandcamp). Discriminates against artists based on their political beliefs.

Finger Lickin' Records

6 Windmill Street
London
W1T 2JB
Email: info@fingerlickin.co.uk
Website: http://www.fingerlickin.co.uk
Website: https://soundcloud.com/fingerlickinmanagement

Genres: Break Beat; Dance; Hip-Hop; Electronic

Record label based in London.

Fired Up Records

Lincoln
Email: sarahc@fireduprecords.com
Website: https://fireduprecords.com
Website: https://soundcloud.com/fireduprecords

Genres: Hard Dance

Contact: Sarah Curtis

Record label based in Lincoln, UK. Specialises in hard dance. Submit demo via online submission form.

First Night Records

Website: http://first-night-records.co.uk

Genres: Soundtracks

Contact: John Craig OBE

Mainly deals in theatre, film and TV soundtracks.

Flair Records

1st Floor
25 Commercial Street
Brighouse
HD6 1AF
Email: info@now-music.com
Website: https://www.now-music.com
Website: https://www.facebook.com/Now-Music-388961064509727/

Genres: Pop

Record label based in West Yorkshire, dealing with pop artists.

Flair Records

25 Commercial Street
Brighouse
HD6 1AF
Email: info@now-music.com
Website: http://www.now-music.com
Website: https://www.facebook.com/Now-Music-388961064509727/

Genres: Mainstream Pop; Acoustic

Contact: John Wagstaff

Pop label based in Brighouse, West Yorkshire.

Folkroom Records

Email: stephen@folkroom.co.uk
Email: ben@folkroom.co.uk
Website: http://folkroom.co.uk
Website: https://www.facebook.com/Folkroom

Genres: Folk

Folk label based in London. Acts are generally discovered by playing at the fortnightly live gigs. Best method of approach is therefore to apply to play at one of the gigs.

Fury Records

PO Box 7187
Ringstead
Kettering
NN16 6DJ
Email: furyrecords@btconnect.com
Website: http://www.fury-records.com

Genres: Rockabilly; Rock and Roll

Record label based in Kettering, Northamptonshire. Specialises in all styles related to Rockabilly and Rock'n'Roll music.

Fuzzkill Records

Email: fuzzkillrecords@gmail.com
Website: https://www.facebook.com/FUZZKILLrecords
Website: https://twitter.com/FUZZKILLRECORDS

Genres: Garage; Lo-fi; Psychedelic Rock; Rock and Roll

Scottish record label and party planner.

Gerry Loves Records

Website: http://gerrylovesrecords.com
Website: https://twitter.com/gerryloves

Genres: All types of music

Describes itself as a "tiny DIY label producing quality musical artifacts". Send query using form on website, including links to streaming tracks. Listens to all demos, but cannot guarantee a response.

Gizeh Records

Manchester
Email: contact@gizehrecords.com
Website: https://gizehrecords.com
Website: https://www.facebook.com/gizehrecords

Genres: All types of music

An independent label based in Manchester.

Glasstone Records

Bath
Email: submit@glasstonerecords.com
Email: info@glasstonerecords.com
Website: https://glasstonerecords.com

Genres: Indie; Rock; Metal; Electronic; Punk; Electronic Punk; Alternative

Contact: Greg Brooker

Independent label based in Bath. Send music, plus EPK if you have one, in an email via dropbox (preferred), soundcloud, or youtube. Listens to everything but cannot guarantee response.

Gravy

Email: info@gravyhq.com
Website: https://www.gravyhq.com
Website: https://www.facebook.com/GravyNorwich

Genres: Dance; Punk

A musical collective born in Norwich, UK.

Green Pepper Junction

Website: https://greenpepperjunction.com

Genres: All types of music

Contact: Asher Halle

Originally founded in the early seventies as a production company, now a record label based in Glasgow.

Greentrax Recordings

Cockenzie Business Hub
Edinburgh Road
Cockenzie
East Lothian
EH32 0XL

Email: info@greentrax.com
Website: https://www.greentrax.com
Website: https://www.facebook.com/greentrax/

Genres: Regional; Traditional; Celtic

Contact: Ian Green

Record label dealing in traditional Scottish, Celtic, and Gaelic music.

Groovin' Records

Email: groovin.records@phonecoop.coop
Website: http://www.groovinrecords.co.uk

Genres: Blues; Rhythm and Blues; Acoustic; Soul

Contact: AL Willard Peterson

Record label based in Merseyside, focusing on rhythm and blues.

Gruuv

Email: demos@gruuv.net
Email: label@gruuv.net
Website: https://soundcloud.com/gruuv
Website: https://www.facebook.com/gruuv

Genres: House; Techno

Send query by email with links to streaming or download links online.

Hand in Hive

Email: contact@handinhive.com
Website: http://www.handinhive.com
Website: https://www.facebook.com/handinhive

Genres: Indie; Pop

An independent music company, formed in 2014 by two friends with a shared love of music, specialising in records, management, publishing and sync.

Handsome Dad Records

Email: handsomedadrecords@gmail.com
Website: http://www.handsomedadrecords.com
Website: https://www.facebook.com/handsomedadrecords

Genres: All types of music

Record label releasing CDs and vinyl.

Hassle Records

Email: mease@fulltimehobby.co.uk
Email: tom@fulltimehobby.co.uk
Website: http://www.hasslerecords.com
Website: https://www.facebook.com/HassleRecords/

Genres: Alternative; Emo; Hardcore; Indie Rock; Punk; Metal; Pop Punk

A fully independent record label based in London, UK. Releases heavy guitar music.

Headcount Records

Email: info@headcountrecords.co.uk
Website: https://www.headcountrecords.co.uk
Website: https://soundcloud.com/headcount-records

Genres: Funk; Hip-Hop; Rap; Soul

An independent record label dedicated to supporting and championing talent across a wide array of genres and releasing limited edition vinyl along with digital content. Send demos by email.

Heavenly Recordings

Email: daisy@heavenlyrecordings.com
Website: https://heavenlyrecordings.com
Website: https://www.facebook.com/HeavenlyRecordings

Genres: Indie; Alternative; Rhythm and Blues; Underground; Country Pop

Send submissions by email.

Hit And Run Records

Email: Joe@hitandrunrecords.com
Website: https://www.facebook.com/hitandrunrecords

Genres: Pop Punk; Rock; Alternative

Independent record label from Birmingham, UK, specialising in Pop Punk, Rock and alternative music.

Holier Than Thou Records

Website: http://holierthanthou.co.uk
Website: https://twitter.com/HTTrecords

Genres: Rock; Indie; Alternative; Metal; Lo-fi; Punk; Hard Rock; Heavy Rock; Alternative Rock; Electronic Rock; Garage Lo-fi Rock; Progressive Rock; Glam; Melodic Metal; Progressive Metal; Power Metal; Gothic Metal; Melodic Thrash

Contact: David Begg, Label Manager

Established in June 1995, an independent record label. We focus on providing music promotion, PR and digital distribution for our clients. Working within a very strong and competitive market we arrange promotion campaigns for single, album releases and quality demos (downloads or CD) Our promotion and management activities generate, radio airplay , interviews, music review, live sessions, gigs and music sales.

Hope Recordings

Unit 4.16 The Paintworks
Bath Road
Bristol
BS4 3EH
Email: la@hoperecordings.com
Website: https://www.hoperecordings.com
Website: https://www.facebook.com/HopeRecordings/

Genres: Dance

Record label based in Bristol. Send demos as WeTransfer or Soundcloud links through online submission form.

Hospital Records

Unit 4 Bessemer Park
250 Milkwood Road
London
SE24 0HG
Fax: +44 (0) 20 8613 0401
Email: Chris@HospitalRecords.com
Email: Dan@HospitalRecords.com
Website: https://www.hospitalrecords.com
Website: https://www.facebook.com/hospitalrecords

Genres: Drum and Bass

Contact: Chris Goss

Record label based in London. Send demos via demo submission page on website. No demos by email.

Houndstooth

Email: houndstooth@fabriclondon.com
Website: https://www.houndstoothlabel.com
Website: https://soundcloud.com/HoundstoothLBL

Genres: Electronic

Artist-led electronic label based at a London nightclub.

I Ka Ching Records

Email: ikaching@hotmail.co.uk
Website: https://ikaching.cymru
Website: https://www.facebook.com/Ikaching

Genres: All types of music

Independent record label based in Wales.

I'm Not From London

The Old Bus Depot
Upstairs 1st Floor
1 Fisher Gate Point
Lower Parliament Street
Nottingham
NG1 1GD
Email: info@imnotfromlondon.com
Website: https://www.imnotfromlondon.com
Website: https://soundcloud.com/imnotfromlondonrecords

Genres: Guitar based

A group of Nottingham based DIY promoters, regularly putting on gigs in Nottingham and sometimes in Leeds, Sheffield and Blackpool. Launched label in 2010 and released first record in 2011.

Iffy Folk Records

Glasgow
Email: iffyfolkrecords@gmail.com
Website: http://www.iffyfolkrecords.com
Website: https://www.facebook.com/iffyfolkrecords

Genres: Country; Folk; Indie; Psychebilly; Rock; Rockabilly

Record label based in Glasgow.

Ignition Records

London
Fax: +44 (0) 20 7258 0962
Website: https://ignitionrecords.co.uk
Website: https://twitter.com/IgnitionMusicUK

Genres: Alternative; Rock

Independent record label with offices in London and LA. Send query via online contact form, including links to as many of your social media accounts as possible.

In At The Eye Records

Email: info@iaterecords.com
Email: a&r@iaterecords.com
Website: http://www.iaterecords.com
Website: https://www.facebook.com/InAtTheEyeRecords

Genres: Alternative; Dance; Electronic; Indie; Pop; Rock; Shoegaze; Acoustic Alternative; Synthpop; Singer-Songwriter; Acoustic; Experimental; New Wave; Mainstream; Leftfield

Contact: Jase Burns

Send submissions by email with info and links. No attachments.

Infidelity Records

Email: demos@infidelityrecords.co.uk
Website: http://infidelityrecords.co.uk
Website: https://www.facebook.com/Infidelityrecords

Genres: Drum and Bass

Record label specialising in D&B. Vocalists and producers can approach through through email.

Infinite Hive

Website: https://infinitehive.com
Website: https://www.facebook.com/infinitehive

Genres: Indie; Metal; Punk; Rock

Contact: Mr John

Edinburgh-based Independent Record Label.

Innerground Records

Website: https://www.innergroundmusic.com
Website: https://soundcloud.com/innergroundmusic

Genres: Dance; Drum and Bass

Record label based in London. Send demo via submission system on website.

Innersense Music

Website: http://www.innersenseworld.com

Genres: All types of music

Releases albums of relaxation and meditation.

Intuitive Productions

37 Cochrane Park Avenue
Newcastle upon Tyne
NE7 7JU
Email: kev@intuitive.productions
Website: http://intuitive.productions
Website: https://www.facebook.com/IntuitiveProductions/

Genres: All types of music

Contact: Kevin Daley

Sound Production, Video Production, TV Production, Record Label, and Music Publisher.

Invisible Hands Music

40 Mortimer Street
London
W1W 7EQ
Email: sales@invisiblehands.co.uk
Website: http://www.invisiblehands.co.uk

Genres: All types of music

An independent record label based in the heart of Soho, London, England.

Iron Man Records

Website: https://ironmanrecords.net
Website: https://twitter.com/IronManRecords

Genres: Alternative; Metal; Rock; Punk

Independent record label working out of Birmingham, Cardiff and London. The label also provides Tour Management Services to Musicians, Theatre groups and Film production companies.

Island Records

4 Pancras Square
Kings Cross
London
N1C 4AG
Website: https://www.islandrecords.co.uk

Genres: All types of music

Record label based in London.

istartedthefire records

Website: http://www.istartedthefire.co.uk
Website: https://www.facebook.com/istartedthefire

Genres: Acoustic; Alternative Country; Folk

Record label based in Cheltenham, Gloucestershire.

Jeepster Recordings Ltd

Email: info@jeepster.co.uk
Website: https://jeepster.co.uk
Website: https://www.facebook.com/jeepsterrecordings

Genres: All types of music

Send demo by email with info and links to your music online.

JohnJohn Records

61b Stepney Green
London
E1 3LE
Email: theboss@johnjohnrecords.com
Website: http://www.johnjohnrecords.com

Genres: Folk; Jazz; World

Contact: Benoit Viellefon

Record label based in London.

Joof Recordings

Email: daniel@joof.co.uk
Email: gary@joof.co.uk
Website: https://www.joof.co.uk
Website: https://www.facebook.com/JOOFRecordings

Genres: Trance

Record label handling Trance only. Send demos by email.

JSNTGM (Just Say No To Government Music)

Email: andy@jsntgm.com
Website: https://jsntgm.com
Website: https://www.facebook.com/pages/category/Musician-Band/Just-Say-No-To-Government-Music-175595205810038/

Genres: Punk; Punk Rock; Ska Punk; Pop Punk; Post Punk; Underground; Psychebilly

Contact: Andy

Small independent non-profit-making label based in Blackpool. Established in the early nineties as a reaction against the mainstream music served up by the music industry.

Jungle Records

Suite B2 Livingstone Court
55 Peel Road
Wealdstone
Harrow
HA3 7QT
Email: enquiries@jungle-records.com
Website: https://www.jungle-records.net
Website: https://www.facebook.com/JungleRecords

Genres: All types of music

Record label based in London. Rarely signs new acts, and the only usually ones with an established sales base. Send query by email with links to music online, or submit CD by post. No MP3s by email.

Just Music

Just House
9 Gladwyn Road
London
SW15 1JY

Email: justmusic@justmusic.co.uk
Website: https://www.justmusic.co.uk
Website: https://soundcloud.com/justmusiclabel

Genres: Electronic; Acoustic; Ambient; Downtempo; Chill

Contact: John Benedict; Serena

Record label founded out of a belief that all music of artistic merit should have the opportunity to "enrich our lives". Accepts demos by post or email, but cannot return material or reply to unsuccessful submissions.

JW Music Limited

Email: https://jwmusic.uk
Website: https://facebook.com/jwmusichq

Genres: Electronic; House; Pop; R&B; Urban

Record label based in Carlisle. Also offers artist management, hosts branded events, and operates YouTube channel and radio show / podcast. Send demo through demo submission form on website.

Killing Moon Records

Email: info@killing-moon.com
Website: https://killing-moon.com
Website: https://www.facebook.com/killingmoonrecords

Genres: Indie; Pop; Rock; Hardcore; Post Hardcore

Record label based in London. Accepts demos electronically.

King Prawn Records

Email: Info@kingprawnrecords.co.uk
Email: demo@kingprawnrecords.co.uk
Website: http://www.kingprawnrecords.co.uk
Website: https://www.facebook.com/kingprawnrecords/

Genres: Alternative; Indie; Metal; Rock

Send demos as streaming links by email.

Kscope

Snapper Music plc
1st Floor
52 Lisson Street
London
NW1 5DF
Website: https://kscopemusic.com
Website: https://soundcloud.com/kscopemusic

Genres: Rock; Post Progressive

Record label based in London. Due to the high level of submissions, cannot answer all demo enquiries.

Kudos Records Limited

77 Fortess Road
Kentish Town
London
NW5 1AG
Email: info@kudosrecords.co.uk
Website: https://kudosrecords.co.uk
Website: https://www.facebook.com/kudosrecords

Genres: House; Leftfield; Hip-Hop; Jazz; Techno

London distributor that will work with artists willing to act as their own label.

Kufe Records Ltd

Fax: +44 (0) 20 8898 8649
Email: info@kuferecords.com
Website: https://www.kuferecords.com

Genres: Reggae; Classic R&B; Country

Specialised in Sixties & Modern R & B, Reggae, Soca and Country Music.

Lab Records

Email: info@labrecs.com
Website: https://labrecs.com
Website: https://www.facebook.com/labrecords/

Genres: Pop Rock; Acoustic; Alternative; Folk; Hip-Hop; Reggae; World

Pop-rock label based in Manchester. Send demo by post.

The Lab

Website: https://www.thelab.cc
Website: http://twitter.com/thelabcc

Genres: Acoustic; Alternative; Indie; Folk; Pop; Rock

We create and work on things that we love. Whether it be print, design, music, creative projects or event collaborations.

Lake

Email: info@fellside.com
Website: https://www.fellside.com
Website: https://www.facebook.com/lakerecords

Genres: Jazz; Mainstream; Traditional;

Contact: Paul and Linda Adams

Label started in 1984 to release Jazz. Focuses mainly (but not exclusively) on British mainstream and traditional styles.

The Leaf Label Ltd

PO Box 272
Leeds
LS19 9BP
Email: contact@theleaflabel.com
Website: http://www.theleaflabel.com
Website: https://www.facebook.com/theleaflabel

Genres: Alternative; Experimental

Record label based in Leeds. Send demo on CD, vinyl, or cassette. No emails with attachments. See website for full details.

Lewis Recordings

95A Hackney Road
London
E2 8ET
Email: info@LewisRecordings.com
Website: http://www.lewisrecordings.com
Website: https://www.facebook.com/LewisRecordingsLDN

Genres: Alternative Hip-Hop; Rap; Electronic; Dubstep

Record label founded in 2001.

Lex Records Ltd

Email: word@lexrecords.com
Website: https://lexrecords.com
Website: https://www.facebook.com/Lexprojects/

Genres: Alternative

A record label, music publisher, and film production company based in London.

Linn Records

Website: https://www.linnrecords.com
Website: https://www.facebook.com/linnrecordsmusic

Genres: Celtic; Classical; Jazz; Traditional

Describes itself as "one of the world's leading audiophile labels specialising in Classical, Jazz and Scottish music."

Lismor Recordings

46 Elliot Street
Glasgow
G3 8DZ
Website: http://www.lismor.com

Genres: Traditional; Regional; Celtic

Record label based in Glasgow. Describes itself as one of the premier Scottish music labels of all time.

Lojinx

BCM Box 2676
London
WC1N 3XX
Website: https://www.lojinx.com
Website: https://soundcloud.com/lojinx

Genres: Alternative; Indie; Punk; Rock

A small, independent label based in London. Releases only a limited number of carefully considered records. No demos by post or email. Submit as Soundcloud links only.

Loose Music

14 Shaftesbury Centre
85 Barlby Road
London
W10 6BN
Email: info@loosemusic.com

Website: https://www.loosemusic.com
Website: https://soundcloud.com/loose-music

Genres: Americana; Alternative Country

Describes itself as Europe's premier Americana and alt Country record label. Send query by email with links to streams. No attachments.

MadTech Records

181 High Street
Harlesden
London
NW10 4TE
Email: demos@madtechrecords.com
Email: tom@championrecords.co.uk
Website: https://www.madtechrecords.com
Website: https://www.facebook.com/madtechrecords

Genres: Contemporary Electronic

London label releasing contemporary electronic music. Send query by email.

MaggotHouse Music

Email: ben@maggothouse.co.uk
Website: http://www.maggothouse.co.uk

Genres: Techno; Remix; Electronic; Experimental

Contact: Ben Neal

A small record label promoting and distributing the work of its artists, based in Cradley Heath in the West Midlands. Particularly interested in experimental music.

Manic Records UK

Email: info@manic-records.co.uk
Website: https://www.manic-records.co.uk

Genres: All types of music

We are an independent label, driven to introduce new and challenging music.

Measured Records

5 Eagle Street
Glasgow
G4 9XA
Email: info@nohalfmeasures.com
Website: https://nohalfmeasures.com
Website: https://www.facebook.com/nohalfmeasures

Genres: All types of music

Record label based in Glasgow, Scotland. Part of a group including artist management and publishing divisions.

Memphis Industries

Email: info@memphis-industries.com
Website: https://www.memphis-industries.com
Website: https://twitter.com/memphisind

Genres: Alternative; Indie

Record label based in London.

Metalbox Recordings

Email: anna@metalboxrecordings.com
Email: larry@metalboxrecordings.com
Website: http://metalboxrecordings.com
Website: http://www.facebook.com/MetalboxRecordings

Genres: Metal; Rock

Contact: Anna Di Laurenzio; Lawrence Paterson

Independent UK label formed in July 2010.

Midge Bitten Records

Website: https://www.fellside.com

Genres: Indie; Rock

Operators are now in semi-retirement, but the company has not been closed or sold.

Moksha Recordings Ltd

PO Box 102
London
E15 2HH
Email: recordings@moksha.co.uk
Website: https://www.moksha.co.uk

Genres: Alternative Electronic Fusion

Record label based in London. Send query by email with links to music online.

Mook Records

Authorpe Road
Leeds
LS6 4JB
Email: mail@mookhouse.ndo.co.uk
Website: http://www.mookhouse.ndo.co.uk

Genres: Alternative; Indie; Punk

Label based in Leeds, founded in 1995 out of a desire to "make records with a live vibe and a minimum of overdubs". Has own recording studios and rehearsal rooms. Send query by email.

Moshi Moshi Records

Email: hello@moshimoshimusic.com
Website: https://moshimoshimusic.com/
Website: https://www.facebook.com/moshimoshimusic

Genres: Alternative

Record label founded in 1998 by three friends who had jobs working for major record labels, to enable them to work with bands they loved but which didn't fit with the agenda of the companies they worked for. Went full-time in 2004.

Mute Records

Email: demos@mute.com
Email: mute@mute.com
Website: https://mute.com
Website: https://www.instagram.com/muterecords/

Genres: Alternative; Electronic

Send query by email with three or four streaming links. No attachments.

National Anthem

Email: hello@national-anthem.co.uk
Website: http://www.national-anthem.co.uk
Website: https://www.facebook.com/nationalanthemmusic

Genres: All types of music

Independent record label specialising in limited edition vinyl releases pressed on high quality 7″, 10″ or 12″ vinyl, also released digitally.

Needwant

Email: demos@needwantmusic.com
Email: info@needwantmusic.com
Website: https://needwantmusic.com
Website: https://soundcloud.com/seanneedwant

Genres: Chill; Electronic; House; Techno; Dance

Send query by email with links to music online.

Nervous Records

5 Sussex Crescent
Northolt
Middx.
UB5 4DL
Email: info@nervous.co.uk
Website: https://www.nervous.co.uk
Website: https://www.facebook.com/Nervous-Records-90855264733/

Genres: Psychebilly; Rockabilly; Rock and Roll

Record label based in Northolt, Middlesex. Aims to to bring rock and roll into the present day – NOT a nostalgia label.

Nettwerk Records

15 Adeline Place, 3rd Floor
London
WC1B 3AJ
Fax: +44 (0) 20 7456 9501
Website: https://nettwerk.com
Website: https://www.facebook.com/nettwerkmusicgroup

Genres: Acoustic; Folk; Singer-Songwriter

Record label with head office in Canada and other offices in Los Angeles, New York City, London, and Hamburg.

New State Music

58 Rochester Place
Camden Town
London
NW1 9JX
Email: info@newstatemusic.com
Website: https://www.newstatemusic.com
Website: https://soundcloud.com/newstatemusic

Genres: Trance; Dance

Record label based in London. Send demos as soundcloud links through online contact form.

9 Volt Records

Email: ac@9voltrecords.com
Email: martin@9voltrecords.com
Website: http://www.9voltrecords.com

Genres: Electronic

Contact: Adrian Collier; Martin Craig; Shaun Herbert; Gina Cole

Electronic label willing to reach out and look beyond the horizons of the genre. Send query by email with links to music online. No MP3 attachments. Response only if interested.

Ninja Tune

PO Box 4296
London
SE11 4WW
Email: demos@ninjatune.net
Website: https://www.ninjatune.net

Genres: Hip-Hop; Electronic; Break Beat; Downtempo; Leftfield; Jazz

Record label with offices in London, UK, and Los Angeles, California. Send demo by email only, with links to MP3 files, soundcloud pages, or websites, but No MP3 attachments. Keep demos short and sweet with your best track first. Do not chase for response.

No Dancing Records

Email: info@nodancing.co.uk
Website: https://www.nodancing.co.uk
Website: https://soundcloud.com/nodancing

Genres: Indie; Rock; Leftfield; Alternative

Record label based in Belfast. Loves to hear new music, but not currently that active.

No Front Teeth

PO Box 27070
London
N2 9ZP
Email: NFTpunx@nofrontteeth.co.uk
Website: https://www.nofrontteeth.co.uk

Genres: Punk Rock

Record label based in London.

Nu Electro

Email: demos@nu-electro.com
Email: nu@nu-electro.com
Website: http://www.nu-electro.com
Website: https://soundcloud.com/nu-electro

Genres: Drum and Bass; Electronic; Techno; New Wave; Synthpop; Punk

Record label based in Maidenhead. Send soundcloud links by email.

One Inch Badge (OIB) Records

Second Floor Central Block
St Augustine's Church
Stanford Avenue
Brighton
BN1 6EA
Email: submissions@oneinchbadge.com
Email: office@oneinchbadge.com
Website: https://www.oneinchbadge.com
Website: https://www.facebook.com/oneinchbadge

Genres: Rock; Pop; Electronic; Folk

Concert promotions, record label and venue management company based in Brighton. Send demos by email.

One Little Independent Records

34 Trinity Crescent
London
SW17 7AE
Email: demos@olirecords.com
Email: contact@olirecords.com
Website: https://www.olirecords.com
Website: https://www.facebook.com/olirecords

Genres: All types of music

Send email with links to MP3 files, SoundCloud pages or websites. Include contact details in the body of the email.

Ostereo

International House
61 Mosley Street
Manchester
M2 3HZ

LONDON
23 Tileyard Studios
Tileyard Road
London
N7 9AH
Email: info@ostereo.com
Website: https://ostereo.com

Genres: All types of music

Record label with offices in Manchester and London.

PAPERecordings

Email: hello@paperecordings.com
Website: https://paperecordings.com
Website: https://soundcloud.com/paperecordings

Genres: House; Disco; Leftfield

Style ranges from deep house and disco to Balearic and leftfield.

Park Records

PO Box 651
Oxford
OX2 9RB
Email: parkoffice@parkrecords.com
Website: https://parkrecords.com
Website: https://www.facebook.com/profile.php?id=100063531371464

Genres: Folk

Folk record label based in Oxford.

Parlophone Records

Website: https://www.parlophone.co.uk
Website: https://www.facebook.com/parlophone

Genres: All types of music

Long-standing label that has boasted such acts as the Beatles, Blur, Radiohead, and Kylie.

Perry Road Records Ltd

75 Perry Road
Buckden
Cambridgeshire
PE19 5XG
Email: enquiries@perryroadrecords.co.uk
Website: https://www.perryroadrecords.co.uk

Genres: Blues; Country; Indie; Rock

Record label based in Cambridgeshire. Send demo by post, or by email with the name of your music page online. No attachments or links.

Phantasy Sound Ltd

5a Bear Lane
Southwark
London
SE1 0UH
Email: demos@phantasysound.co.uk
Email: phantasyhq@gmail.com
Website: https://shop.phantasysound.co.uk
Website: https://www.facebook.com/phantasy.sound

Genres: Alternative; Dance; Electronic

Record label based in London. Send demo by email.

Philophobia Music

Email: philophobiamusic@gmail.com
Website: https://www.facebook.com/philophobiamusic
Website: https://linktr.ee/PhilophobiaMusic?fbclid=IwAR1YJvdfuf9jdiqXeLRhagetk2WtM5mhhOwxkBnLX79RPqmgR2taGFv9WNo

Genres: Indie; Pop

Independent record label based in Wakefield, West Yorkshire.

Pinball Records

Email: frank@pinballrecords.co.uk
Website: http://www.pinballrecords.co.uk
Website: https://soundcloud.com/pinballrecords/

Genres: Electronic; House

Record label focussed on electro and house.

Pinky Swear Records

Website: http://pinkyswearrecords.limitedrun.com
Website: https://www.facebook.com/pinkyswearrecords

Genres: Emo; Hardcore; Pop; Punk

Independant Record Label focussing on vinyl and tape releases.

Play It Again Sam

1 Bevington Path
London
SE1 3PW
Website: http://www.playitagainsam.net
Website: https://www.instagram.com/playitagainsamrecs/

Genres: All types of music

Record company based in London. Part of one of the biggest independent record distributors in Europe.

Polydor Records

4 Pancras Square
London
N1C 4AG
Website: https://www.polydor.co.uk
Website: https://www.facebook.com/polydorrecords

Genres: All types of music

Record label based in London.

Positiva Records

London
Website: https://positivarecords.com
Website: https://soundcloud.com/positivarecords

Genres: Dance

Send submissions as Soundcloud link via online submission system. Response not guaranteed unless interested.

Pretty Neat Records

London / Brighton
Email: prettyneatrecordings@googlemail.com
Website: http://www.8hz.co.uk/prettyneat
Website: https://soundcloud.com/pretty-neat-records

Genres: Chill; Drum and Bass; Dubstep; Electronic; Techno

Contact: Samuel Batt (A&R)

Record label based in London / Brighton. All profits go to charity.

A Priscilla Thing

Email: info@apriscillathing.co.uk
Website: http://apriscillathing.co.uk
Website: https://twitter.com/apriscillathing

Genres: Urban; Garage; R&B; Hip-Hop; House; Soul; Jazz

Independent urban music record label based in London, United Kingdom. The label distributes and produces music across a range of genres including; garage, R&B, hip-hop, house, neo-soul and nu jazz.

Public Pressure

London
Website: https://we.publicpressure.io
Website: https://soundcloud.com/jointhepressure

Genres: Alternative; Heavy Blues; Psychedelic Hip-Hop; Progressive Metal; Electronic

We empower artists and labels connecting them directly to their audience and allowing them to retain control over their work and revenue.

Pumpkin Records

Website: https://pumpkinrecords.co.uk
Website: https://www.facebook.com/pumpkinrecordsuk

Genres: Dub; Garage; Psychebilly; Punk; Rockabilly; Ska; Ska Punk

Describes itself as more of a collective than a record label.

Purple Worm Records

Hull
Website: https://www.facebook.com/

purplewormrecords/
Website: https://twitter.com/purplewormrec

Genres: All types of music

Independent record label based in Hull.

Quatre Femmes Records

London
Email: quatrefemmesrecords@gmail.com
Website: https://quatrefemmesrecords.bandcamp.com
Website: https://www.facebook.com/QuatreFemmesRecords

Genres: Folk; Indie; Pop; Psychedelic; Rock

Record label based in London.

Ram Records

5 Merchant Square
8th Floor
London
W2 1AS
Email: info@ramrecords.com
Website: https://www.ramrecords.com
Website: http://soundcloud.com/ramrecords/

Genres: Drum and Bass

Drum & bass label based in London. Send demos via Soundcloud or Wavo submission on Facebook.

Ramber Records

7 Winfell Drive
Manchester
M40 7BX
Email: rob@ramberrecords.com
Website: https://ramberrecords.com
Website: https://www.facebook.com/Ramberrecords

Genres: Electronic Pop; Garage; Psychedelic Rock

Home-dubbed cassette enthusiasts based in Manchester, specialising in dark-edged electro-pop. Send demos by post or by email.

RareNoiseRecords

Suite 509
Britannia House
1-11 Glenthorne Road
London
W6 0LH
Email: info@rarenoiserecords.com
Website: https://www.rarenoiserecords.com
Website: https://www.facebook.com/rarenoise

Genres: Ambient; Dub; Jazz; Progressive

Record label based in London, with a mission to detect and amplify contemporary trends in progressive music, by highlighting their relation to the history of the art-form, while choosing not to be bound by pre-conceptions of genre. Send query by email with Soundcloud links or equivalent, with bio and background information.

Raven Black Music

Email: info@ravenblackmusic.com
Website: https://www.facebook.com/ravenblackmusic

Genres: All types of music

UK-based record label. Promotes new melodic intelligent music which is both passionate and positively life affirming.

RCA Label Group UK

2 Canal Reach
London
N1C 4DB
Email: reception.enquiries@sonymusic.com
Website: https://www.rca-records.co.uk

Genres: All types of music

UK record label. Accepts demos via post only in USB or CD format. Mark submissions for the attention of a specific label, followed by "demos".

Red Eye Music

Website: http://www.redeyemusic.co.uk

Genres: Alternative Country; Americana; Blues; Folk; Singer-Songwriter

An independent Record Label and Music Production Company.

The Red Flag Recording Co.

The Basement
1 Star Street
London
W2 1QD
Email: info@redflagrecords.com
Email: info@playwrite.uk.com
Website: http://www.redflagrecords.com

Genres: Pop; Rock

Incubation label for its sister company, with a deliberately small roster. Believe in cultivation, development, and the creation of an environment in which artists can produce their best work.

Rekids Ltd

Email: loverekids@gmail.com
Website: https://rekids.com
Website: http://soundcloud.com/rekids

Genres: Electronic; House; Techno

Record label based in UK and Berlin, supporting international artists. Send all demos by email.

REL Records Ltd

86 Causewayside
Edinburgh
EH9 1PY
Fax: +44 (0) 1316 624463
Email: online@relrecords.co.uk
Website: http://www.relrecords.co.uk

Genres: Celtic; Regional

Record label based in Edinburgh, handling Scottish and Celtic music.

Release / Sustain

East London
Email: info@releasesustain.com
Email: gabbi@releasesustain.com
Website: http://www.releasesustain.com
Website: https://www.facebook.com/release.sustain

Genres: Chill; House; Techno; Underground

Contact: Gabriel Arierep; Eduardo Tavares

Record label based in East London.

Relentless Records

Email: demos@relentlessrecs.com
Email: emily@relentlessrecs.com
Website: https://www.relentlessrecs.com
Website: https://www.facebook.com/relentlessrecs/

Genres: Alternative

Record label based in London. Contact A&R team by email.

Remixdj

Email: remixdj01@gmail.com
Website: https://remixdj.co.uk

Genres: Acoustic Alternative Avant-Garde Classic Commercial Electronic Experimental Funky Leftfield Mainstream Modern Non-Commercial Post Psychedelic Progressive Soulful Traditional Twisted Urban Uptempo Underground Tribal Ambient Blues Chill Classical Club Dance Deep Funk Disco Dub Fusion Funk Garage Guitar based Hip-Hop IDM Indie Instrumental Jazz Latin Lounge Pop Nostalgia Remix Soul Swing Techno Trance

An indie publishing outfit specialising in delivering audio products into prime retail positions.

Revolver Records

152 Goldthorn Hill
Wolverhampton
WV2 3JA
Email: submissions@revolverrecords.com
Email: music@revolverrecords.com
Website: https://revolverrecords.com
Website: http://soundcloud.com/revolverrecords

Genres: Rock; Metal; Jazz

Record label based in London. Prefers to receive demos via email, but also accepts via post. When submitting by email, send no more than MP3 or WAV files as attachments. If sending more, use streaming platforms (e.g. Spotify; Soundcloud) or digital storage platform (e.g. Dropbox; Google Drive). Physical discs submitted by post cannot be returned.

Ridge Records Limited

1 York Street
Aberdeen
AB11 5DL
Fax: +44 (0) 1224 572598
Email: office@ridge-records.com
Website: https://www.ridge-records.com

Genres: Celtic; Traditional

Independent record label based in Aberdeen, Scotland.

River Rat Records

The River Lea
London
E5 9HQ
Email: info@riverratrecords.com
Website: https://www.riverratrecords.com
Website: https://www.facebook.com/riverratrecords/

Genres: Alternative; Folk; Blues

Female purveyors of alternative folk and blues music, hosting international live acts and releasing original music.

Roadrunner Records

Website: https://www.roadrunnerrecords.co.uk
Website: https://www.facebook.com/roadrunnerrecordsuk

Genres: Metal; Rock

Hard rock and metal record label.

Rock Action Records

Glasgow
Email: info@rockactionrecords.co.uk
Website: https://rockaction.scot
Website: https://www.facebook.com/rockactionrecords

Genres: Alternative; Electronic; Indie; Rock

Independent record label based in Glasgow. Happy to receive demos, but cannot guarantee individual response or feedback.

ROKiT Records

ROKiT House
Kingswood Business Park
Holyhead Road
Albrighton
Wolverhampton
WV7 3AU
Fax: +44 (0) 1902 374603
Email: info@rokrecords.com
Website: https://rokitrecords.info

Genres: Hip-Hop; Indie; R&B; Rock

Record label based in Wolverhampton. Describes itself as an innovative music company that utilises its advanced technology to support the music industry.

Rose Coloured Records

Email: records@rosecoloured.com
Website: https://www.rosecoloured.com
Website: https://www.facebook.com/RoseColouredRecords/

Genres: All types of music

Small independent label. Tries to listen and respond to all submissions. Send links to videos or tracks by email or through form on website.

Rough Trade Records

66 Golborne Road
London
W10 5PS
Email: demos@roughtraderecords.com
Website: https://roughtraderecords.com
Website: https://www.facebook.com/roughtraderecords

Genres: Indie; Rock

Record label based in London with offices in New York. Send demos by email as links only. No attachments.

Saint Productions

Sheffield
Email: mark@saintproductions.co.uk
Website: http://saintproductions.co.uk

Genres: Dance; Pop

Record label based in Sheffield, Yorkshire.

Sapien Records Limited

Clarendon House
Clayton Street
Newcastle
NE1 5EE
Email: info@sapienrecords.com
Email: david@sapienrecords.com
Website: http://www.sapienrecords.com
Website: https://www.facebook.com/sapienrecords

Genres: Hip-Hop; Metal; Pop; Punk; Rock; R&B

Contact: David Smith; Ollie Rillands

Independent record label based in Newcastle.

Saved Records

Maidstone, Kent
Email: info@savedrecords.com
Website: http://www.savedrecords.com
Website: https://soundcloud.com/savedrecords

Genres: House; Techno; Electronic

Record label based in Maidstone. Send demos by email.

Saving Grace Music

Email: info@saving-grace.co.uk
Website: https://www.saving-grace.co.uk
Website: https://www.facebook.com/housesginc/

Genres: Grime; Hip-Hop; House; Garage; Indie; Folk; Rock; Soul; Pop; Drum and Bass; Dubstep

A creative imprint and talent development hub working with aspiring, developing and established artists alike, releasing, marketing, promoting and distributing creative works in the fields of music, video, art and fashion.

Schnitzel Records Ltd

Leigh On Sea
Email: talent@schnitzel.co.uk
Email: info@schnitzel.co.uk
Website: https://schnitzel.co.uk
Website: https://www.facebook.com/schnitzelrecords

Genres: Alternative; Rock

Record label based in Leigh On Sea. Send submissions by email.

Scotdisc

62 Telford Road
Cumbernauld
B67 2AX
Email: info@scotdisc.co.uk
Website: https://scotdisc.co.uk

Genres: Regional

Record label based in Cumbernauld, specialising in Scottish music.

Scruff of the Neck (SOTN)

36-40 Edge Street
Manchester
M4 1HN
Email: info@scruffoftheneck.com
Website: https://scruffoftheneck.com
Website: https://www.facebook.com/scruffoftheneck

Genres: All types of music

Independent record label and music collective promoting concerts and tours, releasing records and developing artists. Approach via Artist Contact Form on website.

Scylla Records

Email: rich@scyllarecords.com
Website: https://www.scyllarecords.com
Website: https://www.facebook.com/scyllarecords

Genres: Ambient; Metal; Pop; Punk; Rock

An independent UK record label.

Secret Records Ltd

15 Watling St
Fenny Stratford
Bletchley
Milton Keynes
MK2 2BU
Email: mail@secretrecordslimited.com
Website: https://secretrecordslimited.com
Website: https://www.facebook.com/secretrecordsltd/

Genres: Blues; Reggae; Black Origin Blue Beat Blues Fusion Folk Garage Guitar based Indie Instrumental Jazz Punk Reggae Reggaeton Rock Rock and Roll Rhythm and Blues Soul Acoustic Alternative Classic Acid Contemporary Hard Psychedelic Space Thrash Underground

A British independent record label based in London. The label currently specialises in live releases and older releases ranging across a number of genres including blues, reggae, rock, rock 'n' roll, psychedelic, soul and punk.

Originally started as a punk label, created in 1980 with the first release which reached number 20 in the UK album charts. As the 1990s came around the catalogue became less rooted in punk and become broader in genre choice. After 2000 the label began concentrating more on music DVD releases as well as live CD releases and continues to do so to this day.

Seeca Music Ltd

Fax: +44 (0) 20 3475 3101
Email: info@seeca.co.uk
Website: http://www.seeca.co.uk

Genres: Alternative

Publisher, label and Film & TV placement company. Send demo as MP3 attachment (max 7MB) to email giving brief description of band/artist/composer. Response only if interested.

Shabby Doll Records

Email: hello@shabbydoll.co.uk
Website: http://www.shabbydoll.co.uk
Website: https://www.facebook.com/ShabbyDollRecords

Genres: Underground House

Record label specialising in bespoke underground house music.

Signum Records

Unit 14
21 Wadsworth Road
Perivale
Middlesex
UB6 7LQ
Email: info@signumrecords.com
Website: https://signumrecords.com
Website: https://www.facebook.com/signumrecords

Genres: Classical

Independent classical record label based in Perivale, Middlesex.

Skinny Dog Records

Website: http://www.skinnydogrecords.com
Website: https://www.facebook.com/Skinny-Dog-Records-490311811128177/

Genres: Alternative; Punk; Rock

An independent record label based in Manchester, England, set up in 1999.

Skint Entertainment

PO Box 174
Brighton
BN1 4BA
Email: skint.demos@bmg.com
Website: https://www.skintentertainment.com/
Website: https://www.facebook.com/skintrecords

Genres: Dance

Record label based in Brighton. Send demos by email.

SLAM Productions

c/o 3 Thesiger Road
Abingdon
OX14 2DX
Email: slamprods@aol.com
Email: ZirconRover@aol.com
Website: http://www.slamproductions.net

Genres: Contemporary Jazz; Experimental

Independent CD label based in Abingdon, and founded in 1989. Not releasing CDs by any more new artists as at May 2023.

Slapped Up Soul Records

Bristol
Website: https://www.facebook.com/

slappedupsoul/
Website: https://twitter.com/slappedupsouluk

Genres: Soul

Independent record label specialising in music with soul.

Small Pond Record Label

27 Castle Street
Brighton
BN1 2HD
Email: info@smallpondrec.co.uk
Website: https://smallpondrec.com
Website: https://soundcloud.com/small-pond

Genres: All types of music

Unlike many indie labels, we do not work in one particular genre. We love everything from ambient techno to progressive metal. We do, however, like music that is left-field, alternative, and different. We are always looking for that little je ne sais quoi, no matter the genre.

Snapper Music

52 Lisson Street
London
NW1 5DF
Website: https://snappermusic.com

Genres: Alternative; Rock; Metal; Post Progressive

Record label based in London.

So Recordings

Email: info@sorecordings.com
Website: http://sorecordings.com
Website: https://www.facebook.com/SoRecordings

Genres: Alternative; Indie; Rock

Record label founded in 2009. In 2023, celebrated its first number one album in the UK.

Soma Recordings Ltd

Acre House
35 Whitefield Road
Glasgow
G51 2YB
Email: info@somarecords.com
Website: https://www.somarecords.com
Website: https://www.facebook.com/SomaRecords/

Genres: Dance

Record label based in Glasgow, Scotland. Send email with soundcloud link to your two best tracks. No download links or MP3 files or any other kind of attachment.

SOMM Recordings

13 Riversdale Road
Thames Ditton
Surrey
KT7 0QL
Email: sales@somm-recordings.com
Website: https://somm-recordings.com
Website: https://soundcloud.com/siva-oke

Genres: Classical

Classical label based in Thames Ditton, Surrey.

Sonic Cathedral

Office 44
78 Golders Green Road
London
NW11 8LN
Website: https://soniccathedral.co.uk
Website: https://www.facebook.com/soniccathedral.uk

Genres: Electronic; Psychedelic Rock; Shoegaze

Record label based in London.

Sony Music Entertainment UK Ltd

2 Canal Reach
London
N1C 4DB
Email: reception.enquiries@sonymusic.com
Website: https://www.sonymusic.co.uk

Genres: All types of music

London office of large international record label. Accepts demos via post only, in USB or CD format.

Sotones Music Co-Operative

13 Mansion Road
Southampton
SO15 3BQ
Email: demos@sotones.co.uk
Email: andy@sotones.co.uk
Website: http://sotones.co.uk
Website: https://www.facebook.com/sotones

Genres: All types of music

Contact: Andy Harris (Managing Director)

Music collective based in Southampton, generally only working with local acts. Will accept demos, however. See website for more details.

Soul II Soul

Email: info@soul2soul.co.uk
Website: https://soul2soul.co.uk
Website: https://soundcloud.com/soul2souluk

Genres: R&B; Rap; Urban

Record label based in London.

Soul Jazz Records Ltd

7 Broadwick Street
Soho
London
W1F 0DA
Email: info@soundsoftheuniverse.com
Website: https://soundsoftheuniverse.com/sjr/
Website: https://www.facebook.com/Soul-Jazz-Records-Official-Page-118045430258/

Genres: Reggae; Dubstep; Leftfield; House; Techno; Electronic; Classic Disco; Hip-Hop; Post Punk; Funk; Soul; Jazz; Latin; Roots

Record shop, independent record label, book publisher, and occasional film company based in Soho, London.

Soundplate

London
Website: https://soundplate.com
Website: https://www.facebook.com/Soundplate/

Genres: Electronic; House

A London based independent record label and music technology company.

Southern Fried Records

Email: andy@anglomanagement.co.uk
Website: https://www.southernfriedrecords.com
Website: https://soundcloud.com/southernfriedrecords

Genres: Electronic; Dance

A London-based independent electronic dance music record label. Send demos by email.

Southern Records

Website: http://www.southern.com
Website: https://soundcloud.com/southern

Genres: Acoustic; Alternative; Folk; Rock

Independent record label formed in London in 1990.

Southpoint

Email: info@southpointmusic.co.uk
Website: https://www.southpointmusic.co.uk
Website: https://soundcloud.com/southpointmusic

Genres: Dubstep; Garage; Grime

Record label based in Hove, dedicated to promoting local and lesser known talent and reviving Brighton's fading bass and grime scene.

Space Age Recordings

Website: http://www.spaceagerecordings.com

Genres: Experimental; Electronic

Record label based in Corby, Northamptonshire.

Squirrel Records

Leeds
Email: info@squirrelrecords.co.uk
Website: http://www.squirrelrecords.co.uk
Website: https://www.facebook.com/squirrelrecords

Website: http://www.myspace.com/squirrelrecords

Genres: Pop Punk; Rock and Roll; Lo-fi Indie; Guitar based; Alternative; New Wave

Contact: Darren; Caroline; Dicky; Chris Shake

Independent record label based in Leeds, Yorkshire. Specialises in mainly female-fronted bands.

Stereokill Recordings

Email: info@stereokillrecordings.com
Website: http://stereokillrecordings.com

Genres: All types of music

Independent record label run by "long standing music fanatics rather than by sharks and accountants".

Struggletown Records

Glasgow
Email: struggletownrecords@gmail.com
Website: http://www.struggletown.co.uk
Website: https://www.facebook.com/struggletownrecords

Genres: Pop Punk; Hardcore; Emo; Punk Rock

Small record label from Glasgow in Scotland dealing with pop-punk, hardcore, emo and punk rock.

Tangent Recordings

Email: demos@tangent-recordings.com
Email: office@tangent-recordings.com
Website: http://www.tangent-recordings.com

Genres: Drum and Bass

Send Soundcloud links by email.

33 Jazz Records Ltd

Email: info@33jazz.com
Website: http://www.33jazz.com

Genres: Jazz

Record label specialising in jazz.

3 Beat Records

Liverpool
Website: https://www.threebeatrecords.co.uk
Website: https://soundcloud.com/3beat

Genres: Progressive; Dance; Trance; House; Funky House; Techno; Hardcore

Record store founded in 1989 in Liverpool, now also running a label and providing artist management services.

Tongue Master Records

PO Box 76066
London
W6 6LL
Email: info@tonguemaster.co.uk
Website: http://www.tonguemaster.co.uk
Website: https://twitter.com/TongueMasterRec

Genres: Indie

Independent record label based in London.

Tough Love Records

London
Email: info@toughloverecords.com
Website: http://toughloverecords.com
Website: https://www.facebook.com/ToughLoveRecordings/

Genres: Indie

Record label based in London.

Try Harder Records

20 Rosemary Close
High Wycombe
Bucks
HP12 4AG
Email: info@tryharderrecords.com
Website: http://www.tryharderrecords.com
Website: http://www.myspace.com/tryharderrecords

Genres: Alternative

Record label based in High Wycombe, Bucks.

TV Records Ltd

PO Box 34803
London

W8 7OZ
Email: tv.recordsltd@gmail.com
Email: tenor.vossa@gmail.com
Website: http://www.tenorvossa.co.uk
Website: https://www.facebook.com/TenorVossaAndTVRecords

Genres: Alternative Country; Lo-fi; Post Rock; Space Rock

Record label based in London.

Wasted State Records

Email: info@wastedstate.com
Website: http://www.wastedstate.com
Website: https://www.facebook.com/wastedstate/

Genres: Indie; Metal; Psychebilly; Punk; Rock; Rock and Roll; Ska

Not actively looking for new signings, but if you want to get in touch, first check out existing releases to make sure your music fits the bill.

World Circuit Records

Website: https://worldcircuit.co.uk
Website: https://www.facebook.com/WorldCircuitRecords

Genres: World; Regional

Record label formed in the mid 1980s and based in London, producing world music albums, and specialising in music from Cuba and West Africa.

Wrath Records

The Cardigan Centre
145-149 Cardigan Road
Leeds
LS6 1LJ
Email: info@wrathrecords.co.uk
Website: http://www.wrathrecords.co.uk

Genres: Leftfield; Alternative; Pop

A Leeds-based label bent on purveying quality leftfield alternative popular music.

Zube Records

Email: info@zuberecords.com
Website: https://www.zuberecords.com
Website: https://www.facebook.com/ZubeRecords/
Website: https://myspace.com/zuberecords/

Genres: Alternative; Acoustic; Electronic; Indie; Rock; Experimental

Independent record company based in London. Shares costs and profits 50/50 with artists. Releases acts in Rock, Acoustic, Electronica and Experimental. No cover material, pop, dance, garage, R&B, hip hop, techno, urban, rap or metal.

Canadian Record Labels

For the most up-to-date listings of these and hundreds of other record labels, visit https://www.musicsocket.com/recordlabels

*To claim your **free** access to the site, please see the back of this book.*

Beggars Group Canada

333 King Street East
Toronto, Ontario
M5A 0E1
Email: canada@beggars.com
Website: https://www.beggarsgroup.ca
Website: https://twitter.com/BeggarsCanada

Genres: Alternative; Pop; Rock

Record label based in Toronto, Ontario.

Borealis Records

Email: info@linusent.ca
Website: https://borealisrecords.com
Website: https://www.facebook.com/BorealisRecords/

Genres: Americana; Blues; Folk; Roots; Singer-Songwriter; World

A small dedicated independent record company founded by musicians for musicians located in downtown Toronto.

Dine Alone Records

864 Eastern Avenue
Toronto, ON M4L 1A3
Email: info@dinealonerecords.com
Website: https://dinealonerecords.com
Website: https://www.facebook.com/dinealonerecords

Genres: Emo; Indie; Hip-Hop; Post Hardcore; Punk; Rock

Record label with offices in Toronto, Nashville, Los Angeles, and Sydney.

Justin Time Records Inc.

482 av. Lansdowne
Westmount, QC
H3Y 2V2
Email: info@justin-time.com
Website: https://justin-time.com

Genres: Alternative; Blues; Folk; Gospel; Jazz; Rock; World

Record label based in Westmount, Quebec.

Mughal Music Group

3300 Bloor Street West, Suite 3140
11th Floor
Toronto, Ontario, M8X 2X3
Website: http://www.mughalentertainment.com
Website: https://www.facebook.com/mughalmusicgroup

Genres: R&B; Rap; Hip-Hop; Reggae; Urban; Soundtracks

A global music production company focused on music for film, television, fashion film, games and musical artists.

Nettwerk Records

1675 West 2nd Ave, 2nd Floor
Vancouver, BC V6J 1H3

Email: info@nettwerk.com
Website: http://www.nettwerk.com
Website: https://www.facebook.com/nettwerkmusicgroup

Genres: Acoustic; Folk; Singer-Songwriter

Record label with head office in Vancouver and other offices in the United States (Los Angeles, New York, Nashville, Boston), and Europe (London and Hamburg).

NorthernBlues Music Inc.

39 Birch Ave.
Ottawa ON
K1K 3G5
Email: info@northernblues.com
Website: http://www.northernblues.com
Website: https://www.facebook.com/NorthernBlues-Music-209455625926/

Genres: Blues; World; Roots; Gospel

Record label based in Ottowa, Ontario. Aims to be a friendly home to Canadian blues artists.

Sphere Music

Website: http://www.spheremusique.com
Website: https://www.facebook.com/spheremusique

Genres: All types of music

Record label based in Quebec.

True North Records

23 Griffin Street, P.O. Box 170
Waterdown, Ontario
L0R 2H0
Email: geoff@truenorthrecords.com
Email: brooke@truenorthrecords.com
Website: https://truenorthrecords.com
Website: https://www.facebook.com/tnrecords/

Genres: Blues; Country; Folk; Indie; Jazz; Reggae; Rock; Roots

Describes itself as "Canada's oldest independent record label and one of its largest."

Record Labels Index

This section lists record labels by their genres, with directions to the section of the book where the full listing can be found.

You can create your own customised lists of record labels using different combinations of these subject areas, plus over a dozen other criteria, instantly online at https://www.musicsocket.com.

*To claim your **free** access to the site, please see the back of this book.*

All types of music
88 Rising (*US*)
Acid Jazz Records (*UK*)
Adasam Limited (*UK*)
All Star Music Corporation (*US*)
Ambiel (*UK*)
American Eagle Recordings (*US*)
American Recordings (*US*)
Aspenbeat LLC (*US*)
Atlantic Records (*US*)
AvatarDigi (*US*)
Ba Da Bing Records & Management (*US*)
Big3 Records, Inc. (*US*)
Black Dahlia Music (*US*)
Blue Canoe Records (*US*)
Blue Elan Records (*US*)
Cherry Red Records (*UK*)
Circuit Records (*UK*)
Columbia Records (*US*)
Confidential Records (UK) Ltd (*UK*)
Cooking Vinyl (*UK*)
Cruise International Records (*UK*)
Daemon Records (*US*)
East Central One (*UK*)
ESP-Disk' Ltd (*US*)
Estrus Records (*US*)
Fantasy Records (*US*)
Fat Hippy Records (*UK*)
FatCat Records UK (*UK*)
FatCat Records UK (*UK*)
Fever Records (*US*)
Fiction Records (*UK*)
First Access Entertainment (FAE) (*US*)
Gerry Loves Records (*UK*)
Gizeh Records (*UK*)
Green Pepper Junction (*UK*)
Handsome Dad Records (*UK*)
I Ka Ching Records (*UK*)
Innersense Music (*UK*)
Intuitive Productions (*UK*)
Invisible Hands Music (*UK*)
Island Records (*UK*)
Jeepster Recordings Ltd (*UK*)
Jungle Records (*UK*)
!K7 Records (*US*)
Light In The Attic (*US*)
Manic Records UK (*UK*)
Measured Records (*UK*)
Mosley Music Group (*US*)
MRG Recordings (*US*)
National Anthem (*UK*)
Noisy Poet Records (*US*)
One Little Independent Records (*UK*)
The Orchard (*US*)
Ostereo (*UK*)
Parlophone Records (*UK*)
Play It Again Sam (*UK*)
Polydor Records (*UK*)
Purple Worm Records (*UK*)
Ramp Records (*US*)

Rampage Records (*US*)
Raven Black Music (*UK*)
Razor Sharp Records South, Inc. (*US*)
RCA Label Group UK (*UK*)
Renaissance Records (*US*)
Republic Records (*US*)
Rose Coloured Records (*UK*)
The Royalty Network, Inc. (*US*)
Scruff of the Neck (SOTN) (*UK*)
Segue Records (*US*)
Sick House Entertainment (*US*)
Silver Blue Productions / Joel Diamond Entertainment (*US*)
Small Pond Record Label (*UK*)
Sony Music Entertainment UK Ltd (*UK*)
Sony Music Entertainment (*US*)
Sotones Music Co-Operative (*UK*)
Sphere Music (*Can*)
Star Time Intl (*US*)
Stef Angel Music (*US*)
Stereokill Recordings (*UK*)
Stones Throw Records (*US*)
Sumerian Records (*US*)
Surfview Records (*US*)
Symbiotic Records (*US*)
Team Love Records (*US*)
Third Man Records (*US*)
37 Records & Management (*US*)
300 Entertainment (*US*)
Topshelf Records (*US*)
Toucan Cove Entertainment (*US*)
Unfun Records (*US*)
Union Entertainment Group (UEG), Inc. (*US*)
Vagrant Records (*US*)
Warner Music Group (WMG) (*US*)
Warner Records (*US*)
Warrior Records (*US*)

Acid

Backwater Records (*UK*)
Dorado Music (*UK*)
Secret Formula Records, Inc. (*US*)
Secret Records Ltd (*UK*)

Acoustic

Aardvark Records Ltd (*UK*)
Abet Publishing (*US*)
Acoustic Disc (*US*)
The Animal Farm (*UK*)
Arctic Siren Records (*US*)
ATO Records (*US*)
Big Scary Monsters Recording Company (*UK*)
Bohemian Jukebox (*UK*)
Boosweet Records (*US*)
Commercially Inviable Records (*UK*)
Concrete Recordings (*UK*)
Favored Nations Entertainment (*US*)
Fence Records (*UK*)
Flair Records (*UK*)
Groovin' Records (*UK*)
Heartland Recordings (*US*)
In At The Eye Records (*UK*)
istartedthefire records (*UK*)
Just Music (*UK*)
Lab Records (*UK*)
The Lab (*UK*)
Meloden Nashville (*US*)
Nettwerk Records (*UK*)
Nettwerk Records (*Can*)
Remixdj (*UK*)
Secret Records Ltd (*UK*)
Southern Records (*UK*)
West Clark Records (*US*)
Zube Records (*UK*)

Alternative

A&M Records (*US*)
Aardvark Records Ltd (*UK*)
Abet Publishing (*US*)
Alcopop! Records (*UK*)
American Laundromat Records (*US*)
The Animal Farm (*UK*)
Asthmatic Kitty Records (*US*)
Astralwerks Records (*US*)
ATO Records (*US*)
Audiobulb Records (*UK*)
Backwater Records (*UK*)
BackWords Recordings (*US*)
Bar/None Records (*US*)
Beggars Group (US) (*US*)
Beggars Group Canada (*Can*)
Better Looking Records (*US*)
Big Dada Recordings (*UK*)
Big Scary Monsters Recording Company (*UK*)
Bohemian Jukebox (*UK*)
Boosweet Records (*US*)
Buzz Records (*UK*)
Chemikal Underground Records (*UK*)
Clue Records (*UK*)
Dead by Mono Records (*UK*)
Dirty Hit (*UK*)
Dissention Records (*UK*)
Domino Recording Company (*UK*)
Dramatico Entertainment Ltd (*UK*)
Drum With Our Hands (*UK*)
Emperor Jones Records (*US*)
Engineer Records (*UK*)
Esoteric Recordings (*UK*)
Fantastic Plastic (*UK*)
Farmyard Records (*UK*)

Fast Static (*UK*)
Fat Wreck Chords (*US*)
Glasstone Records (*UK*)
Hassle Records (*UK*)
Heavenly Recordings (*UK*)
Hit And Run Records (*UK*)
Holier Than Thou Records (*UK*)
Ignition Records (*UK*)
In At The Eye Records (*UK*)
Iron Man Records (*UK*)
istartedthefire records (*UK*)
Justin Time Records Inc. (*Can*)
King Prawn Records (*UK*)
La Corporación Muzic (*US*)
Lab Records (*UK*)
The Lab (*UK*)
The Leaf Label Ltd (*UK*)
Lewis Recordings (*UK*)
Lex Records Ltd (*UK*)
Lojinx (*UK*)
Loose Music (*UK*)
Manifesto Records, Inc. (*US*)
Meloden Nashville (*US*)
Memphis Industries (*UK*)
Moksha Recordings Ltd (*UK*)
Mook Records (*UK*)
Moshi Moshi Records (*UK*)
Mute Records (*UK*)
No Dancing Records (*UK*)
Phantasy Sound Ltd (*UK*)
Pravda Records (*US*)
Public Pressure (*UK*)
Red Eye Music (*UK*)
Relentless Records (*UK*)
Remixdj (*UK*)
River Rat Records (*UK*)
Rock Action Records (*UK*)
Schnitzel Records Ltd (*UK*)
Secret Records Ltd (*UK*)
Seeca Music Ltd (*UK*)
Shangri-La Projects, Inc. (*US*)
Side One Dummy Records (*US*)
Skate Mountain Records (*US*)
Skinny Dog Records (*UK*)
Snapper Music (*UK*)
So Recordings (*UK*)
Southern Records (*UK*)
Squirrel Records (*UK*)
Strange Music Inc. (*US*)
Thin Man Entertainment (*US*)
Thrive Records (*US*)
Tommy Boy (*US*)
TommyBoy Entertainment LLC (*US*)
Tooth & Nail Records (*US*)
Touch and Go Records (*US*)
Triple Crown Records (*US*)
Try Harder Records (*UK*)
TV Records Ltd (*UK*)
Urband & Lazar (*US*)
West Clark Records (*US*)
Wrath Records (*UK*)
Zube Records (*UK*)

Ambient
Aardvark Records Ltd (*UK*)
Abet Publishing (*US*)
Alex Tronic Records (*UK*)
Audiobulb Records (*UK*)
Blindsight Records (*UK*)
Brain Bomb Productions (BBP) (*UK*)
Burning Shed Limited (*UK*)
Drum With Our Hands (*UK*)
Enhanced Music (*UK*)
Just Music (*UK*)
RareNoiseRecords (*UK*)
Remixdj (*UK*)
Rhombus Records (*US*)
Scylla Records (*UK*)
Six Degrees Records (*US*)
ThrillerTracks (*US*)
Van Richter (*US*)
Waveform Records (*US*)

Americana
Alligator Records (*US*)
Borealis Records (*Can*)
Heartland Recordings (*US*)
Loose Music (*UK*)
Meloden Nashville (*US*)
Memphis International Records (*US*)
Red Eye Music (*UK*)
Rhombus Records (*US*)
Rounder Records (*US*)
Signature Sound Recordings (*US*)
Skate Mountain Records (*US*)
Sub Pop Records (*US*)
Sugar Hill Records (*US*)
Universal Music Group Nashville (*US*)

Avant-Garde
Armellodie (*UK*)
Audiobulb Records (*UK*)
BackWords Recordings (*US*)
K2B2 Records (*US*)
Remixdj (*UK*)
Rhombus Records (*US*)

Black Origin
Secret Records Ltd (*UK*)

Blue Beat
Secret Records Ltd (*UK*)

Blues
Aardvark Records Ltd (*UK*)
Acoustic Disc (*US*)

Alligator Records (*US*)
Basin Street Records (*US*)
Blue Wave Records (*US*)
Boosweet Records (*US*)
Borealis Records (*Can*)
Buzz Records (*UK*)
Dead by Mono Records (*UK*)
Ecko Records (*US*)
Favored Nations Entertainment (*US*)
Fedora (*US*)
Groovin' Records (*UK*)
Harmonized Records (*US*)
Justin Time Records Inc. (*Can*)
K2B2 Records (*US*)
Knitting Factory Records (*US*)
Malaco Music Group (*US*)
Mega Truth Records (*US*)
Megawave Records (*US*)
Meloden Nashville (*US*)
Memphis International Records (*US*)
NorthernBlues Music Inc. (*Can*)
Perry Road Records Ltd (*UK*)
Public Pressure (*UK*)
Red Eye Music (*UK*)
Remixdj (*UK*)
Rhombus Records (*US*)
River Rat Records (*UK*)
Rounder Records (*US*)
SCI Fidelity Records (*US*)
Secret Records Ltd (*UK*)
Shanachie Entertainment (*US*)
Shrapnel Records (*US*)
Skaggs Family Records (*US*)
Skate Mountain Records (*US*)
Sony Music Entertainment – Legacy Recordings (*US*)
Stackhouse & BluEsoterica (*US*)
Sugar Hill Records (*US*)
Summit Records, Inc (*US*)
Sunnyside Records (*US*)
Terminus Records (*US*)
True North Records (*Can*)
Tuff City Music Group (*US*)
Valley Entertainment (*US*)
Wild Records (*US*)
Yep Roc Records (*US*)

Break Beat

Aardvark Records Ltd (*UK*)
Alex Tronic Records (*UK*)
Botchit & Scarper Records (*UK*)
Brain Bomb Productions (BBP) (*UK*)
Finger Lickin' Records (*UK*)
Ninja Tune (*UK*)

Celtic

Aardvark Records Ltd (*UK*)
ARC Music Productions International (*UK*)
Greentrax Recordings (*UK*)
Linn Records (*UK*)
Lismor Recordings (*UK*)
REL Records Ltd (*UK*)
Ridge Records Limited (*UK*)
Valley Entertainment (*US*)

Chill

Aardvark Records Ltd (*UK*)
Abet Publishing (*US*)
AD Music (*UK*)
Brain Bomb Productions (BBP) (*UK*)
Enhanced Music (*UK*)
Just Music (*UK*)
Needwant (*UK*)
NexGen Music Group, LLC (*US*)
Pretty Neat Records (*UK*)
Release / Sustain (*UK*)
Remixdj (*UK*)
Waveform Records (*US*)

Christian

Heartland Recordings (*US*)
Heaven's Disciples, LLC (*US*)
Integrity Music (*US*)
Meloden Nashville (*US*)
Pendulum Records (*US*)
Primarily A Cappella (*US*)
Reunion Records (*US*)
Rockzion Records (*US*)
Skaggs Family Records (*US*)
Vineyard Worship (*US*)
VSR Music Group (*US*)
Word Records (*US*)

Classic

Drum With Our Hands (*UK*)
Esoteric Recordings (*UK*)
Kufe Records Ltd (*UK*)
1-2-3-4 Go! Records (*US*)
Remixdj (*UK*)
Secret Formula Records, Inc. (*US*)
Secret Records Ltd (*UK*)
Skate Mountain Records (*US*)
Soul Jazz Records Ltd (*UK*)

Classical

Abet Publishing (*US*)
Acoustic Disc (*US*)
API Records (*US*)
Arabesque Recordings (*US*)
BackWords Recordings (*US*)
Boosweet Records (*US*)
Caritas Records (*UK*)
Chandos Records Ltd (*UK*)
CRD Records Limited (*UK*)
Divine Art Record Company (*UK*)

Favored Nations Entertainment (*US*)
K2B2 Records (*US*)
Linn Records (*UK*)
Remixdj (*UK*)
Secret Formula Records, Inc. (*US*)
Signum Records (*UK*)
Six Degrees Records (*US*)
SOMM Recordings (*UK*)
Summit Records, Inc (*US*)

Club

Phunk Junk Records Inc (*US*)
Remixdj (*UK*)
Throne of Blood Records (*US*)
West Clark Records (*US*)

Commercial

Aardvark Records Ltd (*UK*)
Amathus Music (*US*)
Amber Artists (*UK*)
Meloden Nashville (*US*)
Remixdj (*UK*)
Secret Formula Records, Inc. (*US*)
Skate Mountain Records (*US*)

Contemporary

Amber Artists (*UK*)
Appleseed Recordings (*US*)
Ecko Records (*US*)
Favored Nations Entertainment (*US*)
5 Points Records (*US*)
Heads Up International (*US*)
Island Records (US) (*US*)
Knitting Factory Records (*US*)
MadTech Records (*UK*)
Meloden Nashville (*US*)
Mountain Apple Company (*US*)
Om Records (*US*)
Primarily A Cappella (*US*)
Rhombus Records (*US*)
Secret Formula Records, Inc. (*US*)
Secret Records Ltd (*UK*)
Silver Wave Records (*US*)
Six Degrees Records (*US*)
SLAM Productions (*UK*)
Surfdog Records (*US*)
Verve Label Group (*US*)
Word Records (*US*)

Country

Alternative Tentacles Records (*US*)
Amazon Records (*UK*)
Atlan-Dec/Grooveline Records (*US*)
Average Joes Entertainment (*US*)
Backwater Records (*UK*)
Boosweet Records (*US*)
Broken Bow Records (*US*)
Buzz Records (*UK*)
Columbia Nashville (*US*)
Commercially Inviable Records (*UK*)
Heartland Recordings (*US*)
Heavenly Recordings (*UK*)
Iffy Folk Records (*UK*)
istartedthefire records (*UK*)
Knitting Factory Records (*US*)
Kufe Records Ltd (*UK*)
Loose Music (*UK*)
Mailboat Records (*US*)
Meloden Nashville (*US*)
Memphis International Records (*US*)
Mercury Nashville (*US*)
New Pants Publishing (*US*)
1-2-3-4 Go! Records (*US*)
Perry Road Records Ltd (*UK*)
Pravda Records (*US*)
Rebel Records (*US*)
Red Eye Music (*UK*)
Robbins Entertainment (*US*)
Saddle Creek (*US*)
Secretly Canadian (*US*)
Shanachie Entertainment (*US*)
Shrapnel Records (*US*)
Skaggs Family Records (*US*)
Skate Mountain Records (*US*)
Sony Music Entertainment – Legacy Recordings (*US*)
Sony Music Nashville (*US*)
Southland Records (*US*)
True North Records (*Can*)
TV Records Ltd (*UK*)
Universal Music Group Nashville (*US*)
Valley Entertainment (*US*)
Warner Music Nashville (*US*)
Word Records (*US*)
Yep Roc Records (*US*)

Dance

76Label Music (*US*)
Aardvark Records Ltd (*UK*)
Alex Tronic Records (*UK*)
Almighty Records Limited (*UK*)
Amathus Music (*US*)
Astralwerks Records (*US*)
Audiobulb Records (*UK*)
Barely Breaking Even Records (*UK*)
Beggars Group (US) (*US*)
Berman Brothers (*US*)
Black Butter Records (*UK*)
Boosweet Records (*US*)
Casablanca Records (*US*)
Chocolate Fireguard Music Ltd (*UK*)
Cr2 Records (*UK*)
Craniality Sounds (*US*)
Critical Music (*UK*)
Dead Happy Records (*UK*)

Defected (*UK*)
Dim Mak Records (*US*)
eenie meenie records (*US*)
Finger Lickin' Records (*UK*)
Fired Up Records (*UK*)
5 Points Records (*US*)
Gravy (*UK*)
Hope Recordings (*UK*)
In At The Eye Records (*UK*)
Innerground Records (*UK*)
Loveslap! Recordings (*US*)
Needwant (*UK*)
New State Music (*UK*)
NexGen Music Group, LLC (*US*)
Om Records (*US*)
Phantasy Sound Ltd (*UK*)
Phunk Junk Records Inc (*US*)
Positiva Records (*UK*)
Remixdj (*UK*)
Robbins Entertainment (*US*)
Saint Productions (*UK*)
Secret Formula Records, Inc. (*US*)
Six Degrees Records (*US*)
Skint Entertainment (*UK*)
Soma Recordings Ltd (*UK*)
Southern Fried Records (*UK*)
Spiral Galaxy Entertainment (*US*)
Subliminal Records (*US*)
3 Beat Records (*UK*)
Thrive Records (*US*)
Thump Records (*US*)
Tommy Boy (*US*)
TommyBoy Entertainment LLC (*US*)
Ultra Music (*US*)
West Clark Records (*US*)

Deep Funk
Remixdj (*UK*)

Disco
Barely Breaking Even Records (*UK*)
PAPERecordings (*UK*)
Remixdj (*UK*)
Soul Jazz Records Ltd (*UK*)
Throne of Blood Records (*US*)

Downtempo
Aardvark Records Ltd (*UK*)
Alex Tronic Records (*UK*)
Audiobulb Records (*UK*)
Brain Bomb Productions (BBP) (*UK*)
Just Music (*UK*)
NexGen Music Group, LLC (*US*)
Ninja Tune (*UK*)
Waveform Records (*US*)

Drum and Bass
Aardvark Records Ltd (*UK*)
Alex Tronic Records (*UK*)
Brain Bomb Productions (BBP) (*UK*)
Critical Music (*UK*)
Dorado Music (*UK*)
Hospital Records (*UK*)
Infidelity Records (*UK*)
Innerground Records (*UK*)
NexGen Music Group, LLC (*US*)
Nu Electro (*UK*)
Pretty Neat Records (*UK*)
Ram Records (*UK*)
Saving Grace Music (*UK*)
Tangent Recordings (*UK*)
West Clark Records (*US*)

Dub
Ariwa Sounds Ltd (*UK*)
Pumpkin Records (*UK*)
RareNoiseRecords (*UK*)
Remixdj (*UK*)

Dubstep
Lewis Recordings (*UK*)
NexGen Music Group, LLC (*US*)
NoFace Records (*US*)
Pretty Neat Records (*UK*)
Saving Grace Music (*UK*)
Soul Jazz Records Ltd (*UK*)
Southpoint (*UK*)
West Clark Records (*US*)

Electronic
76Label Music (*US*)
Abet Publishing (*US*)
AD Music (*UK*)
Alex Tronic Records (*UK*)
Alias Records (*US*)
Alpha Pup Records (*US*)
Amathus Music (*US*)
Aphagia Recordings (*US*)
Ariwa Sounds Ltd (*UK*)
Astralwerks Records (*US*)
Audiobulb Records (*UK*)
Babygrande Records, Inc. (*US*)
BackWords Recordings (*US*)
Beggars Group (US) (*US*)
Bifocal Media (*US*)
Black Acre Records (*UK*)
Blindsight Records (*UK*)
Blue Jackel Entertainment (*US*)
Border Community (*UK*)
Burning Shed Limited (*UK*)
Buzzin' Fly Records (*UK*)
Casablanca Records (*US*)
Chocolate Fireguard Music Ltd (*UK*)
Circus Records (*UK*)
Cityscape Records (*UK*)
Cr2 Records (*UK*)
Criminal Records (*UK*)

Critical Music (*UK*)
Dancing Turtle Records (*UK*)
Dim Mak Records (*US*)
Dorado Music (*UK*)
Drum With Our Hands (*UK*)
eenie meenie records (*US*)
Enhanced Music (*UK*)
Esoteric Recordings (*UK*)
Far Out Recordings (*UK*)
Finger Lickin' Records (*UK*)
5 Points Records (*US*)
Glasstone Records (*UK*)
Harmonized Records (*US*)
Holier Than Thou Records (*UK*)
Houndstooth (*UK*)
In At The Eye Records (*UK*)
Just Music (*UK*)
JW Music Limited (*UK*)
Knitting Factory Records (*US*)
La Corporación Muzic (*US*)
Lewis Recordings (*UK*)
MadTech Records (*UK*)
MaggotHouse Music (*UK*)
Megawave Records (*US*)
Moksha Recordings Ltd (*UK*)
Mute Records (*UK*)
Needwant (*UK*)
NexGen Music Group, LLC (*US*)
9 Volt Records (*UK*)
Ninja Tune (*UK*)
NoFace Records (*US*)
Nu Electro (*UK*)
Om Records (*US*)
One Inch Badge (OIB) Records (*UK*)
Phantasy Sound Ltd (*UK*)
Phunk Junk Records Inc (*US*)
Pi Recordings (*US*)
Pinball Records (*UK*)
Pretty Neat Records (*UK*)
Public Pressure (*UK*)
Ramber Records (*UK*)
Rekids Ltd (*UK*)
Remixdj (*UK*)
Robbins Entertainment (*US*)
Rock Action Records (*UK*)
Ropeadope Records (*US*)
Saddle Creek (*US*)
Saved Records (*UK*)
SCI Fidelity Records (*US*)
Secret Formula Records, Inc. (*US*)
Shanachie Entertainment (*US*)
Six Degrees Records (*US*)
Sonic Cathedral (*UK*)
Soul Jazz Records Ltd (*UK*)
Soundplate (*UK*)
Southern Fried Records (*UK*)
Space Age Recordings (*UK*)
Sub Pop Records (*US*)
Subliminal Records (*US*)
ThrillerTracks (*US*)
Thrive Records (*US*)
Throne of Blood Records (*US*)
Thump Records (*US*)
Tommy Boy (*US*)
TommyBoy Entertainment LLC (*US*)
Ultra Music (*US*)
Waveform Records (*US*)
West Clark Records (*US*)
Zube Records (*UK*)

Emo
Dine Alone Records (*Can*)
Engineer Records (*UK*)
Hassle Records (*UK*)
Pinky Swear Records (*UK*)
Revelation Records (*US*)
Struggletown Records (*UK*)
West Clark Records (*US*)

Ethnic
Sonic Safari Music (*US*)
Sony Music Entertainment – Legacy Recordings (*US*)

Experimental
Actual Size Music (*UK*)
Aphagia Recordings (*US*)
Audiobulb Records (*UK*)
Bohemian Jukebox (*UK*)
D.O.R. (*UK*)
Dancing Turtle Records (*UK*)
Hydra Head Records (*US*)
In At The Eye Records (*UK*)
The Leaf Label Ltd (*UK*)
MaggotHouse Music (*UK*)
NexGen Music Group, LLC (*US*)
Remixdj (*UK*)
SLAM Productions (*UK*)
Space Age Recordings (*UK*)
Zube Records (*UK*)

Extreme
Rotten Records (*US*)

Folk
Aardvark Records Ltd (*UK*)
Acoustic Disc (*US*)
Amazon Records (*UK*)
American Laundromat Records (*US*)
Appleseed Recordings (*US*)
ARC Music Productions International (*UK*)
Backwater Records (*UK*)
Blue Jackel Entertainment (*US*)
Bohemian Jukebox (*UK*)

Boosweet Records (*US*)
Borealis Records (*Can*)
Buzz Records (*UK*)
Commercially Inviable Records (*UK*)
Dancing Turtle Records (*UK*)
Drum With Our Hands (*UK*)
Emperor Jones Records (*US*)
Fellside Recordings (*UK*)
Fika Recordings (*UK*)
Folkroom Records (*UK*)
Heartland Recordings (*US*)
Iffy Folk Records (*UK*)
istartedthefire records (*UK*)
JohnJohn Records (*UK*)
Justin Time Records Inc. (*Can*)
Knitting Factory Records (*US*)
Lab Records (*UK*)
The Lab (*UK*)
Mailboat Records (*US*)
Meloden Nashville (*US*)
Memphis International Records (*US*)
Nettwerk Records (*UK*)
Nettwerk Records (*Can*)
New Pants Publishing (*US*)
NYC Records (*US*)
Oh Boy Records (*US*)
One Inch Badge (OIB) Records (*UK*)
Park Records (*UK*)
Quatre Femmes Records (*UK*)
Rebel Records (*US*)
Red Eye Music (*UK*)
Rhombus Records (*US*)
River Rat Records (*UK*)
Ropeadope Records (*US*)
Rounder Records (*US*)
Saving Grace Music (*UK*)
Secret Records Ltd (*UK*)
Secretly Canadian (*US*)
Shanachie Entertainment (*US*)
Signature Sound Recordings (*US*)
Six Degrees Records (*US*)
Sony Music Entertainment – Legacy Recordings (*US*)
Southern Records (*UK*)
Sub Pop Records (*US*)
Surfdog Records (*US*)
True North Records (*Can*)
Yep Roc Records (*US*)

Funk

Barely Breaking Even Records (*UK*)
Headcount Records (*UK*)
NexGen Music Group, LLC (*US*)
1-2-3-4 Go! Records (*US*)
Remixdj (*UK*)
Secret Formula Records, Inc. (*US*)
Soul Jazz Records Ltd (*UK*)
Tuff City Music Group (*US*)

Funky

Craniality Sounds (*US*)
Meloden Nashville (*US*)
Remixdj (*UK*)
Rhombus Records (*US*)
3 Beat Records (*UK*)

Fusion

Moksha Recordings Ltd (*UK*)
Remixdj (*UK*)
Rhombus Records (*US*)
Secret Formula Records, Inc. (*US*)
Secret Records Ltd (*UK*)

Garage

Barely Breaking Even Records (*UK*)
Champion Records (*UK*)
Dead by Mono Records (*UK*)
Dirtee Stank (*UK*)
Dirty Water Records (*UK*)
Fuzzkill Records (*UK*)
Holier Than Thou Records (*UK*)
NexGen Music Group, LLC (*US*)
1-2-3-4 Go! Records (*US*)
A Priscilla Thing (*UK*)
Pumpkin Records (*UK*)
Ramber Records (*UK*)
Remixdj (*UK*)
Saving Grace Music (*UK*)
Secret Records Ltd (*UK*)
Skate Mountain Records (*US*)
Southpoint (*UK*)
West Clark Records (*US*)
Wicked Cool Records (*US*)
Wild Records (*US*)

Glam

Holier Than Thou Records (*UK*)

Glitch

Aphagia Recordings (*US*)

Gospel

Ecko Records (*US*)
Heartland Recordings (*US*)
Integrity Music (*US*)
Justin Time Records Inc. (*Can*)
Malaco Music Group (*US*)
Megawave Records (*US*)
Meloden Nashville (*US*)
NorthernBlues Music Inc. (*Can*)
Pendulum Records (*US*)
Shanachie Entertainment (*US*)
Sony Music Entertainment – Legacy Recordings (*US*)
Southland Records (*US*)
Spiral Galaxy Entertainment (*US*)

Gothic
Holier Than Thou Records (*UK*)
Invisible Records (*US*)
Thin Man Entertainment (*US*)
Van Richter (*US*)
Grime
Big Dada Recordings (*UK*)
Dirtee Stank (*UK*)
Saving Grace Music (*UK*)
Southpoint (*UK*)
Guitar based
BackWords Recordings (*US*)
Concrete Recordings (*UK*)
Fantastic Plastic (*UK*)
Fika Recordings (*UK*)
I'm Not From London (*UK*)
Meloden Nashville (*US*)
Remixdj (*UK*)
Secret Records Ltd (*UK*)
Shrapnel Records (*US*)
Squirrel Records (*UK*)
West Clark Records (*US*)
Hard
A389 Recordings (*US*)
Fired Up Records (*UK*)
Holier Than Thou Records (*UK*)
Hydra Head Records (*US*)
Secret Records Ltd (*UK*)
Shrapnel Records (*US*)
Southern Lord Recordings (*US*)
Spinefarm Records (*US*)
Suburban Noize Records (*US*)
West Clark Records (*US*)
Hardcore
Alternative Tentacles Records (*US*)
Banquet Records (*UK*)
Bifocal Media (*US*)
Big Scary Monsters Recording Company (*UK*)
Blindsight Records (*UK*)
Boslevan Records (*UK*)
Dine Alone Records (*Can*)
Dog Knights Productions (*UK*)
Engineer Records (*UK*)
Hassle Records (*UK*)
Hydra Head Records (*US*)
Jade Tree (*US*)
Killing Moon Records (*UK*)
Kung Fu Records (*US*)
1-2-3-4 Go! Records (*US*)
Pinky Swear Records (*UK*)
Psychopathic Records (*US*)
Revelation Records (*US*)
Rotten Records (*US*)
Secretly Canadian (*US*)
Side One Dummy Records (*US*)
Struggletown Records (*UK*)
3 Beat Records (*UK*)
Touch and Go Records (*US*)
Victory Records (*US*)
West Clark Records (*US*)
Heavy
Holier Than Thou Records (*UK*)
Public Pressure (*UK*)
Shrapnel Records (*US*)
West Clark Records (*US*)
Hip-Hop
Alex Tronic Records (*UK*)
Alpha Pup Records (*US*)
Asylum Records (*US*)
Atlan-Dec/Grooveline Records (*US*)
Babygrande Records, Inc. (*US*)
Barbarian Productions (*US*)
Barely Breaking Even Records (*UK*)
Bifocal Media (*US*)
Big Dada Recordings (*UK*)
Black Butter Records (*UK*)
Boosweet Records (*US*)
Chocolate Fireguard Music Ltd (*UK*)
Closed Sessions (*US*)
Def Jam Recordings (*US*)
Delicious Vinyl LLC (*US*)
Dim Mak Records (*US*)
Dine Alone Records (*Can*)
Dirtee Stank (*UK*)
Dorado Music (*UK*)
Finger Lickin' Records (*UK*)
Freddie Records (*US*)
Grim Reality Entertainment, LLC (*US*)
Headcount Records (*UK*)
iHipHop Distribution (*US*)
Island Records (US) (*US*)
Kudos Records Limited (*UK*)
Lab Records (*UK*)
Lewis Recordings (*UK*)
Mughal Music Group (*Can*)
NexGen Music Group, LLC (*US*)
Ninja Tune (*UK*)
Om Records (*US*)
1-2-3-4 Go! Records (*US*)
Pendulum Records (*US*)
A Priscilla Thing (*UK*)
Psychopathic Records (*US*)
Public Pressure (*UK*)
Remixdj (*UK*)
Rhymesayers Entertainment (*US*)
ROKiT Records (*UK*)
Sapien Records Limited (*UK*)
Saving Grace Music (*UK*)
Secret Formula Records, Inc. (*US*)

Shady Records (*US*)
Skate Mountain Records (*US*)
Slip-N-Slide Records (*US*)
Sony Music Entertainment – Legacy Recordings (*US*)
Soul Jazz Records Ltd (*UK*)
Spiral Galaxy Entertainment (*US*)
Suburban Noize Records (*US*)
Surfdog Records (*US*)
Thump Records (*US*)
Tommy Boy (*US*)
TommyBoy Entertainment LLC (*US*)
Tuff City Music Group (*US*)
Ultra Music (*US*)
Viper Records (*US*)
Waxploitation Records (*US*)
Word Records (*US*)

Horror

Dead by Mono Records (*UK*)

House

Aardvark Records Ltd (*UK*)
Alex Tronic Records (*UK*)
Alter Ego Records (*UK*)
Amathus Music (*US*)
Brain Bomb Productions (BBP) (*UK*)
Buzzin' Fly Records (*UK*)
Champion Records (*UK*)
Cr2 Records (*UK*)
Craniality Sounds (*US*)
Defected (*UK*)
Gruuv (*UK*)
JW Music Limited (*UK*)
Kudos Records Limited (*UK*)
Loveslap! Recordings (*US*)
Needwant (*UK*)
NexGen Music Group, LLC (*US*)
NoFace Records (*US*)
PAPERecordings (*UK*)
Phunk Junk Records Inc (*US*)
Pinball Records (*UK*)
A Priscilla Thing (*UK*)
Rekids Ltd (*UK*)
Release / Sustain (*UK*)
Saved Records (*UK*)
Saving Grace Music (*UK*)
Shabby Doll Records (*UK*)
Soul Jazz Records Ltd (*UK*)
Soundplate (*UK*)
Strictly Rhythm (*US*)
Subliminal Records (*US*)
3 Beat Records (*UK*)
Throne of Blood Records (*US*)

House

Aardvark Records Ltd (*UK*)
Alex Tronic Records (*UK*)
Alter Ego Records (*UK*)
Amathus Music (*US*)
Brain Bomb Productions (BBP) (*UK*)
Buzzin' Fly Records (*UK*)
Champion Records (*UK*)
Cr2 Records (*UK*)
Craniality Sounds (*US*)
Defected (*UK*)
Gruuv (*UK*)
JW Music Limited (*UK*)
Kudos Records Limited (*UK*)
Loveslap! Recordings (*US*)
Needwant (*UK*)
NexGen Music Group, LLC (*US*)
NoFace Records (*US*)
PAPERecordings (*UK*)
Phunk Junk Records Inc (*US*)
Pinball Records (*UK*)
A Priscilla Thing (*UK*)
Rekids Ltd (*UK*)
Release / Sustain (*UK*)
Saved Records (*UK*)
Saving Grace Music (*UK*)
Shabby Doll Records (*UK*)
Soul Jazz Records Ltd (*UK*)
Soundplate (*UK*)
Strictly Rhythm (*US*)
Subliminal Records (*US*)
3 Beat Records (*UK*)
Throne of Blood Records (*US*)

IDM

Phunk Junk Records Inc (*US*)
Remixdj (*UK*)

Indie

4AD (*US*)
A&M Records (*US*)
Aardvark Records Ltd (*UK*)
Alcopop! Records (*UK*)
Alias Records (*US*)
Alpha Pup Records (*US*)
Alternative Tentacles Records (*US*)
Amazon Records (*UK*)
American Laundromat Records (*US*)
The Animal Farm (*UK*)
Anti (*US*)
Armellodie (*UK*)
ATO Records (*US*)
Babygrande Records, Inc. (*US*)
BackWords Recordings (*US*)
Banquet Records (*UK*)
Bar/None Records (*US*)
Barsuk Records (*US*)
Beggars Group (US) (*US*)
Beggars Group (*UK*)
Boslevan Records (*UK*)

Cityscape Records (*UK*)
Clue Records (*UK*)
Concrete Recordings (*UK*)
Criminal Records (*UK*)
Dancing Turtle Records (*UK*)
Dead Happy Records (*UK*)
Dim Mak Records (*US*)
Dine Alone Records (*Can*)
Downtown Music (*US*)
eenie meenie records (*US*)
Emperor Jones Records (*US*)
Engineer Records (*UK*)
Farmyard Records (*UK*)
Fierce Panda Records (*UK*)
Fika Recordings (*UK*)
Fire Tower Entertainment (*US*)
Glasstone Records (*UK*)
Hand in Hive (*UK*)
Hassle Records (*UK*)
Heavenly Recordings (*UK*)
Holier Than Thou Records (*UK*)
Iffy Folk Records (*UK*)
In At The Eye Records (*UK*)
Infinite Hive (*UK*)
Island Records (US) (*US*)
Killing Moon Records (*UK*)
King Prawn Records (*UK*)
The Lab (*UK*)
Lojinx (*UK*)
Manifesto Records, Inc. (*US*)
Meloden Nashville (*US*)
Memphis Industries (*UK*)
Midge Bitten Records (*UK*)
Mook Records (*UK*)
No Dancing Records (*UK*)
1-2-3-4 Go! Records (*US*)
Perry Road Records Ltd (*UK*)
Philophobia Music (*UK*)
Quatre Femmes Records (*UK*)
Reach Out International Records (ROIR) (*US*)
Relapse Records (*US*)
Remixdj (*UK*)
Rock Action Records (*UK*)
ROKiT Records (*UK*)
Ropeadope Records (*US*)
Rough Trade Records (*UK*)
Saddle Creek (*US*)
Saving Grace Music (*UK*)
Secret Records Ltd (*UK*)
Secretly Canadian (*US*)
Signature Sound Recordings (*US*)
Slumberland Records (*US*)
So Recordings (*UK*)
Squirrel Records (*UK*)
Sub Pop Records (*US*)
Surfdog Records (*US*)
Tee Pee Records (*US*)
Thrive Records (*US*)
Tongue Master Records (*UK*)
Touch and Go Records (*US*)
Tough Love Records (*UK*)
True North Records (*Can*)
Urband & Lazar (*US*)
Victory Records (*US*)
Wasted State Records (*UK*)
West Clark Records (*US*)
Zube Records (*UK*)

Industrial

Aphagia Recordings (*US*)
Thin Man Entertainment (*US*)
Van Richter (*US*)

Instrumental

AD Music (*UK*)
Aphagia Recordings (*US*)
Babygrande Records, Inc. (*US*)
BackWords Recordings (*US*)
Dancing Cat Records (*US*)
Dead by Mono Records (*UK*)
Heads Up International (*US*)
Heaven's Disciples, LLC (*US*)
Remixdj (*UK*)
Secret Formula Records, Inc. (*US*)
Secret Records Ltd (*UK*)
ThrillerTracks (*US*)
Valley Entertainment (*US*)

Jazz

Acoustic Disc (*US*)
Amherst Record Sales, Inc. (*US*)
Arabesque Recordings (*US*)
Arkadia Entertainment Corp (*US*)
Atlan-Dec/Grooveline Records (*US*)
Barely Breaking Even Records (*UK*)
Basin Street Records (*US*)
Blue Jackel Entertainment (*US*)
Boosweet Records (*US*)
Cexton Records (*US*)
Dorado Music (*UK*)
Favored Nations Entertainment (*US*)
Harmonized Records (*US*)
Heads Up International (*US*)
JohnJohn Records (*UK*)
Justin Time Records Inc. (*Can*)
K2B2 Records (*US*)
Knitting Factory Records (*US*)
Kudos Records Limited (*UK*)
Lake (*UK*)
Linn Records (*UK*)
Mack Avenue (*US*)
Malaco Music Group (*US*)

Megawave Records (*US*)
Memphis International Records (*US*)
Ninja Tune (*UK*)
NYC Records (*US*)
1-2-3-4 Go! Records (*US*)
Pi Recordings (*US*)
Posi-Tone (*US*)
Primarily A Cappella (*US*)
A Priscilla Thing (*UK*)
RareNoiseRecords (*UK*)
Remixdj (*UK*)
Revolver Records (*UK*)
Rhombus Records (*US*)
Ropeadope Records (*US*)
Rounder Records (*US*)
Secret Formula Records, Inc. (*US*)
Secret Records Ltd (*UK*)
Shanachie Entertainment (*US*)
Shrapnel Records (*US*)
SLAM Productions (*UK*)
Sony Music Entertainment – Legacy Recordings (*US*)
Soul Jazz Records Ltd (*UK*)
Spiral Galaxy Entertainment (*US*)
Summit Records, Inc (*US*)
Sunnyside Records (*US*)
Thin Man Entertainment (*US*)
33 Jazz Records Ltd (*UK*)
True North Records (*Can*)
Tuff City Music Group (*US*)
Valley Entertainment (*US*)
Verve Label Group (*US*)

Latin

Acoustic Disc (*US*)
ARC Music Productions International (*UK*)
Basin Street Records (*US*)
Blue Jackel Entertainment (*US*)
Boosweet Records (*US*)
Freddie Records (*US*)
Heads Up International (*US*)
La Corporación Muzic (*US*)
Pendulum Records (*US*)
Remixdj (*UK*)
Rhombus Records (*US*)
Six Degrees Records (*US*)
Soul Jazz Records Ltd (*UK*)
Thump Records (*US*)
Tommy Boy (*US*)

Leftfield

Armellodie (*UK*)
Audiobulb Records (*UK*)
Bohemian Jukebox (*UK*)
In At The Eye Records (*UK*)
Kudos Records Limited (*UK*)
Ninja Tune (*UK*)
No Dancing Records (*UK*)
PAPERecordings (*UK*)
Remixdj (*UK*)
Soul Jazz Records Ltd (*UK*)
Wrath Records (*UK*)

Lo-fi

Fuzzkill Records (*UK*)
Holier Than Thou Records (*UK*)
Slumberland Records (*US*)
Squirrel Records (*UK*)
TV Records Ltd (*UK*)
West Clark Records (*US*)

Lounge

Remixdj (*UK*)
Secret Formula Records, Inc. (*US*)

Mainstream

Flair Records (*UK*)
In At The Eye Records (*UK*)
Lake (*UK*)
Meloden Nashville (*US*)
Remixdj (*UK*)
Skate Mountain Records (*US*)
West Clark Records (*US*)

Melodic

BackWords Recordings (*US*)
Gearhead Records (*US*)
Holier Than Thou Records (*UK*)
Meloden Nashville (*US*)

Metal

A389 Recordings (*US*)
Alternative Tentacles Records (*US*)
The Animal Farm (*UK*)
Basick Records (*UK*)
Blindsight Records (*UK*)
Boosweet Records (*US*)
Candlelight Records (*UK*)
Earache London (*UK*)
Favored Nations Entertainment (*US*)
Glasstone Records (*UK*)
Hassle Records (*UK*)
Holier Than Thou Records (*UK*)
Hydra Head Records (*US*)
Infinite Hive (*UK*)
Invisible Records (*US*)
Iron Man Records (*UK*)
Island Records (US) (*US*)
King Prawn Records (*UK*)
Knitting Factory Records (*US*)
Metalbox Recordings (*UK*)
Public Pressure (*UK*)
Relapse Records (*US*)
Revolver Records (*UK*)
Roadrunner Records (*UK*)
Rotten Records (*US*)

Sapien Records Limited (*UK*)
Scylla Records (*UK*)
Shrapnel Records (*US*)
Snapper Music (*UK*)
Southern Lord Recordings (*US*)
Spinefarm Records (*US*)
Sub Pop Records (*US*)
Tee Pee Records (*US*)
Victory Records (*US*)
Wasted State Records (*UK*)
West Clark Records (*US*)
Modern
Better Looking Records (*US*)
Meloden Nashville (*US*)
Remixdj (*UK*)
Signature Sound Recordings (*US*)
Terminus Records (*US*)
MOR
Meloden Nashville (*US*)
Mystical
BackWords Recordings (*US*)
New Age
Aardvark Records Ltd (*UK*)
Favored Nations Entertainment (*US*)
Rhombus Records (*US*)
Secret Formula Records, Inc. (*US*)
Silver Wave Records (*US*)
Sound Feelings (*US*)
Valley Entertainment (*US*)
New Wave
Dead by Mono Records (*UK*)
Gearhead Records (*US*)
In At The Eye Records (*UK*)
Meloden Nashville (*US*)
Nu Electro (*UK*)
Squirrel Records (*UK*)
Non-Commercial
Blue Wave Records (*US*)
Remixdj (*UK*)
Secret Formula Records, Inc. (*US*)
West Clark Records (*US*)
Nostalgia
Remixdj (*UK*)
Pop
76Label Music (*US*)
A&M Records (*US*)
Aardvark Records Ltd (*UK*)
Abet Publishing (*US*)
ABKCO Music & Records Inc. (*US*)
Aeronaut Records (*US*)
Almighty Records Limited (*UK*)
Alpha Pup Records (*US*)
Alternative Tentacles Records (*US*)
Amazon Records (*UK*)
Amber Artists (*UK*)
American Laundromat Records (*US*)
Amherst Record Sales, Inc. (*US*)
The Animal Farm (*UK*)
API Records (*US*)
Asthmatic Kitty Records (*US*)
Atlan-Dec/Grooveline Records (*US*)
ATO Records (*US*)
Backwater Records (*UK*)
Barbarian Productions (*US*)
Basin Street Records (*US*)
Beggars Group Canada (*Can*)
Berman Brothers (*US*)
Boosweet Records (*US*)
Cityscape Records (*UK*)
Delicious Vinyl LLC (*US*)
Dim Mak Records (*US*)
Dirty Water Records (*UK*)
Downtown Music (*US*)
Dramatico Entertainment Ltd (*UK*)
Drum With Our Hands (*UK*)
eenie meenie records (*US*)
Esoteric Recordings (*UK*)
Farmyard Records (*UK*)
Fire Tower Entertainment (*US*)
5 Points Records (*US*)
Flair Records (*UK*)
Flair Records (*UK*)
Gearhead Records (*US*)
Hand in Hive (*UK*)
Hassle Records (*UK*)
Heavenly Recordings (*UK*)
Hit And Run Records (*UK*)
In At The Eye Records (*UK*)
Island Records (US) (*US*)
Jade Tree (*US*)
JSNTGM (Just Say No To Government Music) (*UK*)
JW Music Limited (*UK*)
Killing Moon Records (*UK*)
Kung Fu Records (*US*)
La Corporación Muzic (*US*)
Lab Records (*UK*)
The Lab (*UK*)
Mailboat Records (*US*)
Manifesto Records, Inc. (*US*)
Meloden Nashville (*US*)
New Pants Publishing (*US*)
NexGen Music Group, LLC (*US*)
One Inch Badge (OIB) Records (*UK*)
Pendulum Records (*US*)
Philophobia Music (*UK*)
Pinky Swear Records (*UK*)
Pravda Records (*US*)
Quatre Femmes Records (*UK*)
Ramber Records (*UK*)

The Red Flag Recording Co. (*UK*)
Remixdj (*UK*)
Reunion Records (*US*)
Rhombus Records (*US*)
Robbins Entertainment (*US*)
Saint Productions (*UK*)
Sapien Records Limited (*UK*)
Saving Grace Music (*UK*)
Schoolboy Records (*US*)
Scylla Records (*UK*)
Secretly Canadian (*US*)
Signature Sound Recordings (*US*)
Six Degrees Records (*US*)
Skate Mountain Records (*US*)
Slip-N-Slide Records (*US*)
Slumberland Records (*US*)
Sony Music Entertainment – Legacy Recordings (*US*)
Sound Feelings (*US*)
Southland Records (*US*)
Spiral Galaxy Entertainment (*US*)
Squirrel Records (*UK*)
Struggletown Records (*UK*)
Sub Pop Records (*US*)
Surfdog Records (*US*)
Thump Records (*US*)
Tommy Boy (*US*)
TommyBoy Entertainment LLC (*US*)
Ultra Music (*US*)
Verve Label Group (*US*)
Wax Records Inc. (*US*)
Wrath Records (*UK*)
Yep Roc Records (*US*)

Post

Big Scary Monsters Recording Company (*UK*)
Blindsight Records (*UK*)
Bohemian Jukebox (*UK*)
Concrete Recordings (*UK*)
Dine Alone Records (*Can*)
JSNTGM (Just Say No To Government Music) (*UK*)
Killing Moon Records (*UK*)
Kscope (*UK*)
Remixdj (*UK*)
Secret Formula Records, Inc. (*US*)
Slumberland Records (*US*)
Snapper Music (*UK*)
Soul Jazz Records Ltd (*UK*)
TV Records Ltd (*UK*)

Power

Dirty Water Records (*UK*)
Gearhead Records (*US*)
Holier Than Thou Records (*UK*)

Progressive

Aardvark Records Ltd (*UK*)
Alter Ego Records (*UK*)
Aphagia Recordings (*US*)
Basick Records (*UK*)
Burning Shed Limited (*UK*)
Esoteric Recordings (*UK*)
Holier Than Thou Records (*UK*)
Kscope (*UK*)
Public Pressure (*UK*)
RareNoiseRecords (*UK*)
Remixdj (*UK*)
Rhombus Records (*US*)
Shrapnel Records (*US*)
Snapper Music (*UK*)
3 Beat Records (*UK*)

Psychebilly

Dead by Mono Records (*UK*)
Iffy Folk Records (*UK*)
JSNTGM (Just Say No To Government Music) (*UK*)
Nervous Records (*UK*)
Pumpkin Records (*UK*)
Thin Man Entertainment (*US*)
Wasted State Records (*UK*)

Psychedelic

Backwater Records (*UK*)
BackWords Recordings (*US*)
Bohemian Jukebox (*UK*)
Dead by Mono Records (*UK*)
Esoteric Recordings (*UK*)
Fuzzkill Records (*UK*)
Public Pressure (*UK*)
Quatre Femmes Records (*UK*)
Ramber Records (*UK*)
Remixdj (*UK*)
Secret Records Ltd (*UK*)
Sonic Cathedral (*UK*)

Punk

A-F Records (*US*)
Alternative Tentacles Records (*US*)
Amazon Records (*UK*)
Banquet Records (*UK*)
Beggars Group (US) (*US*)
Bifocal Media (*US*)
Big Scary Monsters Recording Company (*UK*)
Bomber Music Ltd (*UK*)
Boslevan Records (*UK*)
Concrete Recordings (*UK*)
Dead by Mono Records (*UK*)
Dim Mak Records (*US*)
Dine Alone Records (*Can*)
Dirty Water Records (*UK*)
Dischord Records (*US*)

Dissention Records (*UK*)
Dog Knights Productions (*UK*)
Engineer Records (*UK*)
Fat Wreck Chords (*US*)
Gearhead Records (*US*)
Glasstone Records (*UK*)
Gravy (*UK*)
Hassle Records (*UK*)
Hit And Run Records (*UK*)
Holier Than Thou Records (*UK*)
Infinite Hive (*UK*)
Iron Man Records (*UK*)
Island Records (US) (*US*)
Jade Tree (*US*)
JSNTGM (Just Say No To Government Music) (*UK*)
Knitting Factory Records (*US*)
Kung Fu Records (*US*)
Lojinx (*UK*)
Manifesto Records, Inc. (*US*)
Mook Records (*UK*)
Nitro Records (*US*)
No Front Teeth (*UK*)
Nu Electro (*UK*)
1-2-3-4 Go! Records (*US*)
Pinky Swear Records (*UK*)
Pumpkin Records (*UK*)
Reach Out International Records (ROIR) (*US*)
Revelation Records (*US*)
Rotten Records (*US*)
Sapien Records Limited (*UK*)
Scylla Records (*UK*)
Secret Records Ltd (*UK*)
Secretly Canadian (*US*)
Side One Dummy Records (*US*)
Skate Mountain Records (*US*)
Skinny Dog Records (*UK*)
Slumberland Records (*US*)
Soul Jazz Records Ltd (*UK*)
Squirrel Records (*UK*)
Struggletown Records (*UK*)
Sub Pop Records (*US*)
Suburban Noize Records (*US*)
Surfdog Records (*US*)
Tee Pee Records (*US*)
Thin Man Entertainment (*US*)
Touch and Go Records (*US*)
Victory Records (*US*)
Wasted State Records (*UK*)
West Clark Records (*US*)

R&B

A&M Records (*US*)
Aardvark Records Ltd (*UK*)
ABKCO Music & Records Inc. (*US*)
Alternative Tentacles Records (*US*)
Amherst Record Sales, Inc. (*US*)
Atlan-Dec/Grooveline Records (*US*)
Barbarian Productions (*US*)
Basin Street Records (*US*)
Berman Brothers (*US*)
Boosweet Records (*US*)
Def Jam Recordings (*US*)
Dome Records Ltd (*UK*)
Ecko Records (*US*)
Heaven's Disciples, LLC (*US*)
Island Records (US) (*US*)
JW Music Limited (*UK*)
Kufe Records Ltd (*UK*)
Malaco Music Group (*US*)
Memphis International Records (*US*)
Mughal Music Group (*Can*)
New Pants Publishing (*US*)
1-2-3-4 Go! Records (*US*)
Pendulum Records (*US*)
Pravda Records (*US*)
A Priscilla Thing (*UK*)
ROKiT Records (*UK*)
Sapien Records Limited (*UK*)
Shanachie Entertainment (*US*)
Skate Mountain Records (*US*)
Slip-N-Slide Records (*US*)
Sony Music Entertainment – Legacy Recordings (*US*)
Soul II Soul (*UK*)
Spiral Galaxy Entertainment (*US*)
Surfdog Records (*US*)
Thump Records (*US*)
Tuff City Music Group (*US*)
Verve Label Group (*US*)

Rap

Asylum Records (*US*)
Atlan-Dec/Grooveline Records (*US*)
Bifocal Media (*US*)
Boosweet Records (*US*)
Def Jam Recordings (*US*)
Delicious Vinyl LLC (*US*)
Dim Mak Records (*US*)
Dirtee Stank (*UK*)
Freddie Records (*US*)
Grim Reality Entertainment, LLC (*US*)
Headcount Records (*UK*)
Heaven's Disciples, LLC (*US*)
Island Records (US) (*US*)
La Corporación Muzic (*US*)
Lewis Recordings (*UK*)
Mughal Music Group (*Can*)
New Pants Publishing (*US*)
Om Records (*US*)
Pendulum Records (*US*)

Psychopathic Records (*US*)
Shady Records (*US*)
Skate Mountain Records (*US*)
Slip-N-Slide Records (*US*)
Soul II Soul (*UK*)
Surfdog Records (*US*)
Thump Records (*US*)
Ultra Music (*US*)
Viper Records (*US*)
Word Records (*US*)

Reggae
Aardvark Records Ltd (*UK*)
Ariwa Sounds Ltd (*UK*)
Bomber Music Ltd (*UK*)
Delicious Vinyl LLC (*US*)
Easy Star Records (*US*)
Heaven's Disciples, LLC (*US*)
Kufe Records Ltd (*UK*)
La Corporación Muzic (*US*)
Lab Records (*UK*)
Megawave Records (*US*)
Mughal Music Group (*Can*)
1-2-3-4 Go! Records (*US*)
Reach Out International Records (ROIR) (*US*)
Rhombus Records (*US*)
Secret Records Ltd (*UK*)
Shanachie Entertainment (*US*)
Side One Dummy Records (*US*)
Slip-N-Slide Records (*US*)
Sony Music Entertainment – Legacy Recordings (*US*)
Soul Jazz Records Ltd (*UK*)
Surfdog Records (*US*)
True North Records (*Can*)
Ultra Music (*US*)
VP Records (*US*)

Reggaeton
Heaven's Disciples, LLC (*US*)
Secret Records Ltd (*UK*)

Regional
Far Out Recordings (*UK*)
Greentrax Recordings (*UK*)
Lismor Recordings (*UK*)
Mountain Apple Company (*US*)
REL Records Ltd (*UK*)
Scotdisc (*UK*)
Silver Wave Records (*US*)
World Circuit Records (*UK*)

Relaxation
Secret Formula Records, Inc. (*US*)
Sound Feelings (*US*)

Remix
MaggotHouse Music (*UK*)
Remixdj (*UK*)
West Clark Records (*US*)

Rhythm and Blues
Atlan-Dec/Grooveline Records (*US*)
Dead by Mono Records (*UK*)
Dirty Water Records (*UK*)
Groovin' Records (*UK*)
Heaven's Disciples, LLC (*US*)
Heavenly Recordings (*UK*)
Secret Records Ltd (*UK*)

Rock and Roll
Bomber Music Ltd (*UK*)
Dead by Mono Records (*UK*)
Dirty Water Records (*UK*)
Fury Records (*UK*)
Fuzzkill Records (*UK*)
Gearhead Records (*US*)
Meloden Nashville (*US*)
Nervous Records (*UK*)
Secret Formula Records, Inc. (*US*)
Secret Records Ltd (*UK*)
Skate Mountain Records (*US*)
Smog Veil Records (*US*)
Squirrel Records (*UK*)
Wasted State Records (*UK*)
West Clark Records (*US*)
Wicked Cool Records (*US*)

Rock
4AD (*US*)
A&M Records (*US*)
A-F Records (*US*)
A389 Recordings (*US*)
Aardvark Records Ltd (*UK*)
Abet Publishing (*US*)
ABKCO Music & Records Inc. (*US*)
Aeronaut Records (*US*)
Alias Records (*US*)
Alternative Tentacles Records (*US*)
Amazon Records (*UK*)
American Laundromat Records (*US*)
Amherst Record Sales, Inc. (*US*)
The Animal Farm (*UK*)
Anti (*US*)
Aphagia Recordings (*US*)
API Records (*US*)
Armellodie (*UK*)
Atlan-Dec/Grooveline Records (*US*)
ATO Records (*US*)
Babygrande Records, Inc. (*US*)
Backwater Records (*UK*)
BackWords Recordings (*US*)
Bar/None Records (*US*)
Barsuk Records (*US*)
Basin Street Records (*US*)
Beggars Group (US) (*US*)
Beggars Group Canada (*Can*)

Better Looking Records (*US*)
Big Scary Monsters Recording Company (*UK*)
Blindsight Records (*UK*)
Boosweet Records (*US*)
Boslevan Records (*UK*)
Broken Arrow Records (*US*)
Burning Shed Limited (*UK*)
Chocolate Fireguard Music Ltd (*UK*)
Clue Records (*UK*)
Criminal Records (*UK*)
Dead by Mono Records (*UK*)
Delicious Vinyl LLC (*US*)
Dim Mak Records (*US*)
Dine Alone Records (*Can*)
Dirty Water Records (*UK*)
Dischord Records (*US*)
Downtown Music (*US*)
eenie meenie records (*US*)
Esoteric Recordings (*UK*)
Fat Wreck Chords (*US*)
Favored Nations Entertainment (*US*)
Fierce Panda Records (*UK*)
Fuzzkill Records (*UK*)
Gearhead Records (*US*)
Glasstone Records (*UK*)
Harmonized Records (*US*)
Hassle Records (*UK*)
Hit And Run Records (*UK*)
Holier Than Thou Records (*UK*)
Hydra Head Records (*US*)
Iffy Folk Records (*UK*)
Ignition Records (*UK*)
In At The Eye Records (*UK*)
Infinite Hive (*UK*)
Invisible Records (*US*)
Iron Man Records (*UK*)
Island Records (US) (*US*)
Jade Tree (*US*)
JSNTGM (Just Say No To Government Music) (*UK*)
Justin Time Records Inc. (*Can*)
Killing Moon Records (*UK*)
King Prawn Records (*UK*)
Knitting Factory Records (*US*)
Kscope (*UK*)
Kung Fu Records (*US*)
La Corporación Muzic (*US*)
Lab Records (*UK*)
The Lab (*UK*)
Lojinx (*UK*)
Mailboat Records (*US*)
Manifesto Records, Inc. (*US*)
Mega Truth Records (*US*)
Megawave Records (*US*)
Meloden Nashville (*US*)
Metalbox Recordings (*UK*)
Midge Bitten Records (*UK*)
New Pants Publishing (*US*)
Nitro Records (*US*)
No Dancing Records (*UK*)
No Front Teeth (*UK*)
Om Records (*US*)
One Inch Badge (OIB) Records (*UK*)
1-2-3-4 Go! Records (*US*)
Perry Road Records Ltd (*UK*)
Pravda Records (*US*)
Quatre Femmes Records (*UK*)
Ramber Records (*UK*)
Reach Out International Records (ROIR) (*US*)
The Red Flag Recording Co. (*UK*)
Relapse Records (*US*)
Reunion Records (*US*)
Revelation Records (*US*)
Revolver Records (*UK*)
Rhombus Records (*US*)
Roadrunner Records (*UK*)
Rock Action Records (*UK*)
Rockzion Records (*US*)
ROKiT Records (*UK*)
Ropeadope Records (*US*)
Rough Trade Records (*UK*)
Rounder Records (*US*)
Saddle Creek (*US*)
Sapien Records Limited (*UK*)
Saving Grace Music (*UK*)
Schnitzel Records Ltd (*UK*)
SCI Fidelity Records (*US*)
Scylla Records (*UK*)
Secret Formula Records, Inc. (*US*)
Secret Records Ltd (*UK*)
Secretly Canadian (*US*)
Shangri-La Projects, Inc. (*US*)
Shrapnel Records (*US*)
Signature Sound Recordings (*US*)
Six Degrees Records (*US*)
Skate Mountain Records (*US*)
Skinny Dog Records (*UK*)
Slush Fund Recordings (*US*)
Snapper Music (*UK*)
So Recordings (*UK*)
Sonic Cathedral (*UK*)
Sony Music Entertainment – Legacy Recordings (*US*)
Southern Lord Recordings (*US*)
Southern Records (*UK*)
Southland Records (*US*)
Spinefarm Records (*US*)
Struggletown Records (*UK*)

Sub Pop Records (*US*)
Suburban Noize Records (*US*)
Suretone Records (*US*)
Surfdog Records (*US*)
Tee Pee Records (*US*)
Terminus Records (*US*)
Thin Man Entertainment (*US*)
Thrive Records (*US*)
Tooth & Nail Records (*US*)
Touch and Go Records (*US*)
Triple Crown Records (*US*)
True North Records (*Can*)
TV Records Ltd (*UK*)
Universal Music Group Nashville (*US*)
Urband & Lazar (*US*)
Valley Entertainment (*US*)
Victory Records (*US*)
VSR Music Group (*US*)
Wasted State Records (*UK*)
Wax Records Inc. (*US*)
West Clark Records (*US*)
Wicked Cool Records (*US*)
Word Records (*US*)
Yep Roc Records (*US*)
Zube Records (*UK*)

Rockabilly

Bomber Music Ltd (*UK*)
Dead by Mono Records (*UK*)
Fury Records (*UK*)
Iffy Folk Records (*UK*)
Meloden Nashville (*US*)
Memphis International Records (*US*)
Nervous Records (*UK*)
Pravda Records (*US*)
Pumpkin Records (*UK*)
West Clark Records (*US*)
Wild Records (*US*)

Roots

Acoustic Disc (*US*)
Alligator Records (*US*)
Appleseed Recordings (*US*)
Ariwa Sounds Ltd (*UK*)
Blue Jackel Entertainment (*US*)
Borealis Records (*Can*)
Buzz Records (*UK*)
Fellside Recordings (*UK*)
Heartland Recordings (*US*)
Memphis International Records (*US*)
NorthernBlues Music Inc. (*Can*)
Oh Boy Records (*US*)
Rebel Records (*US*)
Round Hill Music (*US*)
Rounder Records (*US*)
Secretly Canadian (*US*)
Signature Sound Recordings (*US*)
Skaggs Family Records (*US*)
Skate Mountain Records (*US*)
Soul Jazz Records Ltd (*UK*)
Sugar Hill Records (*US*)
True North Records (*Can*)
Yep Roc Records (*US*)

Shoegaze

In At The Eye Records (*UK*)
Slumberland Records (*US*)
Sonic Cathedral (*UK*)

Singer-Songwriter

A&M Records (*US*)
Alias Records (*US*)
American Laundromat Records (*US*)
Backwater Records (*UK*)
BackWords Recordings (*US*)
Barbarian Productions (*US*)
Beggars Group (US) (*US*)
Bohemian Jukebox (*UK*)
Borealis Records (*Can*)
Broken Arrow Records (*US*)
Burning Shed Limited (*UK*)
Champion Records (*UK*)
Downtown Music (*US*)
eenie meenie records (*US*)
Fence Records (*UK*)
Heartland Recordings (*US*)
In At The Eye Records (*UK*)
Meloden Nashville (*US*)
Nettwerk Records (*UK*)
Nettwerk Records (*Can*)
Om Records (*US*)
Red Eye Music (*UK*)
Ropeadope Records (*US*)
SCI Fidelity Records (*US*)
Shanachie Entertainment (*US*)
Signature Sound Recordings (*US*)
Skate Mountain Records (*US*)
Sub Pop Records (*US*)
Surfdog Records (*US*)
Touch and Go Records (*US*)
Urband & Lazar (*US*)

Ska

Bomber Music Ltd (*UK*)
JSNTGM (Just Say No To Government Music) (*UK*)
1-2-3-4 Go! Records (*US*)
Pumpkin Records (*UK*)
Side One Dummy Records (*US*)
Wasted State Records (*UK*)
West Clark Records (*US*)

Soul

Aardvark Records Ltd (*UK*)
Dome Records Ltd (*UK*)
Dorado Music (*UK*)

Ecko Records (*US*)
Farmyard Records (*UK*)
Groovin' Records (*UK*)
Headcount Records (*UK*)
Malaco Music Group (*US*)
NexGen Music Group, LLC (*US*)
1-2-3-4 Go! Records (*US*)
Pravda Records (*US*)
A Priscilla Thing (*UK*)
Remixdj (*UK*)
Saving Grace Music (*UK*)
Secret Records Ltd (*UK*)
Skate Mountain Records (*US*)
Slapped Up Soul Records (*UK*)
Soul Jazz Records Ltd (*UK*)
Tuff City Music Group (*US*)
Wild Records (*US*)

Soulful
Remixdj (*UK*)
Skate Mountain Records (*US*)

Soundtracks
Aphagia Recordings (*US*)
Artists' Addiction Records (*US*)
Barbarian Productions (*US*)
First Night Records (*UK*)
Mughal Music Group (*Can*)
Secret Formula Records, Inc. (*US*)
Skate Mountain Records (*US*)
Sony Music Entertainment – Legacy Recordings (*US*)
ThrillerTracks (*US*)
Watertower Music (*US*)

Space
Secret Records Ltd (*UK*)
TV Records Ltd (*UK*)

Spoken Word
BackWords Recordings (*US*)

Surf
Dead by Mono Records (*UK*)
West Clark Records (*US*)
Wild Records (*US*)

Swing
Cexton Records (*US*)
Memphis International Records (*US*)
Remixdj (*UK*)
Southland Records (*US*)

Synthpop
In At The Eye Records (*UK*)
Nu Electro (*UK*)
Van Richter (*US*)

Techno
Aardvark Records Ltd (*UK*)
Astralwerks Records (*US*)
Barely Breaking Even Records (*UK*)
Brain Bomb Productions (BBP) (*UK*)
Buzzin' Fly Records (*UK*)
Cr2 Records (*UK*)
Gruuv (*UK*)
Kudos Records Limited (*UK*)
MaggotHouse Music (*UK*)
Needwant (*UK*)
NoFace Records (*US*)
Nu Electro (*UK*)
Pretty Neat Records (*UK*)
Rekids Ltd (*UK*)
Release / Sustain (*UK*)
Remixdj (*UK*)
Saved Records (*UK*)
Secret Formula Records, Inc. (*US*)
Soul Jazz Records Ltd (*UK*)
Subliminal Records (*US*)
3 Beat Records (*UK*)
West Clark Records (*US*)

Thrash
Holier Than Thou Records (*UK*)
Secret Records Ltd (*UK*)

Traditional
Aardvark Records Ltd (*UK*)
BackWords Recordings (*US*)
Fellside Recordings (*UK*)
Greentrax Recordings (*UK*)
Heads Up International (*US*)
Lake (*UK*)
Linn Records (*UK*)
Lismor Recordings (*UK*)
Mountain Apple Company (*US*)
Remixdj (*UK*)
Rhombus Records (*US*)
Ridge Records Limited (*UK*)
Sonic Safari Music (*US*)
Southland Records (*US*)

Trance
Aardvark Records Ltd (*UK*)
Alter Ego Records (*UK*)
Amathus Music (*US*)
Brain Bomb Productions (BBP) (*UK*)
Dead Happy Records (*UK*)
Enhanced Music (*UK*)
Joof Recordings (*UK*)
New State Music (*UK*)
NoFace Records (*US*)
Phunk Junk Records Inc (*US*)
Remixdj (*UK*)
Secret Formula Records, Inc. (*US*)
3 Beat Records (*UK*)

Tribal
Brain Bomb Productions (BBP) (*UK*)
Remixdj (*UK*)

Trip Hop
Secret Formula Records, Inc. (*US*)

Twisted
Remixdj (*UK*)
Underground
Amathus Music (*US*)
Bomber Music Ltd (*UK*)
Craniality Sounds (*US*)
Grim Reality Entertainment, LLC (*US*)
Heavenly Recordings (*UK*)
JSNTGM (Just Say No To Government Music) (*UK*)
NexGen Music Group, LLC (*US*)
Release / Sustain (*UK*)
Remixdj (*UK*)
Secret Records Ltd (*UK*)
Shabby Doll Records (*UK*)
Smog Veil Records (*US*)
Suburban Noize Records (*US*)
Thin Man Entertainment (*US*)
West Clark Records (*US*)
Uptempo
Remixdj (*UK*)
Urban
Affluent Records (*US*)
Atlan-Dec/Grooveline Records (*US*)
Black Butter Records (*UK*)
Def Jam Recordings (*US*)
Dirtee Stank (*UK*)
Downtown Music (*US*)
Freddie Records (*US*)
Island Records (US) (*US*)
JW Music Limited (*UK*)
La Corporación Muzic (*US*)
Mughal Music Group (*Can*)
Om Records (*US*)
Pendulum Records (*US*)
A Priscilla Thing (*UK*)
Remixdj (*UK*)
Shady Records (*US*)
Slip-N-Slide Records (*US*)
Soul II Soul (*UK*)
Surfdog Records (*US*)
Thump Records (*US*)
Visionary Music Group (*US*)
World
Aardvark Records Ltd (*UK*)
Abet Publishing (*US*)
Acoustic Disc (*US*)
ARC Music Productions International (*UK*)
Arkadia Entertainment Corp (*US*)
Beggars Group (US) (*US*)
Blue Jackel Entertainment (*US*)
Borealis Records (*Can*)
Dancing Cat Records (*US*)
Dancing Turtle Records (*UK*)
Heads Up International (*US*)
JohnJohn Records (*UK*)
Justin Time Records Inc. (*Can*)
Knitting Factory Records (*US*)
Lab Records (*UK*)
Luaka Bop (*US*)
Megawave Records (*US*)
NorthernBlues Music Inc. (*Can*)
Primarily A Cappella (*US*)
Rhombus Records (*US*)
Ropeadope Records (*US*)
Shanachie Entertainment (*US*)
Silver Wave Records (*US*)
Six Degrees Records (*US*)
Sonic Safari Music (*US*)
Sony Music Entertainment – Legacy Recordings (*US*)
Stackhouse & BluEsoterica (*US*)
Sunnyside Records (*US*)
Ultra Music (*US*)
Valley Entertainment (*US*)
World Circuit Records (*UK*)

US Managers

For the most up-to-date listings of these and hundreds of other managers, visit https://www.musicsocket.com/managers

*To claim your **free** access to the site, please see the back of this book.*

21st Century Artists, Inc.

32 W 22nd St, Fl 3
New York, NY 10010
Email: info@21stca.com
Website: https://www.21stca.com

Represents: Artists/Bands

Genres: Folk; Rock; Roots

New York based management company representing artists dealing in folk music, rock, and roots.

25 Artist Agency

25 Music Square West
Nashville, TN 37203
Fax: +1 (615) 687-6699
Email: david@25ent.com
Email: dara@25ent.com
Website: https://www.25ccm.com/
Website: https://www.instagram.com/25artistagency/

Represents: Artists/Bands

Genres: Christian

Contact: David Breen; Dara Easterday; Todd Thomas

Christian record label, based in Nashville, Tennessee.

ACA Music & Entertainment

705 Larry Court
Waukesha, WI 53186
Fax: +1 (262) 790-9149
Email: info@acaentertainment.com
Website: http://acaentertainment.com
Website: https://www.facebook.com/AcaMusicEntertainment/

Represents: Artists/Bands; DJs; Tribute Acts

Genres: All types of music

Describes itself as the oldest and largest provider of live entertainment in the Midwest.

Act 1 Entertainment

28 Price Street
Patchogue, NY 11772
Email: info@act1entertainment.net
Email: karl@act1entertainment.net
Website: http://act1entertainment.net
Website: https://www.facebook.com/Act1Inc/

Represents: Artists/Bands; Comedians; DJs; Tribute Acts

Genres: Jazz; R&B; Soul; Blues; Swing; Roots; Rockabilly; Country; Reggae; Classic Rock

Contact: Karl BD Reamer

Management company based in Patchogue, New York.

Advanced Alternative Media (AAM)

New York / Los Angeles
Email: info@aaminc.com
Website: http://www.aaminc.com
Website: https://www.facebook.com/AdvancedAlternativeMedia

Represents: Artists/Bands; Producers; Songwriters; Sound Engineers

Genres: Alternative; Pop; Rock; Indie

Management company with offices in New York, London, and Los Angeles.

Aesthetic V

Website: https://www.vickyhamilton.com

Represents: Artists/Bands

Genres: All types of music

Contact: Vicky Hamilton

Management by long time Grammy Award-Winning music industry executive and personal manager, responsible for developing or managing such acts as Guns 'N' Roses, Mötley Crüe, Poison, Faster Pussycat and many others. Also offers consultancy service.

Allure Media Entertainment Group

Website: http://indiemusicpublicity.com
Website: https://www.facebook.com/alluremediaent

Represents: Artists/Bands

Genres: Hip-Hop; Pop; Rock; R&B; Alternative Rock

Contact: Ken Cavalier

Provides publicity and marketing solutions for indie artists and labels. Send links to music online via online submission form.

American Artists Entertainment Group

29 Royal Palm Pointe Suite 5
Vero Beach, Florida 32960
Email: online@aaeg.com
Website: https://aaeg.com
Website: https://www.facebook.com/aaegcom/
Website: https://myspace.com/aaeg

Represents: Artists/Bands

Genres: Country; Pop; R&B; Rock

Management company with offices in Vero Beach, Florida, New York, and Hollywood. Has a 45-year history in the performing arts, and today serves over 16 countries and over 100 cities worldwide.

American International Artists, Inc.

356 Pine Valley Road
Hoosick Falls, NY 12090
Fax: +1 (518) 686-1960
Email: cynthia@aiartists.com
Website: https://aiartists.com
Website: https://www.instagram.com/aiartists/

Represents: Artists/Bands; Film / TV Composers

Genres: Classical; Jazz

Contact: Cynthia Herbst

Management company based in Hoosick Falls, NY. Devoted to the building and development of international careers of its world-class composers and jazz and classical performers, and to the development and co-ordination of special projects.

AMW Group Inc.

Website: https://www.amworldgroup.com
Website: https://facebook.com/amwgrp

Represents: Artists/Bands

Genres: All types of music

We have worked with promoting music for over 24 years. We work with different clients including major and independent labels, artists and producers. If you're looking for modern and effective ways to promote your music you have come to the right place.

APA (Agency for the Performing Arts)

10585 Santa Monica Blvd.
Los Angeles, CA 90025
Website: https://www.apa-agency.com

Represents: Artists/Bands

Genres: All types of music

Management company with offices in Los Angeles, Nashville, New York, Atlanta, Toronto, and London.

Arslanian & Associates, Inc.

6671 Sunset Boulevard, Suite 1502
Hollywood, CA 90028
Email: oscar@discoverhollywood.com
Website: http://www.arslanianassociates.com

Represents: Artists/Bands

Genres: Classic Rock

Contact: Oscar Arslanian; Nyla Arslanian

Management company based in Hollywood, California.

Artist Representation and Management (ARM) Entertainment

Email: info@armentertainment.com
Website: https://armentertainment.com

Represents: Artists/Bands

Genres: Blues; Country; Classic Rock; Metal

Entertainment business with a focus on 70s, 80s, and 90s rock.

Backer Entertainment

Email: info@backerentertainment.com
Website: https://backerentertainment.com

Represents: Artists/Bands; Tribute Acts

Genres: All types of music

Manages mainly tribute acts for events.

Backstage Entertainment

Email: staff@backstageentertainment.net
Website: https://backstageentertainment.net
Website: https://www.facebook.com/BackstageEntertainment

Represents: Artists/Bands

Genres: All types of music

Contact: Paul Loggins

Artist management/marketing firm which specialises in working with independent artists, and aims to bridge the gap between radio, print and social media.

BBA Management & Booking

Email: info@bbabooking.com
Website: https://www.bbabooking.com
Website: https://www.facebook.com/bbabooking

Represents: Artists/Bands

Genres: Jazz; Classical; Rock; Latin

Contact: Michael Mordecai; Laura Mordecai

Management and booking for jazz, classical, and versatile party bands in Central Texas.

Big Beat Productions, Inc.

1515 University Drive, Suite 106
Coral Springs, FL 33071
Fax: +1 (954) 755-8733
Email: talent@bigbeatproductions.com
Website: http://www.bigbeatproductions.com
Website: https://www.facebook.com/bigbeatproductions/

Represents: Artists/Bands; Comedians; DJs

Genres: Contemporary; Classic Rock; R&B; Disco; Regional; Jazz; Country

Contact: Richard Lloyd; Gary Ladka; Elissa Solomon

Management company based in Coral Springs, Florida.

Big Hassle Management

New York and Los Angeles
Email: weinstein@bighassle.com
Email: jim@bighassle.com
Website: https://www.bighassle.com

Represents: Artists/Bands

Genres: Indie; Pop; Rock; Alternative

Contact: Ken Weinstein

Management company with offices in New York and Los Angeles.

Big Noise

11 South Angell Street, Suite 336
Providence, RI 02906
Email: algomes@bignoisenow.com
Email: al@bignoisenow.com
Website: http://www.bignoisenow.com

Represents: Artists/Bands

Genres: All types of music

Contact: Al Gomes; A. Michelle

Award-winning Music Firm specialising in artist development, project management, career strategies, and promotion and publicity. Based in Providence, Rhode Island. Looking for artists who are unique, talented, professional, and ready to launch. Considers all genres. Query by phone or email in first instance. Must be at least 18.

Bill Silva Management

Website: https://www.billsilvaentertainment.com

Represents: Artists/Bands; Songwriters

Genres: All types of music

Contact: Bill Silva

Management company, including music management, model management, and music publishing.

Bitchin' Entertainment

1750 Collard Valley Road
Cedartown, GA 30125
Email: Ty@BitchinEntertainment.com
Email: Rodney@BitchinEntertainment.com
Website: http://www.bitchinentertainment.com

Represents: Artists/Bands; Tribute Acts

Genres: Rock; Pop; R&B; Funk; Urban; Hip-Hop; Rap; Instrumental; Jazz; Classical; Ambient; World; Experimental; House; Trance; Electronic; Techno; Alternative; Metal; Punk; Gothic; Country; Americana; Blues; Folk; Singer-Songwriter; Spoken Word

Management company based in Cedartown, Georgia. Send query by email with link to your music online. See website for full submission guidelines, and details of who to approach regarding specific genres. For unsolicited demos, a submission code must be obtained before submitting.

Black Dot Management

Fax: +1 (323) 777-8169
Email: info@blkdot.com
Website: http://www.blkdot.com

Represents: Artists/Bands; Producers; Songwriters; Sound Engineers; Studio Musicians; Studio Technicians

Genres: Jazz; R&B; Urban; Contemporary

Contact: Raymond A. Shields II; Patricia Shields

Management company handling jazz, R&B, and urban.

Blind Ambition Management, Ltd

Atlanta, GA 30307
Email: info@blindambitionmgt.com
Website: http://www.blindambitionmgt.com
Website: https://www.facebook.com/BlindAmbitionManagement

Represents: Artists/Bands; Film / TV Composers; Songwriters

Genres: Blues; Gospel; Roots; Folk; Singer-Songwriter

Management company based in Atlanta, Georgia, providing career management, business management, creative guidance, publicity, legal, and marketing services for recording artists and music-related businesses.

Booking Entertainment

Two Park Avenue 20th Floor
New York, NY 10016
Email: agents@bookingentertainment.com
Website: https://www.

bookingentertainment.com
Website: https://www.facebook.com/profile.php?id=100057634982148

Represents: Artists/Bands

Genres: Pop; Rock; Jazz; R&B; Contemporary

Books big name entertainment for private parties, public concerts, corporate events, and fundraisers.

Brick Wall Management

39 West 32nd Street, Suite 1403
New York, NY 10001
Fax: +1 (212) 202-4582
Website: https://www.brickwallmgmt.com

Represents: Artists/Bands; Producers

Genres: Country; Pop; Rock; Singer-Songwriter

Contact: Michael Solomon; Rishon Blumberg

Management company based in New York.

Brilliant Corners Artist Management

2069 Mission Street, Suite A
San Francisco, CA 94110

SEATTLE OFFICE:
1434-C Elliott Ave W
Seattle, WA 98119
Email: info@brilliantcorners.com
Website: https://brilliantcorners.com
Website: https://www.facebook.com/brilliantcornersmgmt

Represents: Artists/Bands

Genres: Indie; Rock; Singer-Songwriter

Management company with offices in San Francisco and Seattle. Not actively seeking unsolicited demos and strongly discourages sending physical copies. If approaching by email send only to the email address above; do not attach anything; and do not follow up.

Brilliant Productions

Email: nancy@brilliant-productions.com
Website: https://brilliant-productions.com
Website: https://www.youtube.com/user/itsbrilliant

Represents: Artists/Bands

Genres: Blues; Regional; Roots; Americana

Contact: Nancy Lewis-Pegel

Music booking and management for roots / blues / Southern / jam / Americana music.

The Brokaw Company

4135 Bakman Avevenue
North Hollywood, CA 91602
Email: jobrok@aol.com
Email: db@brokawco.com
Website: http://brokawcompany.com

Represents: Artists/Bands

Genres: Country; Hip-Hop; Pop; Christian; Rock

Contact: Joel Brokaw; David Brokaw; Sanford Brokaw

Management company based in North Hollywood, California. As well as handling music artists, has also handled publicity for hit shows such as The Cosby Show and Roseanne.

Bsquared MGMT

Email: bsquaredmgmt@gmail.com
Website: https://www.bsquaredmgmt.com
Website: http://facebook.com/bsquaredmgmt1

Represents: Artists/Bands

Genres: All types of music

Artist Branding, Artist Development, Booking, Playlisting, Social Media MGMT and More...

Bulletproof Artist Management

241 Main Street
Easthampton, MA 01027
Email: patty@bulletproofartists.com
Website: https://bulletproofartists.com
Website: https://twitter.com/bproofmgmt

Represents: Artists/Bands; Producers

Genres: Country; Pop; Rock; Folk

Contact: Patty Romanoff

Management company based in Easthampton, Massachusetts.

Burgess World Co.

PO Box 646
Mayo, MD 21106-0646
Email: info@burgessworldco.com
Website: http://www.burgessworldco.com

Represents: Artists/Bands; Producers; Sound Engineers

Genres: Alternative; Blues; Jazz; Rock; Singer-Songwriter

Management company based in Mayo, Maryland. Originally founded to manage producers and engineers, but in the nineties expanded into artist management.

C Management

Email: info@studioexpresso.com
Website: http://www.studioexpresso.com/CHome.htm

Represents: Artists/Bands; Film / TV Composers; Producers; Songwriters; Sound Engineers; Studio Technicians; Supervisors

Genres: All types of music

Management company representing producers, mixers, engineers, songwriters, arrangers, magicians, and musicians.

Cantaloupe Music Productions, Inc.

157 West 79 Street
New York, NY 10024-6415
Email: ellenazorin@gmail.com
Website: https://www.cantaloupeproductions.com
Website: https://www.facebook.com/CantaloupeMusicProductions

Represents: Artists/Bands

Genres: Regional; Latin; World; Jazz; Blues; Swing

Contact: Ellen Azorin, President

Handles Brazilian music, Argentine tango, and other Latin-American music.

Case Entertainment Group Inc.

119 N. Wahsatch Ave
Colorado Springs, CO 80903
Fax: +1 (719) 634-2274
Email: rac@crlr.net
Website: https://newpants.com
Website: http://www.oldpants.com

Represents: Artists/Bands

Genres: Rock; Pop; Country; Folk; R&B; Rap

Contact: Robert Case

Management company based in Colorado Springs, Colorado.

Celebrity Enterprises (CE) Inc.

137 Saddle Spur Trail,
Tijeras, NM 87059
Email: info@worldstageevents.com
Website: https://www.ent123.com

Represents: Artists/Bands

Genres: All types of music

Provides acts for corporate events and fundraisers, performing arts centres and casinos, and other special events.

Celebrity Talent Agency Inc.

111 East 14th Street Suite 249
New York, NY 10003
Fax: +1 (201) 837-9011
Email: markg@celebritytalentagency.com
Email: alinak@celebritytalentagency.com
Website: https://www.celebritytalentagency.com
Website: https://www.facebook.com/CelebrityTalentAgency/

Represents: Artists/Bands; Comedians; DJs

Genres: Dance; Hip-Hop; R&B; Latin; Reggae; Jazz; Gospel

Contact: Mark Green; Alina Kim

Talent agency with offices in New York and London.

Century Artists Management Agency, LLC
711 West End Avenue, Suite 3CS
New York, New York 10025
Email: centuryartists@gmail.com
Website: https://www.camatalent.com
Website: https://twitter.com/centuryartists

Represents: Artists/Bands; Producers; Songwriters

Genres: All types of music

Contact: Paul E. Horton, President

Offers strategic brand management for artists in music, television, film, and the performing arts. Seeking established and new talent.

Chaney Gig Affairs (CGA)
California
Email: ChaneyGigAffairs@gmail.com
Website: https://www.chaneygigaffairs.com
Website: https://www.facebook.com/ChaneyGigAffairs/

Represents: Artists/Bands

Genres: Jazz; R&B; Soul

Provides Music and Artist Management Services; Web Design, EPKs and Video/Media Content Creation; and Event Management.

Chapman & Co. Management
Fax: +1 (818) 788-9525
Email: info@chapmanmanagement.com
Email: steve@chapmanmanagement.com
Website: https://www.chapmanmanagement.com

Represents: Artists/Bands

Genres: Contemporary Jazz

Contact: Steve Chapman

Management company concentrating on smooth, contemporary jazz.

Ciulla Management, Inc.
Email: mail@ciullamgmt.com
Website: https://ciullamgmt.com

Represents: Artists/Bands

Genres: Rock; Metal

Management company handling rock/metal artists.

Collin Artists
1099 N. Mar Vista Ave
Pasadena, CA 91104
Email: collinartists@gmail.com
Website: http://www.collinartists.com

Represents: Artists/Bands

Genres: Instrumental Jazz; Latin; World; Blues; R&B; Swing; Contemporary Jazz

Contact: Barbara Collin

Management company based in Pasadena, California.

Columbia Artists Music LLC (CAMI Music)
1180 Avenue of the Americas, 8th Floor
New York, NY 10036
Fax: +1 (212) 841-9581
Email: info@camimusic.com
Website: https://www.camimusic.com

Represents: Artists/Bands; Film / TV Composers; Lyricists; Variety Artists

Genres: Classical; Instrumental; Jazz; World

Represents classical, jazz, and popular musicians; orchestras, ensembles, etc.

Concerted Efforts
PO Box 440326
Somerville MA, 02144
Fax: +1 (617) 209-1300
Email: concerted@concertedefforts.com
Website: https://concertedefforts.com

Represents: Artists/Bands

Genres: Blues; Folk; Jazz; Gospel; Soul; Singer-Songwriter; Rock; World

Music booking agency based in Somerville, Massachusetts.

Creative Artists Agency (CAA)
2000 Avenue of the Stars
Los Angeles, CA 90067

Fax: +1 (424) 288-2900
Website: https://www.caa.com
Website: https://www.instagram.com/creativeartistsagency/

Represents: Artists/Bands

Genres: All types of music

Talent agency with offices across the US, as well as in the UK, China, and Europe.

Crush Music Media Management

Email: info@crushmusic.com
Website: https://www.crushmusic.com

Represents: Artists/Bands; Producers; Songwriters

Genres: All types of music

Full service music company based in New York and Los Angeles

Culler Talent Management

Los Angeles
Website: https://www.linkedin.com/in/chandler-culler-913972a8

Represents: Artists/Bands

Genres: All types of music

Contact: Chandler Culler

Provides talent management and event booking for all types of entertainers from all over.

Cumberland Music Collective

Nashville, TN
Email: lee@cmcartists.com
Email: andrew@cmcartists.com
Website: https://www.kcaartists.com
Website: https://www.facebook.com/KeithCaseAndAssociates

Represents: Artists/Bands

Genres: All types of music

Contact: Lee Olsen; Andrew Bestick; Chase Decraene

A new kind of music agency: one that puts the artists, agents and clients first – with the understanding that good business relies on good partnerships founded on mutual respect and integrity, designed for the success of all. To that end, it is a big tent with a boutique approach to artist representation, welcoming all genres of music.

D. Bailey Management, Inc.

17815 Gunn Hwy Suite 5
Odessa, FL 33556
Fax: +1 (813) 960-4662
Email: dennis@dbaileyemanagement.com
Website: https://www.dbaileymanagement.com
Website: https://www.facebook.com/dbaileymanagement

Represents: Artists/Bands

Genres: Pop; R&B; Rock

Contact: Dennis Bailey

Live entertainment, event management, and artist management, based in Odessa, Florida.

DAS Communications Ltd

83 Riverside Drive
New York, NY 10024
Website: https://www.bloomberg.com/profile/company/0835448D:US

Represents: Artists/Bands; Producers; Songwriters

Genres: Hip-Hop; Pop; Rock

Management company based in New York.

Dave Kaplan Management

1126 South Coast Highway 101
Encinitas, CA 92024
Fax: +1 (760) 944-7808
Email: demo@surfdog.com
Website: https://surfdog.com
Website: https://www.facebook.com/surfdogrecords/

Represents: Artists/Bands

Genres: Rock

Contact: Dave Kaplan; Scott Seine

Management company based in Encinitas, California. Also runs associated record label.

Accepts submissions by post marked for the attention of A&R, but prefers links by email (no MP3 attachments).

David Belenzon Management, Inc.

PO Box 5000 PMB 67,
Rancho Santa Fe, CA 92067

Fax: +1 (858) 832-8381
Email: David@Belenzon.com
Website: https://www.belenzon.com

Represents: Artists/Bands; Variety Artists

Genres: Contemporary; Pop; Rock; R&B

Contact: David Belenzon

Management company based in Rancho Santa Fe, California, representing artists, variety artists, plus theatrical and production shows.

Dawn Elder Management

Email: deworldmusic@aol.com
Website: https://dawnelderworldentertainment.com
Website: https://www.facebook.com/DawnElderWorldEntertainment/

Represents: Artists/Bands

Genres: Classical; Jazz; Pop; Rock; Roots; Traditional; World

Have managed, represented and organised international tours for some of the most highly regarded international artists today.

DCA Productions

302A 12th Street, # 330
New York, NY 10014
Fax: +1 (609) 259-8260
Email: info@dcaproductions.com
Website: https://dcaproductions.com
Website: https://www.facebook.com/dcaproductionsplus/

Represents: Artists/Bands; Comedians; Variety Artists

Genres: Pop; Rock; Folk

Contact: Daniel C. Abrahmsen, President; Gerri Abrahamsen, Vice President

Management company founded in 1983, specialising in variety performers, comedians, musical performers, theatre productions, and producing live events.

DDB Productions

Email: ddbprods@gmail.com
Website: https://www.ddbprods.com/
Website: http://www.deedeebridgewater.com

Represents: Artists/Bands; Lyricists; Producers; Songwriters; Studio Vocalists

Genres: Jazz; World; Alternative

Contact: Dee Dee Bridgewater

A boutique record label, music production company and talent management firm, based in Los Angeles, CA and New Orleans, LA. Founded by triple Grammy and Tony award winning Jazz artist.

Deep South Artist Management

RALEIGH
PO Box 17737
Raleigh, NC 27619

NASHVILLE
PO Box 121975
Nashville, TN 37212
Email: Hello@DeepSouthEntertainment.com
Website: http://www.deepsouthentertainment.com
Website: https://www.facebook.com/deepsouthent

Represents: Artists/Bands

Genres: Alternative; Country; Pop; Rock; Americana; Christian

Record label, artist management firm, talent agency, and concert production company based in Raleigh, North Carolina, with offices in both Raleigh and Nashville, Tennessee.

Def Ro Inc.

33 Prospect Street, Suite 1r
Bloomfield, NJ 07003
Email: defroinc@msn.com

Website: http://sirro.tripod.com/index.html
Website: http://defroinc.blogspot.co.uk

Represents: Artists/Bands

Genres: Hip-Hop; Pop; R&B

Contact: Will Strickland

Management company based in Bloomfield, New Jersey. Send up to three tracks by mail only.

Direct Management Group (DMG)

8332 Melrose Ave, Top Floor
Los Angeles, CA 90069
Website: https://directmanagement.com

Represents: Artists/Bands

Genres: Pop

Contact: Martin Kirkup; Bradford Cobb; Steven Jensen

Management company based in West Hollywood, California. Founded in April 1985. Describes itself as an internationally oriented entertainment company with broad-based success in the representation of musical artists.

Dog & Pony Industries

Email: info@dogandponyindustries.com
Website: http://www.dogandponyindustries.com

Represents: Artists/Bands

Genres: All types of music

Specializing in talent management and the coordinating of concert tours and special projects in the Music, TV & Film industries. Contact by email.

Domo Music Group Management

11022 Santa Monica Blvd. #300
Los Angeles, CA 90025
Email: dino@domomusicgroup.com
Website: https://www.domomusicgroup.com
Website: https://www.facebook.com/officialdomomusicgroup

Represents: Artists/Bands; DJs; Film / TV Composers; Producers; Songwriters; Studio Musicians

Genres: Contemporary; Classical; Folk; Indie; New Age; Pop; Rock; Singer-Songwriter; World; Ethnic

Management company based in Los Angeles, California, handling Japanese artists. Prefers links to music online by email or via submission form on website, or send CD by post marked for the attention of A&R.

East Coast Entertainment (ECE)

Email: info@bookece.com
Website: https://www.bookece.com
Website: https://www.facebook.com/EastCoastEntertainment/

Represents: Artists/Bands; Comedians; DJs

Genres: All types of music

Describes itself as the largest full-service entertainment agency in the country.

Elevation Group Inc.

Email: kent@elevationgroup.net
Website: https://www.elevationgroup.net

Represents: Artists/Bands

Genres: All types of music

Contact: Kent Sorrell

Management company based in California.

Emcee Artist Management

Email: liz@emceeartist.com
Email: mfair@emceeartist.com
Website: https://www.emceeartist.com

Represents: Artists/Bands

Genres: Jazz; Blues; Rock

Contact: Liz Penta; Meagan Fair

Management company representing jazz, blues, and rock artists. No hip-hop.

Enlight Entertainment, Inc.

Website: http://www.enlight-ent.com
Website: https://www.facebook.com/tashia.l.stafford

Represents: Artists/Bands; Producers; Songwriters

Genres: R&B; Gospel; Rap

Contact: Tashia Stafford

Offers the following services:

- Producer and Personal Management
- Independent Publishing Company Consulting
- Administrative Assistant Services
- A & R Consulting and Administration
- Personal Assistants
- Song Writing Clinics

Entertainment Services International

1819 South Harlan Circle
Lakewood, CO 80232
Fax: +1 (303) 936-0069
Email: randy@esientertainment.com
Website: http://www.esientertainment.com

Represents: Artists/Bands

Genres: Rock; Classic Rock

Contact: Randy Erwin

Manager based in Lakewood, Colorado.

Entourage Talent Associates, Ltd

Email: info@entouragetalent.com
Website: https://www.entouragetalent.com
Website: https://www.facebook.com/EntourageTalentAssociates

Represents: Artists/Bands

Genres: Pop; Rock; Singer-Songwriter; Jazz

Not currently seeking new acts for representation. However, you can submit your music and information for consideration for support/packaging with one of the existing clients for an upcoming tour. Send submissions by email, or via form on website.

Fat City Artists

1906 Chet Atkins Place, Suite 502 Nashville, TN 37212
Fax: +1 (615) 321-5382
Website: http://fatcityartists.com

Represents: Artists/Bands

Genres: Acoustic; Blues; R&B; Celtic; Country; Folk; Funk; Gospel; Jazz; Pop; Reggae; Rockabilly; Rock and Roll; Ska; Swing; World

Artists management based in Nashville, Tennessee. Not signing new artists as at November 2022.

Fire Tower Entertainment

Los Angeles, CA
Email: artists@firetowerent.com
Email: info@firetowerent.com
Website: https://firetowerent.com
Website: https://www.facebook.com/firetowerent

Represents: Artists/Bands

Genres: Indie; Pop; Singer-Songwriter

Entertainment startup located in Los Angeles focused on artist management and A&R services.

First Access Entertainment

Website: https://www.facebook.com/firstaccessent

Represents: Artists/Bands

Genres: Pop; Rap; R&B; Hip-Hop

Management Company, Record Label, Music Publisher.

First Artists Management

4764 Park Granada, Suite 110
Calabasas, CA 91302
Fax: +1 (818) 377-7760
Email: info@firstartistsmgmt.com
Website: https://www.firstartistsmanagement.com

Represents: Film / TV Composers; Supervisors

Genres: Soundtracks

Management company based in Calabasas, California, specialising in the representation of composers, music supervisors, and music editors for film and television.

5B Artist Management

220 36th St, Suite B442
Brooklyn, NY 11232

LOS ANGELES:
12021 Jefferson Blvd,
Culver City, CA 90230
Email: info@5bam.com
Website: http://5bam.com

Represents: Artists/Bands

Genres: Alternative; Metal; Rock

Management company with offices in New York, Los Angeles and Birmingham (UK).

Fleming Artists

PO Box 1568
Ann Arbor, MI 48106
Email: jim@flemingartists.com
Email: cynthia@flemingartists.com
Website: https://www.flemingartists.com
Website: https://www.facebook.com/flemingartists/

Represents: Artists/Bands

Genres: Contemporary Roots Rock; Blues; Folk; Pop; Rock

Management company with a mission to "represent a high quality, diverse roster of performing artists by providing them with a unique, thoughtful and individualized approach to concert booking."

Fresh Flava Entertainment

2705 12th Street NE
Washington, DC 20018
Email: freshflava17@gmail.com
Website: http://www.freshflava.com

Represents: Artists/Bands

Genres: Hip-Hop; Jazz; Gospel; R&B; Rock

Management company based in Washington DC.

Funzalo Music / Mike's Artist Management

PO Box 2518
Agoura Hills, CA 91376
Email: mike@mikesmanagement.com
Website: https://funzalorecords.com
Website: https://www.facebook.com/funzalorecords

Represents: Artists/Bands; Producers

Genres: All types of music

Contact: Mike Lembo

Record label and management company based in Agoura Hills, California.

Gary Stamler Management

PO Box 34575
Los Angeles, CA 90034
Email: garystamler@me.com
Email: nancysefton@gsmgmt.net
Website: https://www.gsmgmt.net

Represents: Artists/Bands; Producers

Genres: All types of music

Contact: Gary Stamler; Nancy Sefton

Management company based in Los Angeles.

Gayle Enterprises, Inc.

51 Music Square East
Nashville, TN 37203
Email: info@crystalgayle.com
Website: https://crystalgayle.com
Website: https://www.facebook.com/236343614779

Represents: Artists/Bands

Genres: All types of music

Contact: Bill Gatzimos

Management company based in Nashville, Tennessee, dedicated to representing one artist only. No submissions or queries.

Gold Mountain Entertainment

LOS ANGELES
12400 Ventura Blvd., Suite 444
Studio City, CA 91604

NASHVILLE
11 Music Square East, Suite 103
Nashville, TN 37203
Fax: +1 (615) 255-9001
Email: info@gmemusic.com
Website: http://www.gmemusic.com

Represents: Artists/Bands

Genres: Contemporary; Blues; Folk; Indie; Pop; Punk; Reggae; Rock; Singer-Songwriter; World

Management company with offices in Los Angeles, Nasville, and Montreal.

Good Guy Entertainment

Email: aa@goodguyent.com
Website: https://www.facebook.com/GoodGuyEntertainment

Represents: Artists/Bands

Genres: Pop; Urban

Management company specialising in artist and project development, mass media marketing and promotion, independent record promotion, and television production.

The Gorfaine/Schwartz Agency, Inc.

4111 West Alameda Avenue, Suite 509
Burbank, CA 91505
Website: https://www.gsamusic.com
Website: https://www.facebook.com/gorfaineschwartz

Represents: Artists/Bands; Producers

Genres: All types of music

Management agency based in Burbank, California.

Grassy Hill Entertainment

303 West 42nd Street, Suite 614
New York, NY 10036
Fax: +1 (212) 977-1069
Email: managers@grassyhill.net
Email: margo.parks@grassyhillentertainment.com
Website: http://www.grassyhillentertainment.com

Represents: Artists/Bands

Genres: Roots; Americana; Folk; Singer-Songwriter

Contact: Margo Parks; Julia Reinhart

A full service management company based in New York, describing itself as a "talent incubator" for independent artists in the roots / americana genres.

Hard Head Management

PO Box 651
New York, NY 10014
Fax: +1 (212) 337-0708
Email: info@hardhead.com
Website: https://www.hardhead.com

Represents: Artists/Bands

Genres: Americana; Electronic; Rock

Contact: Stefani Scamardo

Management company based in New York.

Hardin Entertainment

Email: info@hardinentertainment.com
Website: http://www.hardinentertainment.com
Website: https://www.facebook.com/hardinbourke/

Represents: Artists/Bands; Film / TV Composers; Lyricists; Producers; Songwriters; Studio Vocalists; Supervisors

Genres: Contemporary; Alternative; Americana; Blues; Christian; Country; Dance; Electronic; Folk; Hardcore; Indie; Latin; Pop; Rock; Roots; Singer-Songwriter; World

Management company with offices in Los Angeles and New York.

HardKnockLife Entertainment

Website: https://hardknocklifeent.com
Website: https://www.instagram.com/hardknocklifeent/

Represents: Artists/Bands

Genres: Acoustic; Hip-Hop; Pop; R&B; Rap

Contact via form on website, including links to your music online.

Harmony Artists

3575 Cahuenga Blvd. W, #560
Los Angeles, CA 90068
Fax: +1 (323) 655-5154
Email: contact_us@harmonyartists.com
Website: https://www.harmonyartists.com
Website: https://www.facebook.com/HarmonyArtistsLA/

Represents: Artists/Bands; Tribute Acts

Genres: Blues; Latin; Jazz; Swing

Specialises in providing top national headline and regional entertainment for venues throughout the world.

Hello! Booking, Inc.

PO Box 18717
Minneapolis, MN 55418
Fax: +1 (763) 463-1264
Email: eric@hellobooking.com
Website: https://www.hellobooking.com
Website: https://www.facebook.com/hellobookingusa

Represents: Artists/Bands

Genres: Country; Folk; Indie; Jazz; Hip-Hop; Acoustic; Rockabilly; Rock; Pop

Contact: Eric Roberts

Show booking company based in Minneapolis.

Hoffman Entertainment

21301 S. Tamiami Trl. STE 320-151
Estero, FL 33928
Email: info@ilovehoffman.com
Email: wayne@ilovehoffman.com
Website: https://ilovehoffman.com/
Website: https://www.facebook.com/ilovehoffman

Represents: Artists/Bands; Comedians; Variety Artists

Genres: All types of music

Contact: Wayne Hoffman

Provides a range of talent for events, including music, celebrities, comedy, variety, and speakers.

Hornblow Group USA, Inc.

Email: info@hornblowgroup.com
Website: https://www.hornblowgroup.com
Website: https://www.facebook.com/hornblowmusic/

Represents: Artists/Bands; Film / TV Composers; Lyricists; Producers; Songwriters; Studio Musicians

Genres: Indie; Pop; Rock; Alternative; Singer-Songwriter

Full-service artist management firm, independent record label, purveyors of cool t-shirts and bumper stickers.

Howard Rosen Promotion, Inc.

Email: info@howiewood.com
Email: Howie@howiewood.com
Website: https://howiewood.com/
Website: https://myspace.com/howardrosen

Represents: Artists/Bands

Genres: All types of music

Contact: Howard Rosen; Alex Louton

Full service radio promotion company based in Ojai, California. Submit music using online submissions system on website.

IMC Entertainment Group

Website: http://www.imcentertainment.com

Represents: Artists/Bands

Genres: Pop; R&B

Entertainment company based in Porter Ranch, California, providing entertainment and production services worldwide. Specialises in music performance, production, publishing and supervision services.

IMG Artists

Pleiades House
7 West 54th Street
New York, NY 10019
Fax: +1 (212) 994-3550
Email: artistsny@imgartists.com

Website: https://imgartists.com
Website: https://twitter.com/imgartistsny

Represents: Artists/Bands

Genres: Classic; Folk; Gospel; Jazz; World; Latin; Singer-Songwriter

Describes itself as the global leader in the arts management business, with offices in New York, London, Paris, Hanover, and Seoul.

Impact Artist Management

Kingston, NY 12401
Email: info@impactartist.com
Website: http://www.impactartist.com
Website: https://www.facebook.com/impactartistmanagement

Represents: Artists/Bands; Film / TV Composers; Songwriters; Supervisors

Genres: Contemporary; Blues; Folk; Indie; Jazz; Latin; R&B; Rock; Roots; Singer-Songwriter; World; Alternative; Alternative Country

Management company based in Kingston, New York.

In De Goot Entertainment

119 West 23rd Street, Suite 609
New York, NY 10011
Fax: +1 (212) 924-3242
Website: https://www.indegoot.com
Website: https://www.facebook.com/Indegoot/

Represents: Artists/Bands

Genres: Indie; Metal; Pop; Rock; Underground

Contact: Michael Iurato

Management company based in New York. Send unsolicited submissions by post.

In Touch Entertainment

309 W 55th St
New York, NY 10019
Email: info@intouchent.com
Website: https://intouchent.com
Website: https://www.facebook.com/intouchentertainment

Represents: Artists/Bands

Genres: All types of music

A worldwide entertainment organisation that manages both established and up-and-coming recording artists, books talent into venues, oversees music recording, and promotes and produces concerts and films. Send electronic press kit by email, including bio, audio, video, tour history, and contact info. Response only if interested.

Ina Dittke & Associates

6538 Collins Avenue, Suite 295,
Miami Beach, FL 33141
Email: ina@inadittke.com
Email: gina@inadittke.com
Website: https://inadittke.com
Website: https://www.facebook.com/inadittkeassociates/

Represents: Artists/Bands

Genres: Jazz; Latin; World

Music agency based in Miami, Florida, representing a varied and international roster of artists.

International Creative Management (ICM) Partners

LOS ANGELES
10250 Constellation Boulevard
Los Angeles, CA 90067

NEW YORK
65 East 55th Street
New York, NY 10022
Email: icmcorporatecommunications@icmpartners.com
Website: https://www.icmpartners.com/
Website: https://www.facebook.com/ICMPartners/

Represents: Artists/Bands; Comedians

Genres: All types of music

Concerts and live appearances department represents artists in all musical genres, including pop, rock, R&B, hip-hop, indie and adult contemporary. Arranges global engagements and tours in a wide variety of settings and venues.

Intrigue Music

Email: staff@intriguegroup.net
Website: https://www.intriguemusic.com
Website: https://www.facebook.com/intriguemusic

Represents: Artists/Bands

Genres: Pop; Rock

Full-service entertainment company based in New Haven, CT. Specialises in worldwide artist management, music publishing, and intellectual property rights management.

Invasion Group, Ltd

333 E 75th St #4A
New York, NY 10021
Fax: +1 (212) 414-0525
Email: info@invasiongroup.com
Website: http://www.invasiongroup.com
Website: https://facebook.com/invasiongroupltd

Represents: Artists/Bands; Film / TV Composers; Lyricists; Producers; Songwriters; Sound Engineers; Studio Musicians; Studio Technicians; Studio Vocalists; Supervisors

Genres: All types of music

Contact: Steven Saporta; Peter Casperson; Steve Dalmer

Management company based in New York.

James Joseph Music Management LA

3229 Rambla Pacifico Street
Malibu, CA 90265
Email: jj3@jamesjoseph.co.uk
Website: http://www.jamesjoseph.co.uk

Represents: Artists/Bands

Genres: All types of music

Management company with offices in Los Angeles, California, and London, UK.

Jampol Artist Management

8033 W. Sunset Blvd., Suite 3250
West Hollywood, CA 90046
Email: assistant@jamincla.com
Website: https://wemanagelegends.com
Website: https://www.facebook.com/jjampol

Represents: Artists/Bands

Genres: All types of music

Manages great legacy artists. Dedicated to the re-introduction of timeless art through modern means, and helps iconic artist legacies make the transition to the digital age with integrity. Does not manage new artists. If you are a legacy artist looking to extend your reach, use new technologies, or place your legacy in a modern context, send query by email.

Jay Anthony's Next Level Booking and Entertainment Agency, LLC

Las Vegas, NV
Email: Jayanthony@nextlevelbookingandentertainment.com
Email: Nextlevelbookingagency@gmail.com
Website: https://www.nextlevelbookingandentertainment.com
Website: https://www.facebook.com/JayAnthonysnextlevel/

Represents: Artists/Bands; Tribute Acts

Genres: All types of music

Always looking for exceptional talent to add to their roster. Looking for: experienced artists that believe in perfecting their craft; acts with great EPK's (no demo sites); and tributes acts that sound and look like the original act.

Jeff Roberts & Associates

Hendersonville, TN 37075
Fax: +1 (615) 851-7023
Website: https://jeffroberts.com
Website: https://www.facebook.com/jrabooking

Represents: Artists/Bands

Genres: Christian

Christina music booking agency, based in Tennessee.

Kari Estrin Management & Consulting

PO Box 60232
Nashville, TN 37206
Email: kari@kariestrin.com
Website: https://www.kariestrin.com
Website: https://www.facebook.com/kariestrinmanagement/

Represents: Artists/Bands

Genres: Americana; Folk; Roots; Acoustic

Based in Nashville, Tennessee. Offers artist management and consulting.

KBH Entertainment

Los Angeles, CA
Email: support@kbhentertainment.com
Website: https://kbhentertainment.com
Website: https://www.facebook.com/KBHEntertainment

Represents: Artists/Bands; Film / TV Composers; Producers; Studio Musicians; Studio Vocalists

Genres: All types of music

Contact: Brent Harvey

A full service entertainment consulting, booking, event production, management and marketing company, based in Los Angeles, California.

Kraft-Engel Management

3349 Cahuenga Blvd. West
Los Angeles, CA 90068
Email: info@Kraft-Engel.com
Website: https://kraft-engel.com

Represents: Film / TV Composers; Songwriters; Supervisors

Genres: Soundtracks

Management company based in Sherman Oaks, California, specialising in representing film and theatre composers, songwriters and music supervisors.

Kuper Personal Management

515 Bomar Street
Houston, TX 77006
Email: info@kupergroup.com
Website: http://www.kupergroup.com

Represents: Artists/Bands

Genres: Alternative; Americana; Folk; Roots Rock

Management company based in Houston, Texas.

The Kurland Agency

173 Brighton Avenue
Boston, MA 02134-2003
Email: agents@thekurlandagency.com
Website: https://www.thekurlandagency.com

Represents: Artists/Bands

Genres: Jazz; Blues

Contact: Ted Kurland

Management company based in Boston, best known for representing jazz artists.

LA Personal Development

Email: Glebe99@yahoo.com
Website: https://www.lapersdev.com
Website: https://www.facebook.com/lapersonaldevelopment/

Represents: Artists/Bands

Genres: All types of music

Contact: Mike Gormley

A management/consulting company started in 1983.

Laffitte Management Group

Email: hello@lmg.me
Website: https://lmg.me
Website: https://www.instagram.com/laffittemgmt/

Represents: Artists/Bands; Producers; Songwriters

Genres: Pop; R&B; Rock

Management company representing over 45 artists, songwriters, and producers.

Lake Transfer Artist & Tour Management

Studio City, CA
Website: http://laketransfermgmt.com
Website: https://twitter.com/LTMusicMgmt

Represents: Artists/Bands

Genres: All types of music

Artist and tour management based in Studio City, California.

Larro Media

Email: steven@larromedia.com
Website: https://larromedia.com
Website: https://www.facebook.com/steven.rosen.969

Represents: Artists/Bands

Genres: All types of music

Contact: Steven Rosen

A full-service music, film and TV, and talent development company specializing in artist synch representation, music supervision and music clearance, talent/brand management, and TV and film production.

Len Weisman Personal Management

357 S. Fairfax Ave. #430
Los Angeles, CA 90036
Fax: +1 (323) 653-7670
Email: persmanmnt@aol.com
Website: https://persmanmnt.com

Represents: Artists/Bands

Genres: R&B; Gospel; Hip-Hop

Represents professional and experienced R&B Artists; Gospel Artists and HipHop Artists to meet promotional, trade show, or corporate event needs.

Leonard Business Management

5777 W. Century Blvd, Suite 1600
Los Angeles, CA 90045
Fax: +1 (310) 458-8862
Email: info@lbmgt.com
Website: http://leonardbusinessmanagement.com
Website: https://www.facebook.com/pages/Leonard-Business-Management/665044716881370

Represents: Artists/Bands

Genres: All types of music

Provides business management services to the entertainment industry, including business management, tour accounting, royalty services, etc.

Lippman Entertainment

Fax: +1 (805) 686-5866
Email: music@lippmanent.com
Email: info@lippmanent.com
Website: http://www.lippmanent.com
Website: https://www.facebook.com/lippmanent
Website: http://www.myspace.com/lippmanentertainment

Represents: Artists/Bands; Film / TV Composers; Producers; Sound Engineers; Studio Technicians

Genres: Pop; R&B; Rap; Hip-Hop; Rock; Singer-Songwriter; Urban

Contact: Michael Lippman; Nick Lippman

Management company based in California. Not accepting submissions as at September 2019.

Loggins Promotion

Nashville, TN
Email: staff@logginspromotion.com
Website: https://logginspromotion.com
Website: https://www.facebook.com/logginspromotion

Represents: Artists/Bands

Genres: R&B; Urban; Rap; Hip-Hop; Dance; Alternative; Rock; Americana; Jazz; Country; Pop

Full service promotion firm based in Nashville, Tennessee. Submit music using online form, or send email for permission to submit by post.

Lupo Entertainment

Email: steve@lupomusic.com
Website: http://www.lupomusic.com

Represents: Artists/Bands

Genres: Country; Pop; R&B; Rock; Hip-Hop

Contact: Steve Corbin

Management company and consulting service founded in 2003.

Madison House Inc.

1401 Walnut St, Suite 500
Boulder, CO 80302
Email: info@madison-house.com
Website: https://madisonhouseinc.com
Website: https://www.facebook.com/MadisonHouseInc

Represents: Artists/Bands

Genres: All types of music

Management company based in Boulder, Colorado.

Magus Entertainment Inc.

268 Water St
New York, NY 10038
Email: info@magusentertainment.com
Website: https://magusentertainment.com
Website: https://www.facebook.com/MagusEntertainment/

Represents: Artists/Bands; Lyricists; Producers; Songwriters; Sound Engineers; Studio Musicians; Studio Technicians; Studio Vocalists

Genres: Contemporary; Electronic; Indie; Latin; Pop; Punk; R&B; Rap; Hip-Hop; Rock; Urban; Singer-Songwriter

A New-York-based, full-service management company, representing both high profile recording artists and a number of mixers and producers.

Maine Road Management

PO Box 1412
Woodstock, NY 12498
Email: mailbox@maineroadmanagement.com
Website: https://maineroadmanagement.com
Website: https://www.facebook.com/maineroadmanagement

Represents: Artists/Bands; Producers

Genres: Country; Folk; Indie; Jazz; Rock

Contact: David Whitehead

New York-based management company.

Major Bob Music, Inc.

Website: https://www.majorbob.com
Website: https://www.facebook.com/majorbobmusic

Represents: Songwriters

Genres: Country; R&B; Soul; Pop

Contact: Bob Doyle; Tina Crawford

Management and publishing company based in Nashville, Tennessee.

The Major Group

33117 Woodward Ave., Suite 331,
Birmingham, MI 48009
Email: contact@themajorgroup.com
Email: bmajor@themajorgroup.com
Website: http://www.themajorgroup.com
Website: https://www.facebook.com/tmgmajorproductions

Represents: Artists/Bands

Genres: Jazz; Rap; Techno; Rock; Pop; R&B

Contact: Brian Major

Management company based in Michigan. Accepts unsolicited material. Submit via online form.

The Management Ark, Inc.

Edward C. Arrendell, II
3 Bethesda Metro Center, Suite 700
Bethesda, MD 20814

Vernon H. Hammond III, CFP
116 Villiage Boulevard, Suite 200
Princeton, NJ 08540
Email: ed@managementark.pro
Email: vernon@managementark.com
Website: http://www.managementark.com

Represents: Artists/Bands

Genres: Jazz

Contact: Edward C. Arrendell, II; Vernon H. Hammond III, CFP

Jazz management company with offices in Bethesda, Maryland, and Princeton, New Jersey.

Mars Jazz Booking

1006 Ashby Place
Charlottesville, VA 22901-4006
Fax: +1 (434) 979-6179
Email: reggie@marsjazz.com
Website: https://marsjazz.com

Represents: Artists/Bands

Genres: Jazz

Contact: Reggie Marshall

Jazz booking agency. Not currently accepting new clients or press kits, but happy to receive CDs and contact details and may contact further down the line if interested.

Mascioli Entertainment

Website: https://masciolientertainment.com

Represents: Artists/Bands

Genres: Country; Jazz; R&B; Swing; Rock

Contact: Paul Mascioli

Full-service entertainment company based in Orlando, Florida, offering artists management and booking for conventions, casinos, arenas, theaters, night clubs, fairs, festivals, and special events.

Mauldin Brand Agency

Email: info@mauldinbrand.com
Website: https://www.mauldinbrandinc.com

Represents: Artists/Bands; Producers; Songwriters

Genres: Hip-Hop; R&B; Rap; Pop

Contact: Michael Mauldin

Your Black American Entertainment Connection with more than 40 years experience in music leadership, management, branding, and marketing. Creates partnerships and enhances branded assets within the consumer marketplace with special focus on teens, young adults, legacy, and the future.

Max Bernard Management

Email: myron@maxbernard.com
Website: https://maxbernard.com
Website: https://www.facebook.com/maxbernardmanagement/

Represents: Artists/Bands; Producers; Songwriters; Studio Musicians; Studio Vocalists

Genres: Urban Indie Jazz R&B Soul Singer-Songwriter; Soundtracks Blues Mainstream Soulful

Contact: Myron Bernard

We, pride ourselves on this blueprint that we specialize in creating a backdrop of musical ambiance featuring the world's finest and unique talent while servicing your entertainment needs.

We actively commit to find quality entertainment and entertainer's that suit your local and international demographic areas and taste.

Offers personal consulting services in all areas of artist development, live entertainment and social media and online network marketing.

Media/PR services are outsourced additions provided to clients. Special event(s) implementation and tour management services are available upon request.

MBK Entertainment

519 8th Ave, 19th Floor
New York, NY 10018
Fax: +1 (212) 629-0035
Email: info@mbkentertainment.com
Website: https://www.mbkentertainment.com

Represents: Artists/Bands; Film / TV Composers; Lyricists; Producers; Songwriters; Studio Musicians; Studio Vocalists

Genres: Contemporary; Gospel; Pop; R&B; Rap; Hip-Hop; Reggae; Urban

Contact: Jeff Robinson

Management company based in New York.

McDonough Management LLC

Email: frank@mcdman.com
Website: http://www.mcdman.com
Website: https://www.facebook.com/mcdmanagement

Represents: Producers; Songwriters; Sound Engineers

Genres: Rock

Contact: Frank McDonough

Management company representing record producers, engineers and mixers.

McGhee Entertainment

Fax: +1 (310) 358-9299
Email: info@mcgheela.com
Website: http://www.mcgheela.com
Website: https://www.facebook.com/McGheeEntertainment

Represents: Artists/Bands; Songwriters

Genres: Country; Metal; Rock; Singer-Songwriter; World

Contact: Don McGhee; Scott McGhee

Management company with offices in Los Angeles and Nashville.

Media Five Entertainment

PO BOX 21300
Lehigh Valley, PA 18002
Email: submissions@medafiveent.com
Email: david.sestak@mediafiveent.com
Website: http://www.mediafiveent.com

Represents: Artists/Bands; Sound Engineers; Studio Musicians; Studio Technicians

Genres: Indie; Punk; Rock

Contact: David Sestak; Patty Condiotti

Approach by email or through contact form on website. Response only if interested.

The MGMT Company

6906 Hollywood Blvd
Hollywood, CA 90028
Email: inquiries@themgmtcompany.com
Website: http://www.themgmtcompany.com

Represents: Artists/Bands

Genres: All types of music

Management company based in Hollywood, California.

Michael Anthony's Electric Events

Post Office Box 280848
Lakewood, CO 80228
Email: info2@electricevents.com
Website: http://www.electricevents.com

Represents: Artists/Bands; Tribute Acts; Variety Artists

Genres: Country; Pop; Dance; Classic Rock

Contact: Michael A Tolerico

Music entertainment booking agency based in Lakewood, Colorado.

Michael Hausman Artist Management Inc.

17A Stuyvesant Oval
New York, NY 10009
Email: info@michaelhausman.com
Website: https://michaelhausman.com

Represents: Artists/Bands

Genres: Contemporary; Pop; Rock; Singer-Songwriter

Contact: Michael Hausman

Management company based in New York.

Mike's Artist Management

PO Box 571567
Tarzana, CA 91357
Email: dan@mikesmanagement.com
Website: https://funzalorecords.com/mikes-artist-management/
Website: https://www.facebook.com/funzalorecords

Represents: Artists/Bands

Genres: Americana; Pop; Rock; Indie; Folk

Contact: Mike Lembo; Dan Agnew

Record label and artist management based in Tarzana, California. Send submissions via contact form on website, including links to music online.

Million Dollar Artists

12 Lake Forest Court West
St. Charles, MO 63301-4540
Fax: +1 (636) 724-1325
Email: info@americaneaglerecordings.com
Email: americaneaglerecordings@earthlink.net
Website: http://www.milliondollarartists.net
Website: https://americaneaglerecordings.com

Represents: Artists/Bands

Genres: All types of music

Contact: Dr. Charles Max E. Million

Management company based in St. Charles, Missouri. Send demos on CD only, with lyrics, bio, and photos / press coverage. Download and complete Preliminary Questionnaire from website. No submissions of MP3s or links by email – these will be ignored.

MM Music Agency

11 Island Avenue, Suite 1711
Miami, FL 33139
Fax: +1 (305) 831-4472
Email: info@mmmusicagency.com
Website: http://www.mmmusicagency.com
Website: https://www.facebook.com/mmmusicagency

Represents: Artists/Bands

Genres: Jazz; Regional; Contemporary

Contact: Maurice Montoya

Music agency based in Florida, handling jazz, Afro-Caribbean, Brazilian and contemporary music.

MOB Agency

6404 Wilshire Blvd
Los Angeles, CA 90048
Fax: +1 (323) 653-0428
Email: Mitch@mobagency.com
Email: joy@mobagency.com
Website: http://www.mobagency.com
Website: https://www.yellowpages.com/los-angeles-ca/mip/mob-agency-471004016

Represents: Artists/Bands

Genres: Alternative; Rock

Agency based in Los Angeles.

Modern Management

Email: info@modmgmt.com
Website: https://www.modmgmt.com
Website: https://www.facebook.com/modernmgmt

Represents: Artists/Bands

Genres: Country

Country management company.

Moksha Entertainment and Music Management (US)

Los Angeles
Email: MyInfoAtMoksha@gmail.com
Email: MokshaMusicManagement@gmail.com
Website: https://www.mokshaentertainment.com/

Represents: Artists/Bands

Genres: Pop; Punk Rock; Psychedelic Punk; Rock

Entertainment, Film, Music Management, Tour Services, and Recording Company, with offices in LA and London. Strives to embolden and embody the human spirit through entertainment, music and film.

Monotone, Inc.

820 Seward Street
Los Angeles, CA 90038
Email: info@monotoneinc.com
Website: https://www.monotoneinc.com

Represents: Artists/Bands

Genres: All types of music

Contact: Ian Montone

Music management company based in Los Angeles, California.

Monqui Presents

PO Box 5908
Portland, OR 97228
Email: monquipresents@gmail.com
Email: web@monqui.com
Website: https://monqui.com
Website: https://www.facebook.com/monquipresents

Represents: Artists/Bands

Genres: Alternative; Indie; Rock; Country; Pop

"Importers of fine live music", serving the Northwest since 1983. Send questions or comments by email and press kits by post.

Morris Higham Management

2001 Blair Blvd
Nashville, TN 37212
Website: https://morrishigham.com
Website: https://www.facebook.com/morrishighammanagement/

Represents: Artists/Bands

Genres: Country

Management company based in Nashville. Does not accept unsolicited material.

MSH Management

Email: mshmgmt@yahoo.com
Website: https://mshmgmt.wixsite.com/music-management

Represents: Artists/Bands

Genres: All types of music

Contact: Marney Hansen

Expertise and relationships in label management, artist development, retail sales, touring, digital sales and marketing, festival development, publicity, radio promotion, and more.

MTS Management

Email: michael@mtsmanagementgroup.com
Website: https://www.mtsmanagementgroup.com

Represents: Artists/Bands

Genres: Commercial Christian Hard Glam Melodic Progressive Power Country Guitar based Metal Pop Rock

Contact: Michael Stover

Full Service Artist Management, Publicity and promotions firm. Reasonable packages with the Indie Artist in Mind. National and International chart success, appearances, press and touring.

Murphy to Manteo (MTM) Music Management

Email: MarkZenow@MTMfirm.com
Website: http://www.mtmfirm.com

Represents: Artists/Bands; Producers; Songwriters

Genres: All types of music

Management company with its roots in Columbia, South Carolina. Contact by phone or by email.

Music + Art Management

15 W. Walnut St. Suite 202
Asheville, NC 28801
Website: https://musicandart.net
Website: https://www.facebook.com/Music-and-Art-Management-163558147005567/

Represents: Artists/Bands

Genres: Electronic; World; Experimental; Rock; Jazz

Full service management and production company specialising in the careers of performing and recording artists. Based in Asheville, North Carolina.

Music City Artists

7104 Peach Ct.
Brentwood, TN 37027
Fax: +1 (615) 266-6223
Email: cray@musiccityartists.com

Website: http://musiccityartists.com
Website: https://www.facebook.com/MusicCityArtists/

Represents: Artists/Bands

Genres: All types of music

Contact: Charles Ray, President / Agent

Full service booking agency representing nationally known artists for performing arts centers, casinos, and corporate entertainment.

Music Gallery International

Email: musicgallerymanagement@gmail.com
Website: http://musicgalleryinternational.com
Website: https://www.facebook.com/musicgalleryinternational

Represents: Artists/Bands; Studio Musicians

Genres: Alternative Hard Heavy Industrial Mainstream Power Americana Emo Garage Gothic Hardcore Metal Punk Rock

Contact: Jamie Moore

Offers management and consulting for a fixed fee (not a percentage).

Music Group Entertainment Worldwide, LLC

Email: musicgroupceo@gmail.com
Website: https://themusicgroupworld.com
Website: https://www.facebook.com/musicgroupworldwide

Represents: Artists/Bands

Genres: All types of music

Celebrity Booking Agency / Independent international Placement / Artist Development.

MusicBizMentors

Email: musicbizmentors@gmail.com
Website: https://musicbizmentors.com
Website: https://www.facebook.com/MusicBizMntrs

Represents: Artists/Bands

Genres: All types of music

Contact: Chris Fletcher

Offers music industry mentoring and coaching.

Myriad Artists

PO BOX 550
Carrboro, NC 27510
Email: trish@myriadartists.com
Email: booking@myriadartists.com
Website: https://www.myriadartists.com
Website: https://www.facebook.com/myriadartists/

Represents: Artists/Bands

Genres: Blues; Folk; Jazz; Americana

Contact: Trish Galfano

Management company based in Carrboro, North Carolina.

Nashville Records, LLC

Nashville, TN
Email: music@nashvillerecordsusa.com
Website: https://nashvillerecordsusa.com

Represents: Artists/Bands; Songwriters

Genres: Christian Acoustic Americana Country Pop Gospel; Americana

Contact: Lincoln Plowman

A full-service Artist Management and Record Label company. If you are serious about your career, so are we.

Females and minorities encouraged to apply.

Nettwerk Management

3900 West Alameda Ave, Suite 850
Burbank, CA 91505

NEW YORK
263 S. 4th St. P.O. Box 110649 Brooklyn, NY 11211
Fax: +1 (747) 477-1093
Website: https://nettwerk.com
Website: https://www.facebook.com/nettwerkmusicgroup

Represents: Artists/Bands; Film / TV Composers; Producers; Songwriters; Sound Engineers; Studio Technicians

Genres: Contemporary; Christian; Electronic; Folk; Indie; Latin; Pop; Punk; Rap; Rock; Hip-Hop; Dance; Singer-Songwriter; World

Media company with offices in New York, London, Vancouver, and Germany. Also label and music publishing company.

New Heights Entertainment

Email: info@newheightsent.com
Website: http://www.newheightsent.com

Represents: Artists/Bands; Producers; Songwriters

Genres: All types of music

Contact: Alan Melina

Privately held personal management and consulting firm, with its core business focusing on Music Producers, Songwriters, Record Label Management, Music Publishing, Brand Development and Strategic Guidance for Entertainment Content and IP Creators. No unsolicited materials.

Nexus Artist Management

Email: info@nexusartists.com
Website: https://www.nexusartists.com
Website: https://www.facebook.com/Nexus.Artist.Management/

Represents: Artists/Bands; DJs

Genres: Hip-Hop; Funk; Reggae; Dubstep; Electronic; House; Techno; Progressive; Break Beat

US management company handling electronic artists.

Nice Management

Email: steve@nicemgmt.com
Website: https://nicemgmt.com
Website: https://www.facebook.com/nicemgmt/

Represents: Artists/Bands; Film / TV Composers; Producers; Songwriters

Genres: Rock

Contact: Steve Nice

Management company representing bands, composers, producers, songwriters, and mixers.

Nightside Entertainment, Inc.

Email: nightsideentertainment@gmail.com
Website: https://www.facebook.com/nightsideentertainment

Represents: Artists/Bands

Genres: All types of music

Full service music booking agency.

NSI Management

2 Threadneedle Alley
Newburyport, MA
Email: contact@newsoundmgmt.com
Website: https://www.newsoundmgmt.com
Website: http://facebook.com/danrussellmusic

Represents: Artists/Bands

Genres: Folk; Indie; Rock; Singer-Songwriter

Contact: Dan Russell

Management company based in Newburyport, Massachusetts.

Once 11 Entertainment

Email: javier@once11ent.com
Website: https://www.once11ent.com
Website: https://www.facebook.com/Once11Ent/

Represents: Artists/Bands

Genres: Latin; World

Arts and entertainment consulting and personal management firm representing all kinds of Latin and World music.

Open All Nite Entertainment

9636 McLennan Avenue
Northridge, CA 91413
Email: info@openallnite.com
Website: https://www.openallnite.com

Website: https://www.facebook.com/openallnite

Represents: Artists/Bands

Genres: All types of music

Contact: Steve Belkin

Consultant for indie/emerging artists and labels in development of all aspects of career and business.

Opus 3 Artists

470 Park Avenue South
9th Floor North
New York, NY 10016
Email: info@opus3artists.com
Website: https://www.opus3artists.com
Website: https://www.facebook.com/opus3artists

Represents: Artists/Bands

Genres: Classical; Jazz

Represents classical and jazz performing artists. Offices in New York and Berlin.

Outrider Music, LLC

Charlottesville, VA
Email: anne@outridermusic.com
Website: http://www.outridermusic.com
Website: https://www.facebook.com/Outridermusic/

Represents: Artists/Bands; Lyricists; Songwriters

Genres: Post Rock; Progressive Rock; Post Metal; Hard Rock; Heavy Rock; Melodic Hardcore; Rock; Punk; Pop Rock; Pop Punk; Electronic Rock; Atmospheric Rock; Alternative; Alternative Rock; Acoustic Rock; Instrumental; Indie; Hardcore; Indie Rock; Ambient; Ambient Rock; Emo; Post Emo

Contact: Anne McGinnis-Townsend

I was born and raised in Charlottesville, and I became obsessed with music at an early age. I spent my early teenage years playing guitar in various pop-punk and alternative rock bands, but it soon became clear to me that I enjoyed the behind-the-scenes work just as much, if not more, than actually playing. After graduating from Charlottesville High School, I got my degree in Music Business from New York University. While at NYU, I spent two semesters interning for Warner Music Group and I had the opportunity to meet and learn from some incredible people. I realized that what I really wanted to do was to help upcoming artists navigate the early stages of their careers. Growing up in Charlottesville, I saw too many of our "hometown heroes" get signed to bad record deals and wash out, and I wanted to help prevent that. I started Outrider Music because I wanted to be an advocate for local bands, to help them navigate both the fun stuff (branding, marketing, touring, booking) and the not-so-fun stuff (contracts, PROs, insurance, taxes). I want to be a part of your team.

Pacific Talent

Email: andy@pacifictalent.com
Website: http://www.pacifictalent.com
Website: https://www.instagram.com/pacifictalentpdx/

Represents: Artists/Bands

Genres: All types of music

Contact: Andy Gilbert

Management company based in Oregon.

Paradigm Talent Agency

8942 Wilshire Boulevard
Beverly Hills, CA 90211
Fax: +1 (310) 288-2000
Website: https://www.paradigmagency.com

Represents: Artists/Bands

Genres: All types of music

Talent agency with offices in Los Angeles, New York, and London.

Paradise Artists

108 E Matilija St.
Ojai, CA 93023
Email: info@paradiseartists.com
Website: http://www.paradiseartists.com

Represents: Artists/Bands

Genres: Rock; Rock and Roll; Pop

Contact: Howie Silverman

Management company with offices in New York and California.

Persistent Management

Los Angeles, CA
Email: pm@persistentmanagement.com
Website: https://www.persistentmanagement.com
Website: https://www.facebook.com/persistentmanagement

Represents: Artists/Bands; Producers

Genres: All types of music

Management company based in Los Angeles. Submit your details through online Artist Submissions form, including links to music online. No postal submissions or phone calls.

Platinum Star Management

Beverly Hills, CA
Website: https://platinumstarmgmt.com
Website: https://www.facebook.com/platinumstarmanagement

Represents: Artists/Bands

Genres: All types of music

Been in the music and entertainment industry for over twenty years, whether it was working for Madonna's record label, Maverick Records (now part of Warner Bros Records) or slogging it out working for larger management firms, entertainment and digital marketing companies or movie studios like Sony Pictures. If you truly believe you or your band has the songs, the drive, the fans and magic to make it to the top then send a query by email.

Position Music

Los Angeles
Email: submissions@positionmusic.com
Email: contact@positionmusic.com
Website: https://www.positionmusic.com
Website: https://soundcloud.com/position_music

Represents: Artists/Bands; Film / TV Composers

Genres: Rap; Hip-Hop; Rock; Alternative; Dance; Electronic; Hardcore; Metal; Pop; R&B; Singer-Songwriter; Urban; World

An independent publisher, record label and management firm. Send streaming links only by email.

PRA [Patrick Rains & Associates]

Email: pra@prarecords.com
Website: https://www.prarecords.com
Website: https://twitter.com/prarecords

Represents: Artists/Bands

Genres: Jazz; Pop; Rock

Contact: Patrick Rains; Stephanie Pappas

Management company based in New York. No unsolicited material.

Pretty Lights

Email: contact@prettylightsmusic.com
Website: http://prettylightsmusic.com
Website: https://soundcloud.com/prettylights

Represents: Artists/Bands

Genres: All types of music

Submit demos using online form, available via website.

Primary Wave

NEW YORK
116 East 16th Street, 9th Floor
New York, NY 10003

LOS ANGELES
10850 Wilshire Blvd., Suite #600
Los Angeles, CA 90024
Email: info@primarywave.com
Website: https://primarywave.com
Website: https://www.facebook.com/PrimaryWave/

Represents: Artists/Bands; Producers; Songwriters

Genres: All types of music

Offers talent management, music publishing, television and film production, and brand marketing.

Prodigal Son Entertainment

Website: https://www.prodigalson-entertainment.com
Website: https://www.facebook.com/ScottWilliamsPSE
Website: https://myspace.com/prodigalsonentertainment

Represents: Artists/Bands

Genres: Alternative; Country; Christian; Instrumental; Rock; Hard Rock

Contact: Scott Williams

Artist management and career consultancy services.

Progressive Global Agency (PGA)

PO Box 50294
Nashville, TN 37205
Fax: +1 (615) 354-9101
Email: info@pgamusic.com
Website: https://pgamusic.com
Website: https://www.facebook.com/progressiveglobalagency

Represents: Artists/Bands

Genres: Pop; Rock; World

Contact: Buck Williams

Management company based in Nashville, Tennessee.

Proper Management

1114 West Main Street
Franklin, TN 37064
Website: http://www.propermgmt.com

Represents: Artists/Bands

Genres: Christian

Christian music management company based in Nashville, Tennessee. Not accepting submissions as at June 2023. Check website for current status.

Pyramid Entertainment Group

377 Rector Place, Suite 21A
New York, NY 10280
Fax: +1 (212) 242-6932
Website: https://pyramid-ent.com

Represents: Artists/Bands

Genres: Gospel; Jazz; Funk; Hip-Hop; R&B; Urban

Contact: Sal Michaels

Management company based in New York.

Q Management

Fax: +1 (615) 599-1235
Website: https://qmanagementgroup.com

Represents: Artists/Bands

Genres: Rock

Rock manager based in Franklin, Tennessee.

Q Prime Management, Inc.

Email: newyork@qprime.com
Email: nashville@qprime.com
Website: https://qprime.com

Represents: Artists/Bands; Producers

Genres: Blues; Folk; Metal; Pop; Rock; Alternative; Singer-Songwriter

Contact: Cliff Burnstein; Peter Mensch

Management company with offices in New York, Nashville and London.

Rainmaker Artists

PO Box 342229
Austin, TX 78734
Fax: +1 (512) 843-7500
Website: https://www.rainmakerartists.com
Website: https://open.spotify.com/playlist/6bgMwK0DD5mlJStc3MaKBo

Represents: Artists/Bands

Genres: Pop; Rock

Management company based in Austin, Texas.

RAM Talent Group

Fort Lee, NJ
Email: ruben@rubenrodriguezentertainment.net
Website: http://ramtalentgroup.com
Website: https://www.facebook.com/RAMTalentGroup/

Represents: Artists/Bands

Genres: Gospel; Latin; Urban

Contact: Ruben Rodriguez

A full service music and entertainment management company with diverse talents.

Red Entertainment Agency

505 8th Avenue Suite 1004
New York, NY 10018
Email: info@redentertainment.com
Email: carloskeyes@redentertainment.com
Website: http://www.redentertainment.com
Website: https://www.facebook.com/RedEntertainmentAgencyGroup

Represents: Artists/Bands

Genres: Funk; Jazz; Gospel; Latin; Hip-Hop; Pop; Rock; R&B; Urban

Contact: Carlos Keyes

Since its founding in 2002, has established itself as a leading entertainment talent agency, guiding the careers of an elite roster of musical artists. Under the leadership of agency President, has carved out a distinctive niche in the entertainment landscape and earned a reputation for putting artists' interests above all else. With a select group of professional agents working side by side, the agency credo is one of team work and availability that translates into successful relationships for all clients.

The select yet diverse client list allows it to effectively compete with other large agencies while guaranteeing personalized attention to every client. With offices in New York City, provides representation to clients across its music, motion picture, television and personal appearances worldwide.

Red Light Management (RLM)

Charlottesville; New York; Nashville; Los Angeles; Atlanta; Seattle
Website: https://www.redlightmanagement.com
Website: http://twitter.com/redlightmgmt

Represents: Artists/Bands; Film / TV Composers; Songwriters; Studio Musicians

Genres: Blues; Christian; Country; Dance; Electronic; Hardcore; Indie; Latin; Metal; Pop; Rap; Hip-Hop; Rock; Singer-Songwriter; World

Management company with offices in Charlottesville, New York, Nashville, Los Angeles, London, Bristol, Atlanta, and Seattle.

Regime Seventy-Two

Email: info@regimeinc.com
Website: https://www.regime72.com

Represents: Artists/Bands

Genres: All types of music

A company based in Art, Music, Fashion and Business.

Riot Artists

Email: staff@riotartists.com
Website: https://www.riotartists.com
Website: https://www.facebook.com/RiotArtists

Represents: Artists/Bands

Genres: World; Traditional; Contemporary

Management company specialising in World music reflecting traditional culture, and incorporating contemporary sounds to varying degrees. Books artists from around the world, with an emphasis on Canada, the US, Mexico, Brazil, and Europe.

Ron Rainey Management Inc.

8500 Wilshire Boulevard, Suite 525
Beverly Hills, CA 90211
Fax: +1 (310) 557-8421
Website: http://www.ronrainey.com

Represents: Artists/Bands

Genres: Contemporary; Blues; Pop; Country; Rock

Management company based in Beverly Hills, California.

RPM Music Productions

420 West 14th Street, Suite 6NW
New York, NY 10014

Email: info@rpm-productions.com
Website: http://rpm-productions.com

Represents: Artists/Bands

Genres: Jazz; Pop

Contact: Danny Bennett

Management company based in New York.

Russell Carter Artist Management

Website: https://www.facebook.com/pages/Russell-Carter-Artist-Management/174050332290?pnref=about.overview
Website: https://twitter.com/RCAM_mgnt
Website: https://myspace.com/rcam

Represents: Artists/Bands

Genres: Contemporary; Alternative; Americana; Blues; Folk; Indie; Jazz; Singer-Songwriter; Pop; Rock

Management company based in Atlanta, Georgia.

Selak Entertainment, Inc.

466 Foothill Blvd. #184
La Canada, CA 91011
Fax: +1 (626)584-8122
Email: steve@selakentertainment.com
Website: https://selakentertainment.com
Website: https://www.facebook.com/selakentertainment/

Represents: Artists/Bands; Comedians; Tribute Acts

Genres: All types of music

Management company based in La Canada, California.

Self Group

Portland, OR
Email: info@selfgroup.org
Website: https://www.selfgroup.org
Website: https://www.facebook.com/selfgroup

Represents: Artists/Bands

Genres: All types of music

An anarcho-syndicalist creative collective. The means of production, control and ownership of rights, royalties and all else governing each individuals artists' career is theirs alone. We come together to form a structure and outlet to present those creations and achieve a communal method through solidarity to carve a more unified means of navigating an industry and world still under the shadow of capitalism where the means of production remains in the hands of the few acting as dictatorial authoritarian governors making overarching decisions as to the welfare of the many. Exclusive and specific to the music community in Portland, Oregon.

Semaphore Mgmt & Consulting

Website: https://www.semaphoremgmt.com
Website: https://www.instagram.com/semaphoremgmt

Represents: Artists/Bands

Genres: Alternative Atmospheric Avant-Garde Electronic Experimental Glam Industrial Heavy Hard Kraut Leftfield New Wave Non-Commercial Post Psychedelic Thrash Underground

Full scale artist management and consulting agency. We offer a la carte consulting and retainer services to bands and labels alike.

September Management (US)

New York / Los Angeles
Email: info@sept.com
Website: https://sept.com

Represents: Artists/Bands; Producers; Sound Engineers

Genres: All types of music

Represents a roster of internationally renowned recording artists, producers and mix engineers who have collectively amassed 44 Grammys, 12 Brit Awards, 2 Oscars, 2 Golden Globes and sold over 100 million albums worldwide. The company has offices in London, New York and Los Angeles.

Sherrod Artist Management

Morehead City, NC
Email: infosherrodartistmanagement@mail.com
Email: sherrodimprove79@gmail.com
Website: http://www.sherrodartistmanagement.com
Website: https://www.facebook.com/sherrodartistmanagement/

Represents: Artists/Bands

Genres: All types of music

Artist Management / Consultant / Artist Development / Music Manager / A&R. Charges $25 to submit.

Silva Artist Management (SAM)

Email: info@sammusicbiz.com
Website: http://www.sammusicbiz.com

Represents: Artists/Bands

Genres: Alternative; Indie; Metal; Pop; Punk; Rock

Management company managing major international rock/indie bands.

Singerman Entertainment

Los Angeles, CA
Email: info@SingermanEnt.com
Website: https://singermanent.com

Represents: Artists/Bands

Genres: Heavy Metal; Thrash; Rock; Hardcore; Rock and Roll

Management company with offices in Los Angeles, California. No unsolicited materials.

SKH Music

540 President Street
Brooklyn, NY 11215
Email: skaras@skhmusic.com
Website: https://skhmusic.com

Represents: Artists/Bands; Lyricists; Producers

Genres: All types of music

Contact: Steve Karas

Management company formed in June 2009.

SMC Artists

Website: https://www.smcartists.com

Represents: Film / TV Composers; Songwriters

Genres: All types of music

Management company representing film and TV composers and songwriters.

Solid Music Company

Email: david@solidmusic.net
Website: https://www.solidmusic.net
Website: https://www.facebook.com/profile.php?id=100070887527477

Represents: Artists/Bands; Songwriters

Genres: All types of music

Contact: David Surnow

A management company for musicians and songwriters.

Sound Management, Inc.

1525 South Winchester Boulevard
San Jose, California 95128
Fax: +1 (408) 741-5824
Email: robert@soundmgt.com
Email: ron@soundmgt.com
Website: https://www.soundmgt.com/
Website: https://www.facebook.com/SoundMgtRecords

Represents: Artists/Bands

Genres: Pop; Rock

Full-Service Artist Management Company based in San Jose, California, navigating the careers of a diverse roster including Multi-Platinum, Grammy Nominated, and Internationally Acclaimed Artists.

Soundtrack Music Associates (SMA)

1601 North Sepulveda Boulevard #579
Manhattan Beach, CA 90266

Email: info@soundtrk.com
Website: https://soundtrk.com

Represents: Film / TV Composers; Supervisors

Genres: Soundtracks

Contact: John Tempereau; Koyo Sonae; Isabel Pappani

Represents award-winning composers, music supervisors and music editors for film, television and all media.

Spectrum Talent Agency

1650 Broadway
New York, NY 10019
Email: chris@spectrumtalentagency.com
Email: jan@spectrumtalentagency.com
Website: https://www.spectrumtalentagency.com
Website: https://www.facebook.com/SpectrumTalentAgency

Represents: Artists/Bands

Genres: Dance; Hip-Hop; Pop; R&B; House

Full service global booking agency.

Spinning Plates

Nashville, TN
Email: Debbie@spinningplatesmgmt.com
Website: https://spinningplatesmgmt.com/

Represents: Artists/Bands; Tribute Acts

Genres: Country; Rock

A boutique management, marketing, and production company based in Nashville, Tennessee, focusing on "making deals happen".

Starkravin' Management

McLane & Wong
11135 Weddington Street, Suite #424
North Hollywood, CA 91601
Fax: +1 (818) 587-6802
Email: bcmclane@aol.com
Website: http://www.benmclane.com

Represents: Artists/Bands; Producers; Songwriters

Genres: Pop; R&B; Rock

Contact: Ben McLane

Management and entertainment law company based in North Hollywood. Provides personal management and legal services.

Sterling Artist Management

Email: mark@sterlingartist.com
Website: http://www.sterlingartist.com

Represents: Artists/Bands; Producers; Songwriters; Studio Musicians

Genres: Blues; Jazz; Singer-Songwriter

Contact: Mark Sterling

Devoted to managing artists whose talent, dedication and drive position them for success in today's music industry.

Steven Scharf Entertainment (SSE)

Website: http://www.stevenscharf.com

Represents: Artists/Bands; Film / TV Composers; Producers; Songwriters; Supervisors

Genres: Alternative; Americana; Blues; Folk; Indie; Jazz; Metal; Pop; Rap; Hip-Hop; Rock; Roots; Singer-Songwriter; World; Soundtracks

Contact: Steven Scharf

Management company handling artists, composers, and producers.

Stiefel Entertainment

21650 Oxnard St # 1925
Woodland Hills, CA 91364
Email: contact@StiefelEnt.com
Website: http://www.stiefelent.com
Website: https://www.linkedin.com/company/stiefel-entertainment

Represents: Artists/Bands

Genres: Contemporary; Dance; Indie; Pop; Rock; Singer-Songwriter

Contact: Arnold Stiefel

Management company based in Woodland Hills, California.

Stiletto Entertainment

Website: https://www.stilettoentertainment.com
Website: https://www.facebook.com/stilettoentertainment

Represents: Artists/Bands; Producers; Songwriters

Genres: All types of music

Broadcasting and media production company.

Street Smart Management

Los Angeles, CA
Website: https://www.facebook.com/streetsmartmanagement
Website: https://twitter.com/streetsmartmgmt

Represents: Artists/Bands

Genres: Indie; Rock; Metal; Pop

Management company based in Los Angeles, California.

Suncoast Music Management

Email: suncoastbooking@aol.com
Email: suncoastoh@hotmail.com
Website: http://www.suncoastentertainment.biz

Represents: Artists/Bands; Tribute Acts

Genres: Disco; Classic Rock; Rock

Contact: Al Spohn; Quinton Coontz; Andy Bowman; Daniel Nathan

Management company specialising in tribute acts.

Sweet! Music Management

Email: ssweet@sweetmusicmanagement.com
Website: https://www.sweetmusicmanagement.com

Represents: Artists/Bands

Genres: Alternative Funky Hard Mainstream Modern Americana Blues Country Deep Funk Folk Fusion Funk Indie Pop Punk Rock Rock and Roll Singer-Songwriter Soul

Contact: Sean Sweet

Represents new Artists/Bands to develop and promote them. Located in Chicago, IL. Please send inquiries by email or phone.

TAC Music Management

Website: https://tacmusicmanagement.com

Represents: Artists/Bands; Songwriters; Studio Musicians; Tribute Acts

Genres: Acoustic; Classic; Hard; Traditional; Regional; Soulful; Heavy; Funky; Commercial; Alternative; Americana; Blues; Country; Folk; Fusion; Funk; Guitar based; Indie; Jazz; Metal; R&B; Rock; Rock and Roll; Roots; Rhythm and Blues; Singer-Songwriter; Rockabilly

Contact: Tracey Chirhart

Services include artist management, booking, promotion and marketing to both local and national artists. Genres include blues, rock, Americana, bluegrass, folk, country, and tributes.

Take Out Management

Email: AlexTakeOutManagement@gmail.com
Website: https://howiewood.com/take-out-management/
Website: https://www.facebook.com/HowardRosenPromotion/

Represents: Artists/Bands; Producers

Genres: All types of music

Contact: Howard Rosen

Has managed independent acts as well as acts signed to Columbia, Curb, Atlantic, etc. Currently focused on working with producers for upcoming major and independent releases. Contact by phone or by email.

Talent Source

The Mill at Nyack
15 North Mill Street
Nyack, NY 10960
Fax: +1 (845) 359-4609
Email: info@talentsourcemanagement.com
Website: http://www.talentsourcemanagement.com

Website: https://www.facebook.com/BoDiddleyOfficial

Represents: Artists/Bands; Variety Artists

Genres: All types of music

Contact: Margo Lewis; Faith Fusillo

Management company based in Nyack, New York.

Tenth Street Entertainment

113 North San Vicente Blvd, 2nd Floor, Suite 241
Beverly Hills, CA 90211

1115 Broadway, 12th Floor
New York, NY 10010
Email: info@10thst.com
Website: http://www.10thst.com

Represents: Artists/Bands; Producers

Genres: All types of music

International company with offices in LA, London, and New York.

That's Entertainment International Inc. (TEI Entertainment)

3820 E. La Palma Ave
Anaheim, CA 92807
Email: thomas@teientertainment.com
Email: jmcentee@teientertainment.com
Website: http://www.teientertainment.com

Represents: Artists/Bands

Genres: All types of music

Contact: John D. McEntee, President

Celebrity Entertainment Resource Company based in Anaheim, California.

Third Coast Talent

PO Box 170
Chapmansboro, TN 37035
Fax: +1 (615) 685-3332
Email: carrie@thirdcoasttalent.com
Website: https://www.thirdcoasttalent.com

Represents: Artists/Bands

Genres: Country

Contact: Carrie Moore-Reed

Management company based in Kingston Springs, Tennessee.

Thirty Tigers

611 Merritt Avenue
Nashville, TN 37203
Website: https://www.thirtytigers.com/
Website: https://www.facebook.com/thirtytigers/

Represents: Artists/Bands

Genres: Indie; Rock; Urban

Contact: David Macias

Management company based in Nashville, Tennessee, with offices in Los Angeles, New York, North Carolina and London.

This Day And Age Management

301 South Perimeter Drive
Nashville, TN 37211
Website: https://www.thisdayandagemanagement.com
Website: https://www.instagram.com/thisdayandagemanagement/

Represents: Artists/Bands

Genres: Pop R&B Rap

Contact: David Patrick Small

We are a management and artist development company located in Nashville, TN. We focus on label pitches, booking and sync licensing pitches.

Threee

Website: https://www.threee.com
Website: https://twitter.com/threee_ent

Represents: Film / TV Composers; Producers; Songwriters

Genres: All types of music

Management company based in Los Angeles, California, representing producers, mixers, songwriters, and composers.

TKO Artist Management

Website: http://www.tkoartistmanagement.com
Website: https://www.facebook.com/TKOArtistMgmt/

Represents: Artists/Bands

Genres: Country

Management company based in Nashville Tennessee.

Tom Callahan & Associates (TCA)

Email: tc@tomcallahan.com
Website: https://www.tomcallahan.com
Website: https://www.linkedin.com/in/tom-callahan-771294/

Represents: Artists/Bands

Genres: All types of music

Full service music consulting company based in Boulder, Colorado, offering record promotion, publicity, internet marketing, production, and more.

A Train Entertainment

PO Box 29242
Oakland, CA 94604
Email: postmaster@a-train.com
Website: http://a-train.com
Website: https://soundcloud.com/a-train-entertainment

Represents: Artists/Bands

Genres: All types of music

Entertainment services, including publishing administration, artist management, physical and digital distribution, international sales and more.

True Talent Entertainment

Email: TRUETALENTENTER@GMAIL.com
Website: http://www.truetalententer.com
Website: https://www.youtube.com/channel/UCXh-_1hDdqY1y92TorFfu7A

Represents: Artists/Bands; Film / TV Composers; Lyricists; Producers

Genres: R&B

Management, promotion, and production company. No unsolicited submissions.

Trunk Bass Entertainment

Email: info@trunkbassent.com
Website: https://www.trunkbassent.com
Website: https://www.facebook.com/TrunkBASSent/

Represents: Artists/Bands

Genres: Alternative; Hip-Hop; Pop; R&B

Offers a range of services, including Podcast Editing, Artist Booking, Music Consultancy, Artist Development, Music Supervision, EPK Building, Campaign Management, Video Production, Tour Management, and Content Creation.

Tsunami Entertainment

1600 E. Desert Inn Road
Las Vegas, NV 89169
Email: Info@tsunamient.com
Website: https://www.tsunamient.com

Represents: Artists/Bands; Producers

Genres: All types of music

A creative and business solutions Company operating in the music, entertainment and media space, providing brand strategy, business development, marketing services, operational support systems and financial management.

Tuscan Sun Music

Nashville, TN
Email: mgmt@angelica.org
Website: http://www.tuscansunmusic.com
Website: http://www.angelica.org

Represents: Artists/Bands

Genres: Ambient; New Age; Pop

Management company based in Nashville, Tennessee.

Uncle Booking

5438 Winding Way Drive
Houston, TX 77091

Email: erik@unclebooking.com
Website: http://www.unclebooking.com

Represents: Artists/Bands

Genres: All types of music

Booking agency based in Texas.

Union Entertainment Group

Email: info@ueginc.com
Website: http://www.ueginc.com

Represents: Artists/Bands

Genres: Rock; Alternative; Blues; Country; Pop; Rap; Hip-Hop

Music management company.

United Talent Agency

9336 Civic Center Drive
Beverly Hills, CA 90210
Website: https://www.unitedtalent.com
Website: https://www.facebook.com/UnitedTalent/

Represents: Artists/Bands

Genres: All types of music

International talent agency with offices in London, Los Angeles, New York, and Nashville.

Universal Attractions Agency

NEW YORK
15 West 36th Street, 8th Floor
New York, NY 10018

LOS ANGELES
22025 Ventura Boulevard, #305
Los Angeles, CA 91364

Fax: +1 (212) 333-4508 / +1 (646) 304-5178
Email: info@universalattractions.com
Website: http://universalattractions.com
Website: https://www.facebook.com/UAAtalent/

Represents: Artists/Bands

Genres: All types of music

Talent agency with offices in New York and Los Angeles.

Universal Tone Management

Email: fanclub@santana.com
Email: merch@santana.com
Website: https://www.santana.com/universal-tone-management-contact-us/

Represents: Artists/Bands; Songwriters

Genres: Blues; Latin; Pop; Rock

Management company based in San Rafael, California.

Val's Artist Management (VAM)

Email: info@vamnation.com
Website: http://www.vamnation.com
Website: https://www.facebook.com/VAMNation-Entertainment-108496975907793/

Represents: Artists/Bands

Genres: Contemporary; Blues; Classical; Country; Dance; Folk; Indie; Jazz; Latin; Pop; Punk; R&B; Rap; Hip-Hop; Rock; Roots; Urban; World

Contact: Valerie Wilson Morris

Aims to identify and cultivate the most elite talent in the entertainment industry. Describes itself as having "a keen understanding of the many facets of the industry gleaned through personal experience and proven professional success".

Variety Artists International

Email: John@varietyart.com
Email: Lloyd@varietyart.com
Website: https://varietyart.com

Represents: Artists/Bands

Genres: Folk; Jazz; Pop; Rap; Rock

Management company providing tour booking services.

Vector Management

PO Box 120479
Nashville, TN 37212

430 W. 15th Street
New York, NY 10011

LOS ANGELES
9350 Civic Center Drive
Beverly Hills, CA 90210
Website: http://www.vectormgmt.com

Represents: Artists/Bands; Songwriters

Genres: Contemporary; Alternative; Americana; Country; Folk; Gospel; Metal; Pop; Rock; Singer-Songwriter

Management company with offices in Nashville, New York, and Los Angeles.

Velvet Hammer Music & Management Group

Website: https://velvethammer.net
Website: https://www.facebook.com/velvethammermusicandmanagementgroup

Represents: Artists/Bands

Genres: All types of music

Contact: David Benveniste (Beno); Mark Wakefield; Samantha Waterman; Taryn Mazza; Kristin Van Trieste; Sara Pacheco; Samantha Surtida; Lauren Horne; Max Kane

Prides itself on identifying quality talent. Submit demos through online submission system.

Walker Entertainment Group

PO Box 7926
Houston, TX 77270
Website: http://www.walkerentertainmentgroup.com
Website: https://facebook.com/walkerentertainmentgrouptx

Represents: Artists/Bands

Genres: All types of music

Global provider of event management, production, and entertainment services.

Waxploitation

Email: artists@waxploitation.com
Website: http://www.waxploitation.com
Website: https://www.facebook.com/WaxploitationRecords/

Represents: Artists/Bands

Genres: Electronic; Indie; Hip-Hop; Rap; Reggae; Rock

Management company based in Los Angeles, California.

Westwood Music Group

2740 Kalsted Street, Suite 200
North Port, FL 34288
Email: westwoodgrp3@gmail.com
Website: https://www.westwoodmusicgroup.com

Represents: Artists/Bands; Film / TV Composers; Songwriters

Genres: Pop; Rock; Country; Blues; Jazz; R&B; Latin; Gospel; Instrumental

Contact: Victor Kaply

Established in 1985, and currently based in North Port, Florida.

Whiplash PR and Management

398 Columbus Ave,
PMB #183,
Boston, MA 02116
Email: Rockergirl363@aol.com
Website: https://www.whiplashprandmanagement.com

Represents: Artists/Bands

Genres: All types of music

An independent PR, brand and marketing agency that services bands, musicians, indie labels and music service companies internationally. Send music by email.

William Morris Endeavor (WME)

BEVERLY HILLS:
9560 Wilshire Blvd
Beverly Hills, CA 90210

9601 Wilshire Blvd
Beverly Hills, CA 90210

131 S Rodeo, 2nd Floor
Beverly Hills, CA 90212

NASHVILLE:

1201 Demonbreun
Nashville, TN 37203

NEW YORK:
11 Madison Avenue
New York, NY 10010
Website: https://wmeagency.com

Represents: Artists/Bands

Genres: All types of music

The world's longest running talent agency, representing music artists, authors, comedians, actors, sportspeople, etc. Has represented iconic names such as Charlie Chaplin, Marilyn Monroe, and Elvis Presley.

Wolfson Entertainment, Inc.

2659 Townsgate Road, Suite 119
Westlake Village, CA 91361
Website: https://www.wolfsonent.com/
Website: https://www.facebook.com/wolfsonentinc

Represents: Artists/Bands

Genres: All types of music

Contact: Jonathan Wolfson

Management company based in Westlake Village, California.

Worldsound, LLC

Seattle, WA 98148
Website: https://www.worldsound.com
Website: https://www.facebook.com/worldsoundllc

Represents: Artists/Bands

Genres: Celtic; Folk; Pop; Rock; World; Rock and Roll

Management company founded in Southern California in 1992, now based in Seattle, Washington.

Wright Entertainment Group (WEG)

Website: https://www.wegmusic.com
Website: https://www.facebook.com/wegmusic

Represents: Artists/Bands

Genres: Hip-Hop; Pop; R&B; Rap; Rock; Singer-Songwriter

Contact: Johnny Wright

Artist management company. Develops and assembles aspiring musical talent and also represents a roster of veteran entertainers.

Yellow Couch Management

Website: https://www.yellowcouchstudio.com
Website: https://www.facebook.com/steven.foxbury

Represents: Artists/Bands

Genres: All types of music

Contact: Steven Foxbury

A boutique artist management company providing comprehensive and creative strategies for those we serve. Our goal is to help shape enduring careers that are both personally and professionally fulfilling.

UK Managers

For the most up-to-date listings of these and hundreds of other managers, visit https://www.musicsocket.com/managers

*To claim your **free** access to the site, please see the back of this book.*

!K7

217 Chester House
Kennington Park
1-3 Brixton Road
London
SW9 6DE
Email: artist-mgmt@k7.com
Website: http://k7.com
Website: https://twitter.com/K7MusicHQ

Represents: Artists/Bands

Genres: All types of music

Represents a varied roster of artists from a wide range of genres.

2-Tone Entertainment (2TE)

91 Peterborough Road
London
SW6 3BU
Email: info@2tone-entertainment.com
Website: https://www.instagram.com/2tone_ent/
Website: https://www.facebook.com/2tone.entertainment

Represents: Artists/Bands

Genres: Dance; Urban; Pop

Record label and talent management based in London.

360 Artist Development

42 Western Avenue
Birstall
WF17 0PF
Email: info@360artistdevelopment.com
Website: https://www.360artistdevelopment.com
Website: https://www.facebook.com/360artistdevelopment

Represents: Artists/Bands

Genres: All types of music

Management / consultancy company based in Wakefield. Submit demos via contact form on website.

4 Tunes Ltd

Website: http://4-tunes.com

Represents: Artists/Bands

Genres: All types of music

Contact: Andy Murray

Now retired, no longer has any management clients or plans for any – but doesn't rule out the possibility completely.

7pm Management

Email: seven@7pmmanagement.com
Email: wolfie@7pmmanagement.com
Website: https://7pmmanagement.com/

Website: https://twitter.com/7pmmanagement

Represents: Artists/Bands; DJs; Producers

Genres: All types of music

Works with music but is not genre specific. In simplest terms if we love it and if we can help make it as a business make money then we work with it.

Also acts as a consultant to top companies within the global industry.

A&R Factory

Email: info@anrfactory.com
Website: https://www.anrfactory.com
Website: https://www.facebook.com/anrfactory

Represents: Artists/Bands

Genres: All types of music

Independent music blog that also offers an artist development program. Send demos through online submission form on website.

A2E – Artists 2 Events

PO Box 64
Ammanford
Carmarthenshire
SA18 9AB
Email: mike@artists2events.co.uk
Email: rob@artists2events.co.uk
Website: http://www.artists2events.co.uk

Represents: Artists/Bands

Genres: Acoustic; Blues; Celtic

Contact: Mike / Rob

Management company based in Ammanford, Carmarthenshire.

ADSRecords

2 Trinity Court
Newsom Place
Manor Road
St Albans
Hertfordshire
AL1 3FT
Email: music@adsrecords.co.uk
Email: podcast@adsrecords.co.uk
Website: https://www.adsrecords.co.uk
Website: https://soundcloud.com/adsrecordsuk

Represents: Artists/Bands

Genres: Acoustic; Alternative; Indie; Pop; Singer-Songwriter

Contact: Alex Dale-Staples

Artist management and composition services. To be considered for Artist Management send query by email, with "Artist Management" in the subject line, links to your music, and a 50-word description.

Aguia Music

Email: luana@aguiamusic.com
Website: https://www.facebook.com/AguiaMusic
Website: https://linktr.ee/aguiamusic

Represents: Artists/Bands

Genres: Americana; Country; Folk; Hip-Hop; R&B; Rap

All about the Vision – we understand the importance of having a coherent plan and supporting our artists in their professional and personal lives, always with the creative vision and approach making sure that every step counts to our future.

AJM

Email: juste@ajmofficial.co.uk
Website: https://www.ajmofficial.co.uk
Website: https://www.facebook.com/ajm.mgmt

Represents: Artists/Bands

Genres: Electronic; Pop

Send query by email with links to music online, bio, links to press shots (Dropbox or similar), your biggest achievements so far, and your goals and ambitions for the next 12 months.

Amber Artists

Email: management@amberartists.com
Email: info@amberartists.com
Website: http://www.amberartists.com

Represents: Artists/Bands

Genres: All types of music

Provides PR and management.

American Artiste (UK)

Cambridge
Email: information@americanartiste.com
Website: https://www.americanartiste.com
Website: https://www.facebook.com/americanartisteltd

Represents: Artists/Bands

Genres: All types of music

Management company with offices in Cambridge, UK, and Hollywood, USA. Send links to music online through online contact form.

Amour:Music

London
Email: info@amourmusic.co.uk
Website: https://amourmusic.co.uk
Website: https://www.facebook.com/AmourMusicUK/

Represents: Artists/Bands

Genres: All types of music

Artist Management and Career Guidance company based in London. Send query by email with links to music online. No downloads.

Amour:Music

Email: info@amourmusic.co.uk
Website: https://amourmusic.co.uk
Website: https://soundcloud.com/amourmusicuk

Represents: Artists/Bands

Genres: Contemporary; Singer-Songwriter

Send query by email with links to streaming music online. No attachments or download links.

Anger Management

Email: info@anger-management.co
Website: https://www.anger-management.co
Website: https://www.facebook.com/AngerManagement100

Represents: Artists/Bands

Genres: All types of music

Provides artist and tour management services.

The Animal Farm

4th Floor, Block A
The Biscuit Factory
100 Clements Road
London
SE16 4DG
Email: info@theanimalfarm.co.uk
Website: http://www.theanimalfarm.co.uk
Website: https://www.facebook.com/theanimalfarmmusic

Represents: Artists/Bands

Genres: All types of music

Send query by email or through online form giving link to website where you can be seen and your music heard. Include reason for approach. No MP3 attachments by email. Do not expect feedback.

AprilSeven Music

London
Email: mike@aprilsevenmusic.com
Email: mail@aprilsevenmusic.com
Website: https://www.aprilsevenmusic.com

Represents: Artists/Bands; Producers

Genres: Jazz; Electronic; Soul

Music consultancy based in London, with expertise in marketing, PR, international and local distribution, and management.

Artistes International Representation (AIR) Ltd

AIR House
Spennymoor
County Durham
DL16 7SE
Fax: +44 (0) 1388 812445
Email: info@airagency.com
Website: http://www.airagency.com

Represents: Artists/Bands; Comedians; Tribute Acts

Genres: All types of music

Management company based in County Durham.

Askonas Holt Ltd

15 Fetter Lane
London
EC4A 1BW
Email: info@askonasholt.co.uk
Website: https://www.askonasholt.com
Website: https://www.facebook.com/askonasholt/

Represents: Artists/Bands

Genres: Classical

Formed in 1998 through an amalgamation of two long-established artist management companies, both based in London but with international connections.

ASM Talent

Email: albert@asmtalent.co.uk
Email: assistant@asmtalent.co.uk
Website: https://www.asmtalent.com

Represents: Artists/Bands

Genres: All types of music

Contact: Albert Samuel

A well-established London-based talent agency with a combination of over 50 years of talent management experience.

Aspire Music Management

Email: mel@aspiremusicmanagement.co.uk
Website: https://www.aspiremusicmanagement.co.uk
Website: https://www.facebook.com/AspireMusicManagement.co.uk/

Represents: Artists/Bands; Songwriters

Genres: Melodic Rock; Pop Rock; Acoustic

Contact: Melanie Perrett

Management company based in northern England, representing unsigned and indie artists and songwriters. Handles a wide range of genres, but particularly interested in Melodic Rock, Pop Rock, and Acoustic. Will consider other genres, however.

Associated London Management

London
Email: martin@associatedlondonmanagement.com
Email: jason@associatedlondonmanagement.com
Website: http://www.associatedlondonmanagement.com
Website: https://facebook.com/ALMgmt

Represents: Artists/Bands

Genres: Alternative

Management company based in London.

ATC Management

The Hat Factory
166-168 Camden Street
London
NW1 9PT
Email: info@atcmanagement.com
Website: https://www.atcmanagement.com
Website: https://www.facebook.com/atcmanagement/

Represents: Artists/Bands

Genres: All types of music

London based management company with offices in Los Angeles, New York, and Copenhagen.

AuthorityMGMT

Second Floor
Unit 14 Tileyard Studios
Tileyard Road
London
N7 9AH
Website: https://www.authoritymgmt.com
Website: http://soundcloud.com/authoritymgmt

Represents: Artists/Bands; Songwriters

Genres: Dance; Pop; Singer-Songwriter

Music management company based in London, with a global outlook. Represents artists and songwriters at all levels. Extensive experience in management, A&R, records, publishing and brands deals.

Autonomy Music Group

6a Tileyard Studios
London
N7 9AH
Email: hi@autonomymusicgroup.com
Website: https://autonomymusicgroup.com

Represents: Artists/Bands; DJs; Producers

Genres: All types of music

Provides bespoke artist and campaign services to artists, bands, producers, record labels and DJs. Send query via email.

Avenoir Records

Email: martin@avenoir.org
Website: https://avenoir.org
Website: https://www.facebook.com/avenoirrecords

Represents: Artists/Bands

Genres: All types of music

Offers various music and entertainment industry consultancy packages that range from advice, simple online marketing and branding through to full musical production, development and managerial services at a cost to suit any budget.

AWA Entertainments

4a Queens Road
Sheffield
S2 4DG
Email: awagency@aol.com
Website: http://www.awaentertainments.co.uk
Website: https://www.facebook.com/AWAentertainments/

Represents: Artists/Bands; Comedians; Tribute Acts

Genres: All types of music

Management company based in Sheffield. Describes itself as one of the UK's leading entertainment agencies, providing top bands, duos, solos, tributes, comedians and more to the entertainment world, including Social Clubs, Corporate Functions, Weddings, Parties, Military Functions, Theatres etc.

B.H. Hopper Management Ltd.

Shepherds Building – Unit G7
Rockley Road
London
W14 0DA
Email: hopper@hopper-management.com
Website: http://www.hoppermanagement.com

Represents: Artists/Bands

Genres: Jazz

Management company based in London handling Jazz artists only.

Bad Apple Music Group

Email: hello@badapplemusic.group
Website: https://www.badapplemusic.group
Website: https://www.facebook.com/badapplemusicgroup

Represents: Artists/Bands

Genres: Alternative; Indie; Rock

With strong experience in the ever-changing industry, we are proud to offer artist management and development, release plan assistance, and more to help you to take the right next steps in your music career.

Bandzmedia

Email: info@bandzmedia.com
Website: http://www.bandzmedia.com
Website: https://www.facebook.com/Bandzmedia

Represents: Artists/Bands

Genres: Acoustic; Pop; Rock; Soul; R&B

Contact: Jude Bumby

Management company based in York. Not accepting demo submissions as at June 2021. Check website for current status.

Bear Music Management

Hampshire
Email: info@bearmusicmanagement.co.uk
Website: https://www.

bearmusicmanagement.co.uk
Website: https://www.facebook.com/bearmusicmanagementuk/

Represents: Artists/Bands

Genres: Indie; Pop; Rock

An artist management company based in Hampshire, UK. Specialises in the indie, rock, americana and pop genres with acts from the UK, pushing their music internationally. Pride themselves on being an artist friendly company whose main focus is on providing our artists with a platform to develop their careers and assist them in reaching their goals.

Big Bear Music

PO BOX 944
EDGBASTON
BIRMINGHAM
B16 8UT
Email: admin@bigbearmusic.com
Website: http://www.bigbearmusic.com
Website: https://www.facebook.com/Bigbearmusic/

Represents: Artists/Bands

Genres: Blues; Jazz; Swing

Contact: Jim Simpson

Represents and tours jazz, blue and swing attractions of the highest quality, mostly those signed to the Record label. We also oranise events and jazz festivals, including a midlands jazz festival established in 1985.

Big Dipper Productions Ltd

Email: contact@wearebigdipper.com
Email: adrian@insideslashout.com
Website: https://wearebigdipper.com/
Website: https://www.instagram.com/bigdipperproductions/

Represents: Artists/Bands

Genres: Indie; Pop; Rock

Established in 2000 to manage an experimental band discovered in Iceland. Have since broadened their horizons, frequently discovering and supporting unsigned talent and guiding them towards the right partners in an ever-changing industry. The modern music business offers artists both unparalleled opportunities and previously unseen challenges. Prides itself in being able to navigate through the new landscape, via a professional lifetime of shared experience and contacts.

Big Hug Management

Email: jeff@bighugmanagement.com
Website: http://www.bighugmanagement.com
Website: https://www.facebook.com/bighugmanagement

Represents: Artists/Bands

Genres: All types of music

Contact: Jeff Powell

One-man music management company. Home to Artists, Songwriters and Creatives. It's about raw talent and the long haul. No quick fixes. Artist Integrity is at the forefront.

Big Life Management

67-69 Chalton Street
London
NW1 1HY
Email: reception@biglifemanagement.com
Website: https://www.biglifemanagement.com

Represents: Artists/Bands; Producers

Genres: All types of music

Management company based in London, representing bands, solo artists, and producers. Send query by email with links to music online.

BiGiAM Promotions & Management

Email: info@bigiam.co.uk
Website: https://bigiam.co.uk
Website: https://www.facebook.com/BiGiAMPR/

Represents: Artists/Bands

Genres: All types of music

We promote, advise and manage businesses, events and personal creativity linked to music and the arts. Our portfolio is relatively wide and relatively varied; we play a significant role in the development, project management, marketing/promotions and sponsorship of a number of Brighton area based events.

If you think we can help your company/band/event etc, please approach us for a no obligation chat; we may well be less expensive than you think. Our aim is to provide unrivalled value and excellence in everything we do.

Black Fox Management

Email: generalenquiries@blackfoxmanagement.com
Website: http://blackfoxmanagement.com
Website: https://twitter.com/pollyrocker5

Represents: Artists/Bands

Genres: All types of music

Management company based in London.

BLOCS

Email: info@blocshq.com
Website: https://blocshq.com
Website: https://www.facebook.com/BLOCSHQ/

Represents: Artists/Bands

Genres: All types of music

A new model new music company with bases in Cardiff, Carmarthen, Swansea and Wrexham, and working with artists across the areas of management, live, and releases, with each working relationship tailored to meet the particular needs of each artist project.

Blue Raincoat Music

Unit G2
1 Leonard Circus
64 Paul Street
EC2A 4DQ
Email: info@blueraincoatmusic.com
Email: artists@blueraincoatmusic.com
Website: https://www.blueraincoatmusic.com
Website: https://www.facebook.com/WeAreBRM

Represents: Artists/Bands

Genres: All types of music

Management company based in London.

Bold Management

85 Bold Street
Liverpool
L1 4HF
Fax: +44 (0) 1517 091895
Email: martin@bold-management.com
Website: https://www.bold-management.com
Website: https://www.facebook.com/boldmanagement

Represents: Artists/Bands; Producers; Songwriters

Genres: Pop; Rock; Indie

Develops and manages the careers of a large and varied number of clients including TV personalities, music artists, songwriters and sports people.

Brian Yeates Associates Ltd

Website: https://www.yeatesentertainment.co.uk
Website: https://www.facebook.com/yeatesentertainment

Represents: Artists/Bands; Comedians; DJs; Tribute Acts

Genres: All types of music

Contact: Ashley Yeates

Management company based in the Midlands, with 30 years experience representing a variety of acts.

Brighthelmstone Promotions

Email: brighthelmstonepromotions@gmail.com
Email: james@brighthelmstonepromotions.co.uk
Website: https://www.brighthelmstonepromotions.co.uk
Website: https://www.facebook.com/brighthelmstonepromotions/

Represents: Artists/Bands

Genres: Americana; Folk; Indie

Management company based in Brighton, specialising in Americana and Roots.

Bulldozer Media Ltd

Email: info@bulldozermedia.com
Website: https://www.bulldozermedia.com
Website: https://soundcloud.com/bulldozermedia

Represents: Artists/Bands; DJs

Genres: All types of music

Artist management agency and music publisher.

BUT! Management

Email: jamesie@butgroup.com
Email: Nick.lyp@gmail.com
Website: http://www.butgroup.com
Website: https://www.facebook.com/butmusic/

Represents: Artists/Bands; Producers; Songwriters

Genres: Alternative; Pop; Rock; Singer-Songwriter

Contact: Allan James; Nick Robinson

Management, label, and publishing company based in Brighton. Founded to promote and develop new UK talent both domestically and internationally. Has a policy of listening to and providing feedback on anything received.

Catalyst Management

Website: https://www.facebook.com/officalcatalystmanagment/
Website: https://instagram.com/catalyst.management

Represents: Artists/Bands; Producers

Genres: All types of music

Management and marketing for UK artists aiming for mainstream success.

Chaos & Bedlam Management

Email: liza@chaosandbedlam.com
Website: https://www.musicglue.com/chaos-and-bedlam-consultancy/
Website: https://www.facebook.com/chaosandbedlam/

Represents: Artists/Bands

Genres: Rock

Contact: Liza Buddy

Rock management and consultancy company.

Closer Artists Management & Publishing

Matrix Studios
91 Peterborough Road
London
SW6 3BU
Email: info@closerartists.com
Website: https://www.closerartists.co.uk
Website: https://soundcloud.com/closer-artists

Represents: Artists/Bands

Genres: All types of music

Contact: Paul McDonald; Ryan Lofthouse

Management, record label and publishing company based in London.

CMP Entertainment

Email: info@cmpentertainment.com
Website: http://www.cmpentertainment.com
Website: https://www.facebook.com/CMPEntertainment

Represents: Artists/Bands; Tribute Acts

Genres: All types of music

Contact: Chas Cole; Rob Stringer

Management company based in Liverpool. Will consider all types of music, but works mainly with pop acts.

Conchord

London
Email: info@conchordmanagement.com
Website: https://conchordmanagement.com

Website: https://www.facebook.com/conchordmgmt

Represents: Artists/Bands

Genres: All types of music

Management company based in London.

Consolidated Artists

PO Box 87
Tarporley
CW6 9FN
Fax: +44 (0) 1829 730499
Email: alecconsol@aol.com
Email: ross@consolidatedartists.co.uk
Website: http://www.consolidatedartists.co.uk

Represents: Artists/Bands

Genres: Pop; Rock

Contact: Alec Leslie

Management company based in Tarporley.

Covert Talent Management

Email: covertdemos@gmail.com
Email: simon@coverttalent.com
Website: http://www.coverttalent.com
Website: https://www.instagram.com/coverttalent

Represents: Artists/Bands; Producers; Songwriters

Genres: All types of music

Contact: Simon King

A music management and publishing company that focuses on the creative, strategic and brand development of its hand-picked roster of clients.

Craft Management

Email: enquiries@craftmgmt.com
Website: https://craftmgmt.com

Represents: Artists/Bands; Producers

Genres: Alternative

Represents alternative artists and producers.

Create Management

Email: info@createmanagement.com
Website: http://www.createmanagement.com
Website: http://www.thecreategroup.co.uk

Represents: Artists/Bands; Producers

Genres: Commercial; Pop; Singer-Songwriter

Management company representing primarily singer-songwriters.

Creative International Artist Management

Email: info@cruisin.co.uk
Website: http://www.cruisin.co.uk

Represents: Artists/Bands

Genres: Metal; Pop; Rock

Management company set in 250 acres of countryside on the Wiltshire/Somerset border.

Creative Sounds UK

Email: ariches2@hotmail.co.uk
Website: https://www.creativesoundsuk.com
Website: https://www.facebook.com/CSUK1/

Represents: Artists/Bands

Genres: All types of music

Send query by email with links to your music online, a bio / onesheet / press kit, and your full contact information.

Creeme Entertainments

First Floor
293 Darwen Road
Bromley Cross
Bolton
BL7 9BT
Email: anthony@creeme.co.uk
Email: victoria@creeme.co.uk
Website: https://creeme.co.uk
Website: https://www.facebook.com/creemeentertainmentsltd

Represents: Artists/Bands; Comedians; Other Entertainers; Tribute Acts

Genres: All types of music

Contact: Anthony Ivers

Manages acts including music, tribute acts, lookalikes, comedians, after-dinner speakers, etc. for corporate events, and the pub and club circuits.

Crockford Management

Email: info@crockfordmanagement.com
Website: http://www.crockfordmanagement.com
Website: https://www.facebook.com/crockfordmgmt/

Represents: Artists/Bands

Genres: All types of music

Manager with over 35 years of experience. His clients have sold over 250 million albums worldwide.

Crossfire

3rd Floor
207 Regent Street
London
W1B 3HH
Email: info@crossfiremanagement.com
Website: http://www.crossfiremanagement.com

Represents: Artists/Bands

Genres: Classical; Dance; Pop; House

Management company based in London, describing itself as "an award winning music, creative and media management firm".

Crown Talent & Media Group

The Townhouse
52-54 Davies Street
Mayfair
London
W1K 5JF
Email: info@crowntalentgroup.com
Website: https://www.crowntalentgroup.com
Website: https://www.facebook.com/CrownTalentMedia

Represents: Artists/Bands; Producers

Genres: Commercial; Pop; Indie

Management company with offices in London and Los Angeles, handling chart-topping acts.

dandomanagement

Northamptonshire
Website: https://twitter.com/managementdando
Website: https://www.facebook.com/introducing.dandomanagement

Represents: Artists/Bands

Genres: Indie Rock; Singer-Songwriter

Contact: Martin Dando

Management company based in Northamptonshire.

Danny Brittain Band Management (DBBM)

5 Grand Parade
St Leonards on Sea
East Sussex
TN38 0DD
Email: danny@dbbm.co.uk
Website: http://www.dbbm.co.uk

Represents: Artists/Bands

Genres: All types of music

Contact: Danny Brittain

Management company based in St Leonards on Sea. Describes itself as "The premier live music booking agency for any occasion".

Darkspin Music Management

Email: info@darkspin.co
Website: https://www.darkspinmusic.com
Website: https://linktr.ee/darkspin.co

Represents: Artists/Bands

Genres: All types of music

Contact: Laura Mckay

Independent artist management and unsigned artist development.

Dawson Breed Music

Website: http://www.dawsonbreedmusic.com
Website: https://twitter.com/DawsonBreed

Represents: Artists/Bands

Genres: Americana; Folk; Indie; Pop; Acoustic

Contact: Debra Downes

A live music agency, we work with emerging acts and established acts, but only acts we are passionate about.

Deathless MGMT

Website: https://deathless-mgmt.com
Website: https://www.instagram.com/deathless_mgmt/

Represents: Artists/Bands

Genres: Metal; Rock

A UK based artist management and consultancy service with a focus on rock and metal music. Works with artists through all aspects of their music career including planning appropriate music and show design for live performances, PR, advertising, promotion, use of digital media, image and branding, booking agencies on behalf of the artist, and selection of other key members of the artists' team.

DEF (Deutsch Englische Freundschaft)

Email: info@d-e-f.com
Website: https://d-e-f.com
Website: https://www.facebook.com/DEFallesistgut

Represents: Artists/Bands

Genres: Dance; Electronic

Concentrates on electronic dance, but willing to consider all types of music.

Defenders Ent

Email: music@defendersent.com
Website: https://www.defendersent.com
Website: https://www.facebook.com/DefendersEnt/

Represents: Artists/Bands

Genres: Dance; Reggae; R&B; Rap

Formed in 2001 as an independent record label, has since been involved in managing, releasing and consulting for many acts/brands.

Deltasonic Records

Liverpool
Email: annheston@live.com
Website: http://deltasonicrecords.co.uk
Website: https://soundcloud.com/deltasonic-records

Represents: Artists/Bands

Genres: All types of music

Management company based in Liverpool and France. Send query via online form on website, with soundcloud links.

Deluxxe Management

Email: info@deluxxe.co.uk
Website: https://www.deluxxe.co.uk/
Website: http://www.facebook.com/DeluxxeArtistManagement

Represents: Artists/Bands

Genres: All types of music

Happy to receive new artist submissions. Send email with link to four songs, and social media links. Include message about why you think this is the right time to work with a manager. Response not guaranteed.

Deuce Management & Promotion

Email: rob@deucemusic.com
Website: https://www.deucemusic.com
Website: https://www.facebook.com/deucepr/

Represents: Artists/Bands

Genres: All types of music

Contact: Rob Saunders

Has established itself as one of the leading companies to offer services to unsigned/newly signed bands and artists worldwide. With a growing reputation of being at the forefront of the best new music on the scene and with its idyllically placed office in London, they aim to ensure bands and artists are offered ways and means to get their music heard to a wider audience.

For a FREE evaluation on your music please send a link to your material by email.

DFJ Artists

Studio 114
17 Amhurst Terrace
London
E8 2BT
Website: http://www.dfjartists.com

Represents: Artists/Bands; Producers; Songwriters

Genres: Jazz

Music management and consultancy services across jazz and related music genres.

Dissention Records + Artist Management

Website: https://www.dissentionrecords.com

Represents: Artists/Bands; Film / TV Composers; Other Entertainers

Genres: Alternative; Punk

Contact: Matthew Harris

Record label and artist management company originally founded in the States but now based in the UK. Send query by email with files or links to music online.

DMF Music Ltd

51 Queen Street
Exeter
Devon
EX4 3SR
Email: info@dmfmusic.co.uk
Website: https://dmfmusic.co.uk
Website: https://www.facebook.com/DMFMusicTeam

Represents: Artists/Bands

Genres: Ska; Folk; Indie; World; Jazz; Reggae

Contact: David Farrow; Laura Farrow

Undertake a diverse range of services including album campaign management, artist management, live agency, festival organisation and programming. Work with a range of established and upcoming artists from the UK, Europe and the US across genres including ska, folk, indie, world music, jazz and reggae.

Don't Try

107-111 Fleet St
London
EC4A 2AB
Email: ben@donttrymusic.com
Website: https://www.donttrymusic.com
Website: https://www.facebook.com/donttryuk

Represents: Artists/Bands; Producers

Genres: Alternative; Indie; Rock

Music company based in London, managing artists and producers.

Down For Life

Email: info@downforlifemusic.co.uk
Website: https://www.downforlifemusic.co.uk
Website: https://www.facebook.com/downforlifemusic

Represents: Artists/Bands

Genres: Alternative; Hardcore; Metal; Rock

UK based artist and event management company.

Duroc Media

Beechurst
Farnham Park Lane
Farnham Royal
Buckinghamshire
SL2 3LP
Email: info@durocmedia.com
Website: http://www.durocmedia.com

Represents: Artists/Bands

Genres: All types of music

Management and public relations consultants.

East City Management

London
Email: demo@eastcitymanagement.com
Email: hello@eastcitymanagement.com
Website: https://eastcitymanagement.com
Website: https://www.facebook.com/eastcitymanagement

Represents: Artists/Bands

Genres: Alternative; Dance; Indie

Manager based in London. Send query by email with links to streaming music online.

Elephant Management

Manchester
Email: elephantmgmt@outlook.com
Website: https://elephantmanagement.site123.me
Website: https://www.facebook.com/elephantmanagement/

Represents: Artists/Bands

Genres: Alternative; Psychedelic Rock; Shoegaze

Music management and promotion company based in Manchester.

Empire Artist Management

16 Tileyard Studios
Tileyard Road
London
N7 9AH
Fax: +44 (0) 20 8968 5999
Email: info@empire-management.co.uk
Website: http://www.empire-management.co.uk
Website: https://twitter.com/EmpireMGMT_

Represents: Artists/Bands; Producers; Songwriters

Genres: All types of music

Management company based in London, representing well-known artists, as well as producers and writers.

End of the Trail Creative

Email: kelly@endofthetrailcreative.co.uk
Website: https://www.endofthetrailcreative.co.uk
Website: https://www.facebook.com/endofthetrailcreative

Represents: Artists/Bands

Genres: All types of music

Management company and record label.

Enso Music Management

Email: submissions@ensomgmt.com
Email: info@ensomgmt.com
Website: https://ensomgmt.com
Website: https://www.facebook.com/ensomanagement/

Represents: Artists/Bands

Genres: Metal

Southwest based band management, booking and PR company. Specialises in Metal. Send query by email with links to music online.

Epic Venom

Email: sarah@epicVenom.com
Website: https://www.epicvenom.com
Website: https://www.facebook.com/EpicVenom/

Represents: Artists/Bands

Genres: Rock

Contact: Sarah Furbey

Rock band management including PR, bookings, travel management, event scheduling, and financial record keeping.

Equator Music

London
Website: http://www.equatormusic.com

Represents: Artists/Bands

Genres: Indie; Pop; Rock

London-based management company which has been managing the affairs of major artists and writers for over 35 years.

Everybody's Management Ltd

31 Corsica Street
Highbury
London
N5 1JT
Email: info@everybody-s.com
Website: https://www.everybody-s.com
Website: https://www.facebook.com/everybodysmgmt

Represents: Artists/Bands

Genres: All types of music

Management company based in London.

F&G Management

Unit D
63 Salusbury Road
London
NW6 6NJ
Email: gavino@fgmusica.com
Website: http://www.fgmusica.com
Website: https://www.facebook.com/fgdjtrade

Represents: Artists/Bands; DJs

Genres: Alternative; Dance; Electronic; Experimental; House; Techno

Contact: Gavino Prunas

Started as a DJ booking agency in the late eighties. Interested in music which is eclectic, different, or quirky. Send demo by email.

Fave Sounds

Email: hello@favesounds.com
Website: https://www.favesounds.com
Website: https://www.facebook.com/favesounds/

Represents: Artists/Bands

Genres: All types of music

A platform that features and connects music artists with their audience using effective branding, social media management, and artist management. Send submissions via contact form on website.

Feed Your Head

Website: https://www.fyhpresents.com

Represents: Artists/Bands

Genres: Alternative; Electronic; Dance; Indie

Management company founded in 2008.

Feraltone

Email: rene@feraltone.co.uk
Website: http://www.feraltone.co.uk

Represents: Artists/Bands

Genres: All types of music

Artist management, records, and consulting.

Ferocious Talent

Email: ferocioustalent@gmail.com
Website: http://www.ferocioustalent.com
Website: https://www.facebook.com/ferocioustalentlondon/

Represents: Artists/Bands

Genres: All types of music

Artist service company offering artist management, music consultancy, music business development, agency and rights management, label services, and in-house production.

Finger Lickin' Management

67-69 Chalton Street
Somers Town
London
NW1 1HY
Email: info@fingerlickin.co.uk
Email: amie@fingerlickin.co.uk
Website: http://www.fingerlickinmanagement.co.uk
Website: https://soundcloud.com/fingerlickinmanagement

Represents: Artists/Bands

Genres: Dance; Electronic; Hip-Hop; Break Beat

World recognised booking and artist management agency, currently managing a number of award winning artists and labels.

Flat Cap Music

Email: mike@flatcapmusic.com
Website: https://uk.linkedin.com/company/flat-cap-music
Website: https://twitter.com/mikeflatcap

Represents: Artists/Bands

Genres: All types of music

Independent manager based in London.

Flat50

Email: info@flat50.co.uk
Website: http://www.flat50.co.uk
Website: https://www.youtube.com/user/pmj83hatl/videos

Represents: Artists/Bands

Genres: Pop; Rock; Rap

Artist representation, promotion, and management company based in London. Send demos or queries by email.

Flow State Music

Edinburgh
Email: kyle@flowstatemusic.co.uk
Website: https://flowstatemusic.co.uk
Website: https://www.facebook.com/flowstateedinburgh/

Represents: Artists/Bands; DJs

Genres: Alternative Dance; Electronic

Music company based in Edinburgh, offering Event Production; Artist & Tour Management; Live Music Promotion; Music Programming; Digital Communications (Social Media / Direct Marketing). Send query by email with links to music online.

FP / Fantastic Plastic Music

Unit 6 Trident House
London
SE1 8QW
Email: info@fpmusic.org
Website: https://www.fpmusic.org
Website: https://www.facebook.com/fpmusicco

Represents: Artists/Bands

Genres: Alternative

Music company including record label, publishing, and management services.

Freaks R Us

Email: freaks@freaksrus.net
Website: https://www.facebook.com/freakartists
Website: https://twitter.com/freakartists

Represents: Artists/Bands

Genres: Alternative; Electronic; Experimental; Post Punk

Record label and management company.

Freedom Management

Website: http://www.frdm.co.uk

Represents: Artists/Bands; Producers; Songwriters

Genres: Indie; Pop; Commercial

Provide a broad range of skills and experience including artist / producer / writer management and development, online and audio / visual support, marketing and promotion, touring, publishing, business affairs & finance.

Friends Vs Music Ltd

London
Email: pip@friendsvsmusic.com
Website: https://www.friendsvsmusic.com
Website: https://twitter.com/pipvsrecords

Represents: Artists/Bands; Producers

Genres: All types of music

Artist and producer management company and music consultancy based in London. Approach via form on website.

From the Whitehouse

Email: bookings@fromthewhitehouse.com
Email: katie@fromthewhitehouse.com
Website: http://www.fromthewhitehouse.com
Website: https://www.facebook.com/fromtheWhiteHouse/

Represents: Artists/Bands

Genres: Electronic; Folk; Indie; Singer-Songwriter; World

An award-winning music management, artist development, booking and promotion agency, covering all aspects of strategic artist development for musicians.

Front Room Songs

Website: https://frontroomsongs.com
Website: https://twitter.com/Frontroomsongs

Represents: Artists/Bands

Genres: Folk; Pop; Roots; World

Provides artist and project management for a growing roster of emerging artists spanning the folk / roots / world and pop genres. Send query through online contact form with links to music online.

Fruition Music

Website: http://www.fruitionmusic.co.uk

Represents: Artists/Bands

Genres: Dance; Indie

Offers artist management and music and media PR.

Future Songs

London
Email: michael@futuresongs.co.uk
Website: https://www.facebook.com/futuresongspublishing
Website: https://soundcloud.com/future-songs

Represents: Artists/Bands; Producers; Songwriters; Sound Engineers

Genres: Pop; R&B; Singer-Songwriter

A music company specializing in management and music publishing. The company was founded in 2015 and represents a talented roster of clients which includes Grammy Nominated songwriters, producers and mix engineers.

Ganbei Records

Email: paul@ganbeirecords.com
Website: https://ganbeirecords.com
Website: https://www.facebook.com/ganbeirecords

Represents: Artists/Bands

Genres: Alternative; Folk; Post Punk; Psychedelic Rock

Record label and artist management company that aims to help musicians release and promote their music. Query through contact form on website.

Golden Arm

Email: louise@goldenarm.me
Email: milo@goldenarm.me
Website: http://www.goldenarm.me

Represents: Artists/Bands

Genres: Alternative; Indie; Pop; Rock

Management company based in London.

Goo Music Management Ltd

Email: contact@goomusic.net
Website: https://www.goomusic.net
Website: https://www.facebook.com/goomusic

Represents: Artists/Bands

Genres: Alternative; Indie; Rock

Contact: Ben Kirby

Built from a background of gig promotion, festival production and artist liaison. Has trusting relationships with many industry contacts including record labels, publishers, booking agents and tour managers.

Graphite Media

5-6 Greenfield Crescent
Edgbaston
Birmingham
B15 3BE
Email: info@graphitemedia.net
Email: ben@graphitemedia.net
Website: https://www.graphitemedia.net
Website: https://twitter.com/Graphite1

Represents: Artists/Bands; DJs; Producers

Genres: Dance; Electronic

Contact: Ben Turner

A music management and brand services company, based between London and Los Angeles.

Grizzly Management

25 Newman Street
London
W1N 1NP
Email: info@grizzlymanagement.com
Email: andy@grizzlymanagement.com
Website: https://www.grizzlymanagement.com
Website: https://www.facebook.com/grizzlymanagement

Represents: Artists/Bands

Genres: All types of music

Contact: Andrew Viitalahde-Pountain

Artist management company with offices in London, Manchester, and Helsinki.

Guvnor Management

Email: info@guvnormanagement.co.uk
Website: https://www.guvnormanagement.co.uk
Website: https://www.facebook.com/GuvnorManagement/

Represents: Artists/Bands; Comedians; Other Entertainers; Tribute Acts

Genres: Pop; Rock

An Entertainments Agency established in 2006, covering all aspects of the entertainments business from, cabaret artists, tribute shows, function bands, comedians, sporting and after dinner speakers.

Hal Carter Organisation

41 Horsefair Green
Stony Stratford
Milton Keynes
Bucks
MK11 1JP
Email: artistes@halcarterorg.com
Website: https://www.halcarterorg.com
Website: https://www.facebook.com/halcarterorg/

Represents: Artists/Bands; Tribute Acts

Genres: All types of music

Management company based in Milton Keynes.

Hand in Hive Independent Records & Management

London
Email: contact@handinhive.com
Email: tristan@handinhive.com
Website: https://www.handinhive.com
Website: https://soundcloud.com/hand-in-hive

Represents: Artists/Bands

Genres: Indie; Pop; Rock

Independent music company, formed in 2014 by two friends with a shared love of music, specialising in records, management, publishing and sync.

Handshake Ltd.

2 Holly House
Mill Street,
Uppermill
Greater Manchester
OL3 6LZ
Fax: +44 (0) 1457 810052
Email: info@handshakegroup.com
Website: http://www.Handshakegroup.com
Website: https://www.facebook.com/handshakeltd/

Represents: Artists/Bands; Comedians; DJs; Tribute Acts; Variety Artists

Genres: Pop; Rock and Roll; Commercial

Contact: Stuart Littlewood

Artistes Representation, and Concert Promotion Company, touring shows and events in the UK.

Also offering certain productions on a worldwide basis.

Hannah Management

Matix Studio
91 Peterborough Road
Fulham
London
SW6 3BU
Email: info@hannahmanagement.co.uk
Website: http://www.

hannahmanagement.co.uk
Website: https://soundcloud.com/hannahmanagement

Represents: Artists/Bands; Producers

Genres: All types of music

Contact: A&R

A London based artist and producer management company.

The founder has been successfully managing artists and working in music publishing since 1978. The management team manage record producers as well as up and coming bands.

They have purposely kept their roster small with the intention of working with the best talent and helping them develop all aspects of their career.

Happy House Management & Marketing Services

Email: happyhousemanagement@gmail.com
Email: dannydeathdisco@googlemail.com
Website: http://happyhousemanagement.weebly.com
Website: https://www.facebook.com/happyhousemgmt

Represents: Artists/Bands

Genres: All types of music

Contact: Danny Watson

Management, marketing and product management company.

Heard and Seen

Greens Court
West Street
Midhurst
West Sussex
GU29 9NQ
Email: enquiries@heardandseen.com
Website: http://www.heardandseen.com
Website: https://www.facebook.com/Heard-and-Seen-Ltd-197097010394361/

Represents: Artists/Bands

Genres: All types of music

Offers a range of services to artists, including management. See website for full details.

Heist or Hit

12 Hilton Street
Manchester
M1 1JF
Email: submissions@heistorhit.com
Email: team@heistorhit.com
Website: http://www.heistorhit.com
Website: https://www.facebook.com/heistorhit

Represents: Artists/Bands

Genres: Acoustic; Alternative; Indie

Management company based in Manchester. Send demos by email.

Holier than Thou (HTT) Music

Email: David@httmusic.co.uk
Website: http://www.holierthanthou.co.uk
Website: http://www.httmusic.co.uk

Represents: Artists/Bands; Tribute Acts

Genres: Rock; Metal; Electronic; Alternative; Melodic Metal; Progressive Metal; Gothic Metal; Melodic Thrash

Offers music management, digital distribution, new release promotions, and music publishing admin. Handles Rock, Metal, and sub-genres including Electronic Crossovers.

Hope Management

Unit 4.16 The Paintworks
Bath Road
Bristol
BS4 3EH
Email: info@hopemanagement.co.uk
Website: http://www.hopemanagement.co.uk

Represents: Artists/Bands

Genres: Alternative; Dance

Management company based in Bristol, with US offices in Los Angeles.

Hot Gem

Glasgow
Email: sync@hotgem.co.uk
Website: http://www.hotgem.co.uk
Website: https://soundcloud.com/hotgemtunes

Represents: Artists/Bands

Genres: Ambient; Dance; Electronic; Experimental; Pop

Musician management and label based in Glasgow. Accepts demos, but must have difference / unique sound. No indie guitar bands. Send demos by email as MP3 attachments, or via soundcloud.

On hiatus as at April 2023.

Hot House Music Ltd

33 Duke Street
Marylebone
London
W1U 1JY
Email: info@hot-house-music.com
Website: https://www.hot-house-music.com
Website: https://www.facebook.com/HotHouseMusicLtd/

Represents: Film / TV Composers; Supervisors

Genres: All types of music

Management company based in London, representing film and TV composers / music supervisors / score co-ordinators.

Hot Vox

London
Email: info@hotvox.co.uk
Website: https://hotvox.co.uk
Website: https://www.facebook.com/hotvox

Represents: Artists/Bands

Genres: All types of music

We work hard to create events that showcase the talents of our acts across the full range of genres, creating a great atmosphere for both musician and fan alike.

We also specialise in management, video production and work as consultants for branding, advertising, TV and film.

House of Us

London
Email: us@houseofus.co.uk
Website: https://www.facebook.com/houseofusmanagement/

Represents: Artists/Bands

Genres: Dance; House; Indie; Pop

London-based music management, consultancy, and PR company.

HQ Familia

38 Charles Street
Leicester
LE1 1FB
Email: yasin@hqrecording.co.uk
Email: yasinelashrafi1980@live.co.uk
Website: http://www.hqrecording.co.uk/hq-familia/
Website: http://soundcloud.com/hqrecording

Represents: Artists/Bands

Genres: Electronic; Urban

Contact: Yasin El Ashrafi

Collective of like minded artists with associated record label and recording studio.

Humans & Other Animals

Website: https://humansandotheranimals.com
Website: https://instagram.com/listentohumans

Represents: Artists/Bands

Genres: Indie; Rock; Folk; Electronic

We offer a range of services to help raise the profile of independent recording artists and record labels, from one-off consultancy and advice sessions to strategic campaign and label management. We work with artists and labels to raise your profile. We only work with those we believe can compete at the highest level of the music industry. In other words, we become strategic partners in your musical journey.

ie:music

111 Frithville Gardens
London
W12 7JQ
Email: info@iemusic.co.uk
Website: https://iemusic.co.uk
Website: https://www.facebook.com/iemusic-150700438296856

Represents: Artists/Bands

Genres: All types of music

Management company with offices in London, Los Angeles, and Sydney.

Ignition Management

London
Website: https://www.ignition.co.uk
Website: https://twitter.com/IgnitionMusicUK

Represents: Artists/Bands

Genres: Alternative; Indie; Pop; Rock

Management company with offices in London and LA. Approach via online contact form, including as many links to your social media as possible. Response not guaranteed.

Impact Artist Management

Website: http://impactartist.com/#artist-management-banner
Website: https://www.facebook.com/impactartistmanagement

Represents: Artists/Bands

Genres: All types of music

Our focus is on guiding the long-term career of our artists towards critical and commercial success by linking our clients' unique vision to satisfying and successful projects on a global scale.

Incendia Music

Email: Lulu@incendia-management.co.uk
Website: https://www.incendiamusic.co.uk
Website: https://soundcloud.com/incendia-music-management

Represents: Artists/Bands; Songwriters

Genres: Metal; Rock; Progressive; Experimental; Heavy

Contact: Lulu Davis

Artist Management, Publicity, and Consultancy services for Rock, Prog and Metal bands and artists.

Indevine

Email: sean@indevine.com
Website: https://www.indevine.com
Website: https://twitter.com/indevine

Represents: Artists/Bands; Songwriters

Genres: All types of music

Manager of a songwriter and several bands.

Innate – Music Ltd

Email: nathan@soundvault.tv
Website: https://www.innate-music.com/

Represents: Artists/Bands

Genres: All types of music

Contact: Nathan Graves

Creative strategy, project management, marketing and media consultancy established in 2003.

Insomnia Music UK

Email: management@insomniamusic.co.uk
Website: http://insomniamusic.co.uk
Website: https://www.facebook.com/InsomniaMusicUK/

Represents: Artists/Bands

Genres: Commercial; Pop

Music management company specialising in pop and commercial.

Intertalent Rights Group

First Floor, Malvern House
15-16 Nassau Street
London
W1W 7AB
Website: https://intertalentgroup.com
Website: https://twitter.com/InterTalent

Represents: Artists/Bands

Genres: Classical; Pop

Represents a range of talent, including musicians.

Intune Addicts

Email: info@intuneaddicts.com
Website: https://www.intuneaddicts.com
Website: https://www.facebook.com/intuneaddicts

Represents: Artists/Bands

Genres: All types of music

Contact: Mark Smutz Smith

A cutting-edge artistic development company. Provides handpicked musicians with holistic and forward-thinking management services.

Involved Management

London
Email: info@involvedmanagement.com
Website: https://involvedmanagement.com

Represents: Artists/Bands

Genres: Chill; Electronic; House; Trance; Progressive House

Management company with offices in London and Los Angeles.

JA Artist Management

Email: info@jaartistmanagement.com
Website: https://www.jaartistmanagement.com
Website: https://www.facebook.com/JAArtistManagement

Represents: Artists/Bands

Genres: All types of music

Artist Management for South Coast UK bands and solo artists.

James Joseph Music Management

85 Cicada Road
London
SW18 2PA
Email: jj3@jamesjoseph.co.uk
Website: http://www.jamesjoseph.co.uk

Represents: Artists/Bands

Genres: All types of music

Contact: James Joseph

Management company with offices in London, UK, and Los Angeles, California.

JBLS Management

Unit 13, The Tay Building
2A Wrentham Avenue
London
NW10 3HA
Email: louise@jblsmanagement.com
Email: jo@jblsmanagement.com
Website: http://www.jblsmanagement.com
Website: https://www.facebook.com/JBLSManagement/

Represents: Artists/Bands; Producers; Songwriters

Genres: Electronic; Alternative; Pop; Singer-Songwriter

Contact: Louise Smith

London management company representing artists, producers, remixers, mixers, and writers.

Jelli Records

Email: jellirecords@yahoo.co.uk
Website: https://www.jelli-records.com
Website: https://www.facebook.com/Jelli.Records/

Represents: Artists/Bands

Genres: Acoustic; Folk; Roots

Record label and entertainment agency offering stage management, open mic nights and songwriter evenings, and consultancy services, as well as hosting two radio shows every weeks.

Jude Street Management

Email: info@judestreet.com
Email: paul@judest.com
Website: https://judestreet.com
Website: https://twitter.com/judestreetmusic

Represents: Artists/Bands; Film / TV Composers; Producers

Genres: Alternative; Pop; Indie; Classical

Contact: Paul Devaney

Music services and management company based in East London and established in 2005. Provides professional representation for bands, artists, producers and composers/arrangers in the fields of Alt/Pop/Indie, Classical, Games, Film and TV. Send query by email and follow up with demos upon request.

Kaleidoscope

3-5 Stepney Bank
Newcastle upon Tyne
NE1 2PW
Email: info@kaleidoscope-music.co.uk
Website: https://www.kaleidoscope-music.co.uk
Website: https://www.facebook.com/KaleidoscopeUK/

Represents: Artists/Bands

Genres: All types of music

An artist management company and record label established in 2015 and based in Newcastle upon Tyne, UK. Established a sister company in Bangkok, Thailand, in 2021.

Karma Artists Music LLP

Unit 31, Tileyard Studios
Tileyard Road
Kings Cross
London
N7 9AH
Email: info@karmaartists.co.uk
Website: https://www.karmaartists.co.uk
Website: https://www.facebook.com/karmaartistsuk

Represents: Artists/Bands; Producers; Songwriters

Genres: All types of music

Contact: Jordan Jay; Ross Gautreau; Jess Miller

Multi-faceted entertainment company based in London, representing a roster with combined sales of over 400 million units.

Key Music Management

Suite 403, Bonded Warehouse
18 Lower Byrom Street
Manchester
M3 4AP
Email: contact@kmmltd.com
Email: contact@keymusicmanagement.com
Website: https://www.keymusicmanagement.com
Website: https://www.facebook.com/keymusicmanagement

Represents: Artists/Bands

Genres: Alternative

Contact: Richard Jones; Ryan Terpstra; Will Hanson; Marcus Jones

Management company based in Manchester.

KMY (Keep Me Young)

Website: https://www.keepmeyoung.uk
Website: https://www.instagram.com/KeepMeYoungUK/

Represents: Artists/Bands

Genres: Pop

Art first collective.

KRMB Management & Consultancy

Metropolis Studios
70 Chiswick High Road
London
W4 1SY
Email: kreynolds@krmbmanagement.com
Website: https://www.krmbmanagement.com
Website: https://www.facebook.com/krmbmanagement

Represents: Artists/Bands

Genres: All types of music

Contact: Kevin Reynolds

Management and consultancy company offering artist development, creative direction, talent management, corporate entertainment, and consultancy.

Laissez Faire Club

London
Email: jeremy@laissezfaireclub.com
Website: https://laissezfaireclub.tumblr.com
Website: https://www.facebook.com/jilloyd

Represents: Artists/Bands

Genres: All types of music

Contact: Jeremy Lloyd

Originally a live promotions company, now focuses solely on artist management.

Lazy Daze

Email: studio@lazydaze.co.uk
Website: http://www.lazydaze.co.uk
Website: https://www.facebook.com/LazyDazeRecs

Represents: Artists/Bands

Genres: Indie; Rock; Rock and Roll

Provide music management and label services for up and coming bands.

Legacy Records

Cambridge
Email: jeremy@legacyrecords.uk
Email: info@legacyrecords.uk
Website: https://www.legacyrecords.uk
Website: https://www.facebook.com/OfficialLegacyRecords

Represents: Artists/Bands

Genres: All types of music

With over 20 years industry experience we can help you take the next step towards your goal, with direct contacts to labels, producers, song writers and more our team can not only help you but we can put you with the right people for you.

Line-Up pmc

10 Matthew Close
Newcastle upon Tyne
NE6 1XD
Email: chrismurtagh@line-up.co.uk
Website: http://www.line-up.co.uk

Represents: Artists/Bands

Genres: World

Contact: Chris Murtagh

Promotions and marketing consultancy company with over 25 years of experience specialising in live arts performance, ethnic and World Music. May not necessarily offer representation, but may pass your demo on to relevant contacts if potential is seen.

Liquid Management

Email: david@liquidmanagement.net
Email: steve@Liquidmanagement.net
Website: https://www.musicglue.com/liquidmanagement
Website: https://twitter.com/liquidmgmnt

Represents: Artists/Bands; DJs; Producers

Genres: All types of music

Contact: David Manders; Steve Dix

Management company with 20 years of managing artists through all levels of the music industry.

Listen to This Management

Email: info@lttmusicmanagement.com
Email: grant@lttmusicmanagement.com
Website: https://lttmusicmanagement.com
Website: https://www.facebook.com/listentothisuk

Represents: Artists/Bands

Genres: Alternative; Alternative Country; Rock; Indie

Contact: Grant Tilbury; Charlotte Final

Artist and tour management company with offices in London and Nashville.

Lonewolf Talent Management

Email: rob@theboywiththelionhead.co.uk
Website: https://www.lonewolftalentmanagement.com
Website: https://www.facebook.com/lonewolftalent

Represents: Artists/Bands

Genres: Alternative; Ambient; Indie; Post Punk; Punk; Punk Rock

An artist management company focused on developing and supporting new and emerging artists to achieve their goals and help them through the various stages of their career in the music industry. Contact through form on website. No reply unless interested.

The Lost Atlantis Records

Email: Thelostatlantisrecords@gmail.com
Website: https://www.thelostatlantisrecords.com
Website: https://twitter.com/crystalchild01

Genres: Hip-Hop; House; Rap; Soul; Techno; Urban

Contact: Charlene Jones

Artist development and management. Send query by email.

LSH Management

7 The Courtyard
50 Lynton Road
London
N8 8SL
Email: info@lshmanagement.com
Website: https://www.lshmanagement.com
Website: https://soundcloud.com/lshmanagement

Represents: Artists/Bands

Genres: Indie; Jazz; Pop

Management company based in London.

Lucky House Management

Bristol
Email: luckyhousemanagement@gmail.com
Website: https://www.luckyhousemanagement.com/
Website: https://www.facebook.com/luckyhousemanagement

Represents: Artists/Bands

Genres: Grime; Hip-Hop; Rap; Soul; Urban

Contact: Jade Fearon

Personalised artist management, booking and casting agency.

Lucky Number Music Limited

Unit 1.6, Islington Studios
Marlborough Rd
London
N19 4NF
Email: contact@luckynumbermusic.com
Website: https://www.luckynumbermusic.com/
Website: https://www.facebook.com/luckynumbermusic/

Represents: Artists/Bands

Genres: Indie; Pop; Electronic

Provide management and producer services, and also operate a record label.

Lyricom

Website: https://lyricom.co.uk

Represents: Artists/Bands; Producers; Songwriters

Genres: Indie; Singer-Songwriter; Urban

Managing a roster that spans both independent and major label Recording Artists, Digital Talents, Producers and Writers.

Offering expertise across Production, Distribution, Digital, Promotion, Brand & Franchise Extensions, Live, Merch, Team Architecture and Administration.

M24 Management

Manchester
Email: mgmt@m24management.com
Website: https://www.m24management.com
Website: https://www.facebook.com/M24ManagementAgency

Represents: DJs

Genres: House

Management company based in Manchester, representing House DJs.

MaDa Music Entertainment

London
Email: Adam@Madamusic.com
Website: https://madamusic.com
Website: https://soundcloud.com/mada-music

Represents: Artists/Bands; Producers

Genres: All types of music

London based multi divisional entertainment company specialising in Artist and Producer Management, Events, PR and Consultancy. Particularly interested in pop, indie, and rock, but will consider most genres.

Major Labl

Website: https://www.majorlabl.com
Website: https://www.facebook.com/MajorLabl/

Represents: Artists/Bands

Genres: All types of music

Offers marketing and management services for unsigned and independent artists. Apply through online form.

Manners McDade Artist Management

3rd floor, 12 Greenhill Rents
London
EC1M 6BN
Email: submissions@mannersmcdade.co.uk
Email: info@mannersmcdade.co.uk
Website: http://mannersmcdade.co.uk
Website: https://www.facebook.com/mannersmcdademusic/

Represents: Film / TV Composers

Genres: All types of music

Management company based in London, representing composers for film and TV. Send submissions by email. Response only if interested.

MBM (Music Business Management Ltd)

Labrican
Healey Dell Nature Reserve
Rochdale
OL12 6BG
Email: anne@mbmcorporate.co.uk
Email: phil@mbmcorporate.co.uk
Website: https://www.mbmcorporate.co.uk
Website: https://www.facebook.com/MBMCorporate

Represents: Artists/Bands; DJs; Tribute Acts

Genres: All types of music

Contact: Anne Barrett; Phil Barrett

Entertainment consultancy and artiste management. Specialises in Tributes and Tribite shows.

Memphia Music Management

Bristol
Email: jp@memphia.com
Website: https://www.memphia.com
Website: https://www.facebook.com/MemphiaMM/

Represents: Artists/Bands

Genres: Indie; Rock

Management company based in Bristol. Query by email or via contact us page on website.

Metal Music Bookings

Fax: +44 (0) 20 7084 0323
Email: contact@metalmusicbookings.com
Website: http://www.metalmusicbookings.com
Website: https://www.facebook.com/MetalMusicBookings

Represents: Artists/Bands

Genres: Alternative; Metal; Rock

Contact: Denise Dale

Independent Booking Agency specialising in representing artists in the Heavy Metal and Rock genres, but willing to consider other genres. Offers self-management subscription services.

Miller Music Management

Fax: +44 (0) 20 8964 4965
Email: info@m-music-m.com
Website: http://www.m-music-m.com

Represents: Artists/Bands

Genres: Indie; Rock; Singer-Songwriter

Contact: Carrie Hustler

Management company with offices in London and Los Angeles.

MJM Agency

Email: demos@mjmagency.co.uk
Email: info@mjmagency.co.uk
Website: http://www.mjmagency.co.uk

Represents: Artists/Bands; DJs; Other Entertainers

Genres: All types of music

Contact: Mike Jones

Management agency run on a part-time basis. Handles musical entertainers and performing acts. Send demos and/or band details by email.

Moksha Management

PO Box 102
London
E15 2HH
Email: info@moksha.co.uk
Website: https://www.moksha.co.uk
Website: https://twitter.com/mokshamgt

Represents: Artists/Bands

Genres: Alternative Electronic Fusion; Contemporary; Dance

Demos preferred as streaming weblinks.

Morningstar

Email: enquiries@morningstarpro.co.uk
Email: artists@morningstarpro.co.uk
Website: https://www.morningstarpro.co.uk
Website: https://www.facebook.com/Mstarliveevents

Represents: Artists/Bands

Genres: Indie; Rock

Management agency based on the key values of honesty and a more personal touch with everyone they choose to represent.

Mother Artist Management

Email: info@motherartists.com
Website: https://www.motherartists.com
Website: https://www.facebook.com/motherartistsltd/

Represents: Artists/Bands

Genres: All types of music

Artist management and live music agency.

Music by Design

48 Home Hill
Hextable
Kent
BR8 7RR
Email: info@musicbydesign.co.uk
Website: http://www.musicbydesign.co.uk

Represents: Artists/Bands

Genres: All types of music

"Innovative out of the box thinkers required. Send us your idea, receive a song. Let's create something good together".

Music Media Events

Website: http://www.musicmediaevents.com
Website: https://twitter.com/musicmediasean

Represents: Artists/Bands

Genres: Pop; Acoustic; Alternative; Folk

We have booked artists in to arenas, clubs, art centres, theatres, colleges, stadiums, festivals, Christmas switch-ons, store openings, charity, private and corporate events.

N.O.W. Music Management

1st Floor
25 Commercial Street
Brighouse
HD6 1AF
Email: info@now-music.com
Website: https://www.now-music.com

Represents: Artists/Bands; Tribute Acts

Genres: Pop; Rock

A management company based in Brighouse, West Yorkshire, with strong connections in

Europe and with a small independent record company.

Nettwerk Management UK

15 Adeline Place, Ground Floor
London
WC1B 3AJ
Fax: +44 (0) 20 7456 9501
Email: info@nettwerk.com
Website: http://www.nettwerk.com
Website: https://www.facebook.com/nettwerkmusicgroup

Represents: Artists/Bands

Genres: All types of music

Management company headquartered in Vancouver, with offices in London, Hamburg, LA, and New York.

New Champion Management

Oh Yeah Centre
Belfast
BT1 2LG
Email: newchampionmanagement@gmail.com
Website: https://www.facebook.com/newchampionmanagement/
Website: https://www.instagram.com/newchampionmanagement/

Represents: Artists/Bands

Genres: Electronic; Folk; Indie; Pop; Punk

Provides artist management, PR and music consultancy services. Based in Northern Ireland.

New Level Music Management

Oxford
Email: newlevelmgmt@gmail.com
Website: https://www.facebook.com/NewLevelMgmt
Website: https://twitter.com/NewLevelMgmt

Represents: Artists/Bands

Genres: All types of music

Music management based in Oxford, with contacts with UK and international record labels, publishers, promoters, and booking agents. Provides artist management, tour booking / management, professional guidance, PR, release campaigns, and contract negotiation.

NewLevel Management

Oxford
Email: newlevelmgmt@gmail.com
Website: https://www.facebook.com/NewLevelMgmt
Website: https://twitter.com/NewLevelMgmt

Represents: Artists/Bands

Genres: All types of music

Music management company based in Oxford. Offers artist management, tour booking, professional guidance, tour management, PR, label mailouts, release campaign co-ordination, and contract negotiation.

No Half Measures Ltd

1st Floor
5 Eagle Street
Glasgow
G4 9XA
Email: info@nohalfmeasures.com
Website: https://nohalfmeasures.com/
Website: https://www.facebook.com/nohalfmeasures

Represents: Artists/Bands

Genres: All types of music

A company registered in Scotland, U.K. and based in Glasgow. The firm has a general structure based on its artist management, music publishing, record label and photography divisions. Works with a diverse range of artists and operates in huge variety of areas. These include artist management; intellectual property and rights management; music composition and publishing; audio and audio visual recording, mixing, and mastering; design, manufacturing, distribution and sale of audio and audio visual products, merchandise, clothing, apparel, and printed products; photography; marketing, promotion and advertising of these goods; sponsorship and branding; live entertainment performances, presentations and touring; event logistics, consultancy, management and promotion; sale of tickets; training and education.

Northern Music Co. Ltd

5A Victoria Road
Saltaire
Shipley
West Yorkshire
BD18 3LA
Fax: +44 (0) 1274 593546
Email: demos@northernmusic.co.uk
Email: info@northernmusic.co.uk
Website: http://www.northernmusic.co.uk
Website: https://www.facebook.com/NMCLtd

Represents: Artists/Bands

Genres: Metal; Rock

Contact: Andy Farrow

Send query by email with your band/act's name in the subject line, with details on what you are looking for; links to stream your music; a brief bio of your band/act; links to your website / social media / videos; and any details of existing industry partners / releases / live dates, etc.

Off the Chart Promotions

Email: tim@offthechart.co.uk
Website: https://www.offthechart.co.uk
Website: https://www.facebook.com/offthechartmanagement

Represents: Artists/Bands

Genres: Folk; Pop; Rock; Indie; Singer-Songwriter

Management company based in Cambridge. Works with artists from the East of England and London.

OnDaBeat Talent Management

4 Wandsworth Plain
Church Row
London
SW18 1ES
Email: mgmt@odbentltd.com
Website: https://ondabeat.co.uk
Website: https://soundcloud.com/ondabeatmgmt

Represents: Artists/Bands

Genres: Drum and Bass; Electronic; House; Hip-Hop; Rap; Techno

Management company and record studios based in London.

One Fifteen

A&R
1 Globe House
Middle Lane Mews
London
N8 8PN
Fax: +44 (0) 20 8442 7561
Email: demos@onefifteen.com
Email: contact@onefifteen.com
Website: https://www.onefifteen.com

Represents: Artists/Bands

Genres: All types of music

If submitting by email prefers links to your SoundCloud, YouTube or Facebook page. If you insist on sending MP3s, send no more than two. Include short bio, photo, social media links, and upcoming gig listings. CDs cannot be returned. Aims to listen to everything, but response not guaranteed if not interested.

141a Management

Email: admin@art19.co.uk
Website: https://www.141amanagement.co.uk
Website: https://www.facebook.com/141amanagementcompany/?fref=ts

Represents: Artists/Bands

Genres: All types of music

Music management company representing artists from all music genres.

140dB Management Limited

London
Email: ros@140db.co.uk
Website: https://www.biglifemanagement.com/140db
Website: https://www.facebook.com/140dBManagement/

Represents: Artists/Bands; Producers

Genres: All types of music

Contact: Ros Earls

Management company based in London. Represents artists and producers.

Opre Roma

Email: info@opreroma.co.uk
Website: https://opreroma.co.uk
Website: https://www.facebook.com/OpreRomaSounds

Represents: Artists/Bands

Genres: Acoustic; Americana; Folk; Guitar based; Indie

Contact: Nayfe Slusjan

Aims to help artists build long-term stability into their music careers, with 24/7 access to business management services and global representation. Send links to your music through online submission form.

Orean Music Ltd

Email: adrian@oreanmusic.com
Email: ah@oreanmusic.com
Website: https://oreanmusic.com
Website: https://www.facebook.com/oreanmusic/

Represents: Artists/Bands

Genres: Alternative; Dance; Electronic; Indie; Pop

Artist management company dedicated to helping independent artists grow and succeed in the music industry.

Ornadel Management

Email: info@ornadel.com
Email: guy@ornadel.com
Website: https://ornadel.com
Website: https://www.facebook.com/OrnadelMGM/

Represents: Artists/Bands; DJs

Genres: Dance

Contact: Guy Ornadel

Mainly works with DJs.

Park Promotions

Website: http://www.parkrecords.com
Website: https://www.facebook.com/Park-Promotions-141933172641365/

Represents: Artists/Bands

Genres: Folk; Singer-Songwriter; Roots; Acoustic; Folk Rock

Music company including record label and management and PR services.

Perfect Havoc Ltd

Email: info@perfecthavoc.com
Email: Adam.Griffin@perfecthavoc.com
Website: https://perfecthavoc.com
Website: https://www.facebook.com/perfecthavocmusic/

Represents: Artists/Bands

Genres: Dance; Disco; House

London-based music entertainment management, record label, and events. Submit demos as soundcloud links using online form on website.

Petty Music Management

Email: hello@pettymanagement.com
Website: https://pettymanagement.com

Represents: Artists/Bands

Genres: All types of music

UK management company.

Phono Sounds UK

Email: phonosounds@gmail.com
Website: https://phono.uk/
Website: https://www.facebook.com/phonosounds

Represents: Artists/Bands

Genres: Electronic; Pop; House; Trance; Dance

Independent minded label, also providing publishing, management, and distribution. Send demos by email.

Pieces of 8 Music

London
Email: info@piecesof8music.com
Website: https://piecesof8music.com
Website: https://www.facebook.com/Piecesof8Music

Represents: Artists/Bands; Producers; Songwriters; Sound Engineers

Genres: All types of music

Boutique management company set up to represent artists, producers, engineers, mixers and songwriters on a professional level.

Pierce Entertainment

Pierce House
London Apollo Complex
Queen Caroline Street
London
W6 9QH
Email: info@pierce-entertainment.com
Website: https://www.pierce-entertainment.com
Website: https://www.facebook.com/PierceEnt/

Represents: Producers; Sound Engineers

Genres: Pop; R&B

Management company based in London, home to award winning producers and engineers.

Pillar Artists

Newcastle upon Tyne
Email: pillar.artists@gmail.com
Website: https://www.musicglue.com/pillar-artists
Website: https://facebook.com/PillarArtists

Represents: Artists/Bands

Genres: Acoustic; Alternative; Guitar based; Indie

Management agency based in Newcastle Upon Tyne. Also involved with independent gig promotion, PR, and booking.

Plus Music

Hoxton
London
Email: info@plusmusic.co.uk
Website: http://www.plusmusic.co.uk

Represents: Artists/Bands

Genres: Funk; Pop; R&B; Soul

Contact: Desmond Chisholm

Looking for male or female singers aged 16-23. Send MP3 with recent photo(s) and social media links by email. See website for full details.

PMS Music Management

122 London Road
Rayleigh
Essex
SS6 9BN
Fax: +44 (0) 1268 784807
Email: pmsmusicmgt@yahoo.co.uk
Website: https://pmsmusicmanagement.weebly.com

Represents: Artists/Bands; Tribute Acts

Genres: All types of music

Contact: Peter Scott

Send demo by post or email. MP3 preferred but not essential. Currently managing Indie/pop/rock but open to all genres. 'If I like it, I can represent it!' Welcomes all submissions in the form of CD, MP3 or video on DVD together with a biography and links to your Website, and any other relevant links. Particularly keen to work with unsigned bands.

Program Music, Ltd

197 Queen's Crescent
London
NW5 4DS
Email: info@program-music.co.uk
Website: https://www.program-music.co.uk
Website: https://www.facebook.com/programproducts

Represents: Artists/Bands; DJs

Genres: All types of music

Specialises in the production of immersive video domes and 3D experiences, large-scale audiovisual work and interactive installations, and voice-activated applications.

Prolifica Management

London
Email: info@prolifica.co.uk
Website: http://www.prolificamanagement.co.uk
Website: https://www.instagram.com/prolificamanagement/

Represents: Artists/Bands

Genres: All types of music

London-based Music Management and Production Company.

Psycho Management Company

Email: patrick@psycho.co.uk
Website: https://www.psycho.co.uk/
Website: https://twitter.com/psychomanco

Represents: Artists/Bands; Comedians; DJs; Other Entertainers; Tribute Acts

Genres: All types of music

Management company representing circus acts, entertainment acts, lookalikes, music acts, name acts, and tribute acts.

Push Music Management

London
Email: info@pushmusicmanagement.com
Website: https://pushmusicmanagement.com
Website: https://twitter.com/pushmusicmgmt

Represents: Artists/Bands

Genres: All types of music

Management company based in London.

Quest Management

London
Email: quest@maverick.com
Website: http://www.quest-management.com
Website: https://www.instagram.com/questartistmgmt/

Represents: Artists/Bands

Genres: All types of music

A collective of experienced management executives with offices in London, Los Angeles, and Milan, renowned for innovations in creating lasting revenue strategies for artists.

Radius Music Ltd

PO Box 46375
London
SW17 9WJ
Email: info@radiusmusic.co.uk
Website: https://www.radiusmusic.co.uk
Website: https://www.facebook.com/radiusmusic

Represents: Artists/Bands; Producers; Songwriters

Genres: All types of music

UK based music industry management representing Songwriters and Producers.

Raw Power Management

London
Website: https://rawpowermanagement.com/
Website: https://www.facebook.com/rawpowermanagement

Represents: Artists/Bands

Genres: Punk Rock; Alternative; Metal; Rock

Punk rock management company with offices in London and Los Angeles.

Reaction Management

Email: jay.burnett@reaction-management.com
Email: jedd.lefthander@reaction-management.com
Website: https://www.reaction-management.com
Website: https://www.facebook.com/ReactionManagement

Genres: Alternative; Guitar based; Indie; Metal; Pop Punk; Rock; Singer-Songwriter

Joining the roster isn't a fast track to success but what we will do will set you up for a professional career in music. There are no contracts and you can stay with us for as long or short a period of time as you feel necessary. We have great contacts across the industry and have built up solid relationships with bookers, promoters, venues, PR and media not only in the UK, but across the globe.

Real Media Music

Email: info@realmediamusic.co.uk
Website: https://www.realmediamusic.co.uk
Website: https://www.facebook.com/RealMediaMusic

Represents: Artists/Bands

Genres: All types of music

International artist booking and management.

Rebel Rebel Artists

Email: nick@rebelrebelartists.co.uk
Email: nickconnett@hotmail.co.uk
Website: https://rebelrebelartistsa.wixsite.com/rebelrebelartists
Website: https://www.facebook.com/rebelrebelartists

Represents: Artists/Bands

Genres: Alternative; Electronic; Indie; Pop

Bespoke artist management / PR / bookings / consultancy. Submit through Spotify playlist, or by email.

Reckless Yes

Email: pete@recklessyes.com
Email: sarah@recklessyes.com
Website: https://recklessyes.com/artist-management/
Website: https://www.facebook.com/RecklessYes/

Represents: Artists/Bands

Genres: Acoustic; Alternative; Guitar based; Indie

Contact: Pete; Sarah

Independent record label, management and live music agency. Closed to submissions as at July 2022.

Red Afternoon Music

Email: info@redafternoonmusic.co.uk
Email: lewis@redafternoonmusic.co.uk
Website: https://www.redafternoonmusic.co.uk
Website: https://www.facebook.com/RedAfternoonMusic/

Represents: Artists/Bands

Genres: All types of music

Contact: Lewis Forrest

An Independent Record Company based in Central Scotland and London, UK. Provides label services, distribution, music publishing, specialist consultancy, artist development, artist management and live/ touring services. All genres accepted, but with a particular background in indie/ alternative, pop, EDM/house, Americana, country, jazz and R&B.

Red Grape Music

82 Chestnut Grove
New Malden
Surrey
KT3 3JS
Email: info@redgrapemusic.com
Website: https://www.redgrapemusic.com

Represents: Artists/Bands

Genres: Acoustic; Folk; Pop; Singer-Songwriter

Management company and record label based in New Malden, Surrey. Not accepting submissions as at September 2021. Check website for current status.

Revolt Artist Management

Email: demos@revoltartists.com
Website: https://www.revoltartists.com

Represents: Artists/Bands; Film / TV Composers; Lyricists; Producers; Songwriters; Studio Musicians; Studio Vocalists

Genres: Emo; Garage; Guitar based; Hardcore; Indie; Metal; Nostalgia; Pop; Punk; Rock; Rock and Roll; Singer-Songwriter; Surf

Contact: Lisa Mckeown

Artist Management and Development company based in the UK, providing exclusive worldwide representation to musicians. We offer services in artist management, social media management and artist development.

We've worked with 80's legend 'Tiffany', known for the 1987 Billboard #1 'I Think We're Alone Now', as well as 'Cellar Door Moon Crow', 'The Last Internationale', 'GUN', 'The Graveltones' and 'Silverkord' (just to name a few!)

Our artists have played Download Festival, Lollapalooza, Hellfest, Nova Rock, BST Hyde Park, Venoge Festival, Rock Werchter, Pinkpop Festival, Let's Rock 80's Festival, Forever Young Festival, Impact Festival.

Our artists have supported KISS, Rage Against The Machine, Deep Purple, The Picturebooks, Skindred.

Our artists have had their music featured in Umbrella Academy, TED, The Tonight Show Featuring Jimmy Fallon, The Masked Singer, McDonald's adverts.

Our artists have made TV appearances across the world including I'm a Celebrity Get Me Out of Here!, Strictly Come Dancing: It Takes Two, Lorraine, Loose Women, Good Morning Britain, This Morning, The Morning Show, Celebrity Boot Camp, Wogan.

Please send your music and social links by email.

Rhythmic Records Management and Production

Email: info@rhythmic-records.co.uk
Website: https://www.rhythmic-records.co.uk
Website: https://www.facebook.com/rhythmicrecordsuk

Represents: Artists/Bands

Genres: Dance; Hip-Hop; House; Pop

Contact: Zac Bikhazi

Independent record label and management company based in London. Submit query with links to music online through form on website or by email.

Rock Hippie Management & Music

Website: https://www.facebook.com/rockhippiem/
Website: https://twitter.com/RockHippieM

Represents: Artists/Bands; Comedians; DJs; Songwriters; Tribute Acts

Genres: All types of music

Management company based in London.

Rock People Management (RPM)

Email: terri@rockpeoplemanagement.com
Email: heidi@rockpeoplemanagement.com
Website: https://www.rockpeoplemanagement.com
Website: https://www.facebook.com/rockpeoplemanagement/

Represents: Artists/Bands

Genres: Blues; Rock

Contact: Terri Chapman; Heidi Kerr

With almost 14 years of experience in the music industry and a hands on approach, we can offer a wealth of knowledge, skills and opportunities to todays artists and bands.

Over those 14 years we have amassed a wealth of invaluable industry contacts from Radio to Press, Festivals to Merch Design and everything in between. We take immense pride and care in what we do, and always put your needs and requirements first.

Get in touch today to see how we can help you.

Rockstar Management

Email: hello@rockstar.management
Website: http://www.rockstar.management
Website: https://twitter.com/RockstarMGMT

Represents: Artists/Bands

Genres: All types of music

As an artist-centric, full-service management firm, we offer always-on support to new talent and established stars alike. We build careers from the ground up, engaging with the best in the business to empower the full scope of our clients' creative vision, amplifying their art to a global audience.

Rollover Productions

29 Beethoven Street
London
W10 4LG
Fax: +44 (0) 20 8968 1047
Email: a-r@rollover.co.uk
Website: http://www.rollover.co.uk
Website: https://www.facebook.com/RolloverMusicLondon

Represents: Artists/Bands

Genres: All types of music

Contact: Phillip Jacobs

Specialises in four areas of the music industry: studios, production, management, and publishing.

Rollover

29 Beethoven Street
London
W10 4LG
Fax: +44 (0) 20 8968 1047
Website: http://www.rollover.co.uk

Represents: Artists/Bands

Genres: All types of music

Management company based in London.

Rosier Artist Management (RAM)

Hillgrove House Winbrook
Bewdley
DY12 2BA
Website: https://twitter.com/steverosier
Website: https://suite.endole.co.uk/insight/company/13784719-rosier-artist-management-ltd

Represents: Artists/Bands

Genres: Americana; Rock

Contact: Steve Rosier

UK manager focusing on Rock and Americana.

Roundface Music Management

Scotland
Email: george@roundfacemusic.com
Website: https://www.roundfacemusic.com
Website: https://www.facebook.com/RFmusicmanagement/

Represents: Artists/Bands

Genres: All types of music

Contact: George Murray

Music management company based in Scotland.

Run the Sound

Manchester
Website: https://www.runthesound.com/
Website: https://www.instagram.com/runthesoundmgmt/

Represents: Artists/Bands

Genres: Commercial; Hip-Hop; Pop; Rap

Contact: Zak Akram

A full-service entertainment company, based in the heart of Manchester inclusive of artist and management, label, publishing, touring, film / TV and new ventures. Provides aspiring stars with the opportunities and support they need to bring their talents directly into the spotlight. Also offers consultancy services.

Running Media Group Ltd

Isle of Man
Website: https://www.runningmedia.com

Represents: Artists/Bands

Genres: Singer-Songwriter

Contact: Bob Miller

Artist management company based in the Isle of Man.

S&B Creative

Email: info@snbcreative.com
Website: http://www.snbcreative.com
Website: https://www.facebook.com/SnBCreative/

Represents: Artists/Bands; Film / TV Composers; Producers; Songwriters

Genres: All types of music

Talent management, record label, brand consultancy, and scores for film and TV.

Saga Entertainment

35 Berkeley Square
Mayfair
London
W1J 5BF
Email: info@sagaentertainment.tv
Website: https://www.sagaentertainment.tv
Website: http://www.facebook.com/SagaMusicUK

Represents: Artists/Bands

Genres: Electronic; Pop; Rock

Operates a production company, publishing house and record label with offices in London, England. Specialising in music management, artist development and label services.

Salvation Records

Email: thesoundofsalvation@hotmail.co.uk
Website: https://www.facebook.com/thesoundofsalvationrecords
Website: https://soundcloud.com/salvationrecords

Represents: Artists/Bands

Genres: Electronic; Garage; Psychedelic Rock; Punk

A UK based record label, management company and publisher releasing physical product "in a world of digital noise".

SAS Entertainment

Email: serena@sas-ents.com
Email: steve@sas-ents.com
Website: https://www.sas-ents.com
Website: https://www.facebook.com/SASbackstage

Represents: Artists/Bands

Genres: Americana; Dance; Indie; Pop; Rock

Contact: Steve Hughes; Serena Catapano

Offers Artist Management, Tour Management, Music Consultancy, and Event / Festival Booking.

Saviour Management

London
Email: james@svrmgmt.com
Email: jay@svrmgmt.com
Website: https://www.svrmgmt.com
Website: https://www.facebook.com/saviourmanagement

Represents: Artists/Bands

Genres: Alternative; Metal; Pop Punk

Contact: James Illsley; Jay Harris

Management company based in London. Send query via form on website.

SB Management

Email: info@sb-management.com
Website: https://www.sb-management.com/
Website: https://twitter.com/sbmanagement

Represents: Artists/Bands; Producers; Songwriters

Genres: All types of music

Artist, writer, and producer management.

Scope Music Management

Email: info@scopemusicmanagement.com
Website: http://www.scopemusicmanagement.com
Website: https://www.facebook.com/ScopeMusicMgmt/

Represents: Artists/Bands

Genres: All types of music

Management company founded in 2012, boasting an eclectic roster of artists and bands. Send query by email with SoundCloud or YouTube links.

Second Sun Management

Bristol
Email: enquiries@ secondsunmanagement.co.uk
Website: https://www.instagram.com/ secondsunmgmt/
Website: https://linktr.ee/secondsunmgmt

Represents: Artists/Bands

Genres: All types of music

Management company based in Bristol.

September Management (UK)

London
Email: info@sept.com
Website: https://sept.com

Represents: Artists/Bands; Producers; Sound Engineers

Genres: All types of music

Represents a roster of internationally renowned recording artists, producers and mix engineers who have collectively amassed 44 Grammys, 12 Brit Awards, 2 Oscars, 2 Golden Globes and sold over 100 million albums worldwide. The company has offices in London, New York and Los Angeles.

Serious

Pill Box
Unit 503
115 Coventry Road
London
E2 6GG
Website: https://serious.org.uk
Website: https://www.facebook.com/ seriouslivemusic

Represents: Artists/Bands

Genres: Jazz; World; Contemporary

Management company based in London producing jazz, international, and contemporary music, and offering management, music publishing and the production of concerts, tours and special events.

74 Promotions

Brighton
Email: andy@74promotions.com
Website: http://www.74promotions.com
Website: https://www.facebook.com/74-Promotions-181204548583646/

Represents: Artists/Bands

Genres: All types of music

Contact: Andy Hollis

Management company based in Brighton.

SGM Music Group Ltd

Unit 4, Forest Industrial Park,
Crosbie Grove
Kidderminster
Worcestershire
DY11 7FX
Email: info@sgmmusicgroup.com
Website: https://www.sgmmusicgroup.com
Website: https://www.facebook.com/ sgmmusicgroup/

Represents: Artists/Bands

Genres: Pop; Rock

Contact: Scott Garrett

Over 20 years experience working in the music industry, primarily in the areas of live event production, management, record label services, and education.

SGO Ltd

Website: https://www.sgomusic.com
Website: https://www.facebook.com/ SGOMusic

Represents: Artists/Bands

Genres: All types of music

Offers music publishing, rights management, and label services.

Shaw Thing Management

20 Coverdale Road
London
N11 3FG
Email: info@shawthingmanagement.com
Website: https://www. shawthingmanagement.com

Website: https://www.facebook.com/profile.php?id=100067377485649

Represents: Artists/Bands

Genres: Pop

Management company based in London. Send submissions and enquiries by email.

Sidewinder Management Ltd

Email: sdw@sidewindermgmt.com
Website: http://www.sidewindermgmt.com

Represents: Artists/Bands

Genres: All types of music

Contact: Simon Watson

An Artist management company with over twenty five years experience managing a broad range of bands and solo artists.

Silverword Music Group

Website: https://www.silverword.co.uk

Represents: Artists/Bands

Genres: Urban; Dance; Pop; Rock; Jazz; Soul; Classical; Country; Gospel; R&B

Part of music group incorporating record label, promotion, publishing, distribution, etc.

Siren Artist Management (UK)

Email: ace@sirenmanagement.com
Email: adam@sirenmanagement.com
Website: https://www.sirenmanagement.com
Website: https://www.facebook.com/profile.php?id=100063474578473

Represents: Artists/Bands

Genres: Alternative; Rock

UK office of US management company based in California.

Solar Management

Unit 10 Union Wharf
23 Wenlock Road
London
N1 7SB
Email: info@solarmanagement.co.uk
Website: https://www.solarmanagement.co.uk
Website: https://www.facebook.com/solarmanagement/

Represents: Artists/Bands; Producers

Genres: All types of music

Eexperience in producer and artist development, recording, touring, budgeting and all producer and artist contracts.

Sound Consultancy

Resound Media
PO Box 1324
Cheltenham
GL50 9EU
Email: hey@soundconsultancy.co.uk
Website: https://www.soundconsultancy.co.uk
Website: https://www.facebook.com/soundconsultancy

Represents: Artists/Bands

Genres: All types of music

Cheltenham music company offering artist development, mentoring, and promotion packages. Considers all genres, but mainly acoustic, rock, and folk.

The Soundcheck Group

29 Wardour Street
London
W1D 6PS
Email: info@thesoundcheckgroup.com
Website: https://www.thesoundcheckgroup.com
Website: https://www.facebook.com/thesoundcheckgroup1

Represents: Artists/Bands

Genres: All types of music

Contact: Daniel Hinchliffe

Has grown from a purely music PR company to an all-round PR and Management company representing pop and theatre artists as well as projects in the world of events, literary and branding.

Steve Allen Entertainments

The Coach House
163 Broadway
Peterborough
PE1 4DH
Email: sales@sallenent.co.uk
Website: https://steveallenentertainments.co.uk
Website: https://www.facebook.com/steveallenentertainments/

Represents: Artists/Bands; Comedians; Other Entertainers; Tribute Acts

Genres: All types of music

Contact: Steve Allen

Based in Peterborough, in Cambridgeshire. Supplies entertainers and entertainments for private events and corporate occasions. Client base includes many National companies as well as most of the major Hotel Chains.

Storm5 Management

Resound Media
Brincliffe House
59 Wostenholm Road
Sheffield
S7 1LE
Email: info@storm5management.com
Website: http://www.storm5management.com
Website: https://www.facebook.com/storm5management/

Represents: Artists/Bands

Genres: All types of music

Management company based in Sheffield.

Stormcraft Music

Email: info@stormcraftmusic.com
Website: https://www.stormcraftmusic.com
Website: https://www.facebook.com/stormcraftmusic

Represents: Artists/Bands

Genres: Alternative Pop; Singer-Songwriter; Guitar based

We specialise in the management and development of up and coming artists. Covering a wide range of the musical spectrum we strive to develop the careers of the next generation of original musicians.

With over 10 years worth of industry experience we are able to closely work with each artist to help shape their career and be their gateway into both the music industry and into the public eye.

Sugar House Music

Email: info@sugarhousemusic.co.uk
Email: ros@140db.co.uk
Website: https://www.sugarhousemusic.co.uk
Website: https://www.facebook.com/sugarhousemusic/

Represents: Artists/Bands

Genres: Indie; New Wave; Pop; Rock

Contact: Lee McCarthy; Ady Hall

Record Making / Music Production / Songwriting / Artist Development / Taste Makers.

Tap Music

Email: info@tapmgmt.com
Website: https://tap-music.com
Website: https://www.facebook.com/tapmusicofficial/

Represents: Artists/Bands; Producers; Songwriters

Genres: All types of music

Music management company with offices in London, Berlin, LA and Sydney.

Tape

London
Email: dangarber@taperec.com
Website: http://www.taperec.com
Website: https://twitter.com/taperec

Represents: Artists/Bands

Genres: All types of music, except: Metal; Techno

Management company with offices in London and Barcelona. Contact through form on website.

Third Bar Artist Development

C/O Oh yeah Music Centre
15-21 Gordon Street
Belfast
BT1 2LG
Email: davy@thirdbar.co.uk
Email: candice@thirdbar.co.uk
Website: http://thirdbar.co.uk
Website: https://twitter.com/thirdbarbelfast

Represents: Artists/Bands

Genres: All types of music

Contact: Davy Matchett

Artist development business based in Belfast. Send music via online file transfer system (see website).

This Is Music Ltd

408 Brickfields
37 Cremer Street
London
E2 8HD
Email: simon@thisismusicltd.com
Website: http://thisismusicltd.com
Website: https://www.soundcloud.com/this-is-music

Represents: Artists/Bands; Producers

Genres: Electronic; Underground; Indie; Pop

Contact: Simon Gold

Music company based in London and Los Angeles. Provides management and label services for artists and producers.

Tone Management

Email: hello@tonemgmt.com
Website: http://tonemgmt.com
Website: https://www.instagram.com/tonemanagement/

Represents: Artists/Bands

Genres: Metal; Rock; Pop; Post Rock; Hardcore; Punk

Management company with offices in Leeds, London, Bristol, and New York. Contact by email.

Toonteen Industries: Management & Promotions

Bury St Edmunds
Suffolk
Email: demos@toonteen.co.uk
Email: joe@toonteen.co.uk
Website: https://www.toonteen.co.uk
Website: https://www.facebook.com/toonteenAM

Represents: Artists/Bands

Genres: Acoustic Alternative Heavy Progressive Ambient Emo Hardcore Indie Metal Pop Punk Rock

Contact: Joe Weaver

Management company based in Bury St Edmunds. Promotes shows with various bands in venues all over East Anglia, but mainly focused within Bury St Edmunds. Also manages bands and solo artists. Send query by email with links to music online. No attachments. Response not guaranteed.

Transgressive

Email: general@transgressiverecords.com
Website: https://transgressiverecords.com
Website: https://www.facebook.com/transgressiverecords

Represents: Artists/Bands

Genres: All types of music

An independent music group comprising a record label, publisher and management company.

Travelled Music

Email: alan@travelledmusic.co.uk
Email: ian@travelledmusic.co.uk
Website: https://www.travelledmusic.co.uk
Website: https://twitter.com/travelledmusic

Represents: Artists/Bands

Genres: Alternative; Rock; Electronic; Indie

Contact: Alan Thompson; Ian Thompson

Music company offering artist and tour management, websites and social media, direct-to-fan marketing, bookings and promotions, event management.

Trinifold Management

12 Oval Road
London
NW1 7DH
Website: https://www.trinifold.co.uk

Represents: Artists/Bands

Genres: All types of music

Submit demo via form on website.

UAC Management

Email: hristo@uacmanagement.co.uk
Email: thrasher@uacmanagement.co.uk
Website: https://uacmanagement.co.uk
Website: https://www.facebook.com/uacmanagement/

Represents: Artists/Bands

Genres: All types of music

Contact: Hristo Penchev; Kevin Thrasher

Designed and projected to perform as a world class management and consulting agency and to establish strong capacity and potential to provide high-level of professional expertise in the different aspects of the entertainment industry.

Underplay

Email: chrisbellam@underplay.co.uk
Website: https://www.underplay.co.uk
Website: https://www.instagram.com/u_n_d_e_r_p_l_a_y/

Represents: Artists/Bands

Genres: All types of music

Contact: Chris Bellam

Artist management and promotion.

Up On Mars

Brighton
Email: hello@uponmars.com
Website: https://uponmars.com
Website: https://www.linkedin.com/company/up-on-mars/

Represents: Artists/Bands

Genres: Electronic; Pop

Artist management company based in Brighton. Send demos via form on website.

Upside Management Ltd

18 Cherrington Gardens
Stourbridge
West Midlands
DY9 0QB
Email: denise@upsideuk.com
Email: simon@upsideuk.com
Website: https://www.upsideuk.com
Website: https://www.facebook.com/upsideuk

Represents: Artists/Bands

Genres: Dance; Pop

Contact: Denise Beighton; Simon Jones

Management company based in Stourbridge, West Midlands.

Various Artists Management

37 Lonsdale Road
London
NW6 6RA
Email: info@variousartistsmanagement.com
Website: https://variousartistsmanagement.com
Website: https://www.facebook.com/variousartistsmanagement

Represents: Artists/Bands; Producers

Genres: All types of music

Management company with offices in London, Los Angeles, and Hong Kong.

Verdigris Management

Email: info@verdigrismanagement.com
Website: https://www.verdigrismanagement.com

Represents: Artists/Bands; Producers; Sound Engineers

Genres: All types of music

A full service management company with a roster of Mercury and Grammy-nominated artists, producers and mixers.

Viral Music

Brunswick Mill
Manchester
M40 7EZ
Email: info@viralmusicuk.com
Website: https://www.viralmusicuk.com
Website: https://www.facebook.com/ViralMusicUK/

Represents: Artists/Bands; DJs

Genres: Dance; House; Commercial

Management company providing conservatoire-trained, professionally-accomplished musicians to the nightlife entertainment industry, as well as for a wide range of other events, including weddings and private/corporate functions.

We Like Oliver

London
Email: olly@welikeoliver.com
Website: https://welikeoliver.com
Website: https://www.facebook.com/welikeoliver

Represents: Artists/Bands

Genres: All types of music

Contact: Olly Andrews

Offers "Complete digital Marketing & IT Solutions for your creative business".

The Weird and the Wonderful

London
Email: info@theweirdandthewonderful.com
Website: https://www.andthewonderful.com
Website: https://www.facebook.com/theweirdandthewonderfulofficial

Represents: Artists/Bands

Genres: Electronic; Folk; House; Techno; Urban

An international, multi-faceted talent consultancy, record label, events curation and management collective, dealing with all things weird and wonderful.

Wildlife Entertainment Ltd

Email: info@wildlife-entertainment.com
Website: https://www.wildlife-entertainment.com

Represents: Artists/Bands

Genres: Indie; Rock; R&B

Management company based in South West London.

XIX Entertainment Ltd

259a Pavilion Road
London
SW1X 0BP
Email: info@xixentertainment.com
Website: https://www.xixentertainment.com
Website: https://twitter.com/XIX_NEWS

Represents: Artists/Bands

Genres: All types of music

Management company responsible for such shows as American Idol and Little Britain USA. Has offices in London and Los Angeles.

XVII Music Group

Email: info@xviimusic.com
Website: https://xviimusic.com
Website: https://soundcloud.com/xviimusicgroup

Represents: Artists/Bands

Genres: All types of music

Artists development and record label.

Yellowbrick Music

Email: info@yellowbrickmusic.com
Email: meredith@yellowbrickmusic.com
Website: https://yellowbrickmusic.com
Website: https://twitter.com/YellBrickMusic

Represents: Artists/Bands

Genres: All types of music

Label service company based in London, offering artists a creative range of support and tools. Send query by email or via online contact form.

YMU Group

Clifton Works
23 Grove Park Terrace
Chiswick
London
W4 3QE

180 Great Portland Street
London
W1W 5QZ

3rd Floor Colwyn Chambers
19 York Street
Manchester
M2 3BA
Email: enquiries@ymugroup.com
Website: https://www.ymugroup.com

Represents: Artists/Bands; DJs; Producers; Songwriters

Genres: Alternative Rock; Dance; Electronic; Pop

Management company with offices in London, Manchester, Washington DC, California, and New York.

Young Guns

2 Princes Street
Mayfair
London
W1B 2LB
Email: hello@younggunsgroup.com
Website: https://www.younggunsgroup.com
Website: https://www.facebook.com/YoungGunsLtd

Represents: Artists/Bands; Producers; Studio Musicians

Genres: Classical; Jazz; Pop; Fusion

A music agency that creates acts and sources musicians from all genres for the events, record and TV industries.

Youthquake

Email: contact@youthquake.london
Website: https://youthquake.london/
Website: https://www.instagram.com/youthquakemgmt/

Represents: Artists/Bands

Genres: Alternative; Guitar based

Artist management company based in Isleworth.

Z Management

Email: alex@zman.co.uk
Website: http://www.zman.co.uk
Website: https://www.facebook.com/zmanagementuk

Represents: Artists/Bands; DJs; Producers; Songwriters

Genres: All types of music

Management company based in London, handling song writers, producers, mixers, remixers, and artists. Send demo by email.

Zero Myth

Website: https://www.zeromyth.co.uk
Website: https://twitter.com/ZeroMythUK

Represents: Artists/Bands

Genres: Alternative; Pop; Rock

A creative music management company, specialising in artist development and project management. Aims to create sustainable artist led campaigns by managing strategic development, distribution and partnerships. Offers fixed-fee consultation sessions.

Canadian Managers

For the most up-to-date listings of these and hundreds of other managers, visit https://www.musicsocket.com/managers

*To claim your **free** access to the site, please see the back of this book.*

Bedlam Music Management

290 Gerrard St East
Toronto, ON M5A 2G4

LOS ANGELES
4525 Russell Ave #1
Los Angeles CA 90027

NASHVILLE
1300 Clinton St, Suite 205
Nashville, TN 37203
Email: info@bedlammusicmgt.com
Website: http://www.bedlammusicmgt.com

Represents: Artists/Bands

Genres: All types of music

A full service artist management company based in Toronto, Canada, with offices in Los Angeles and Nashville.

Bruce Allen Talent

#500-425 Carrall Street
Vancouver, BC
V6B 6E3
Fax: +1 (604) 688-7118
Email: info@bruceallen.com
Website: https://www.bruceallen.com

Represents: Artists/Bands; Producers

Genres: All types of music

Contact: Bruce Allen

Talent agency based in Vancouver, British Columbia. Not accepting unsolicited material as at July 2021.

Coalition Music

1731 Lawrence Ave East
Toronto, Ontario, M1R 2X7
Fax: +1 (866) 206-6370
Email: info@coalitionmusic.com
Website: https://www.coalitionmusic.com
Website: https://www.facebook.com/CoalitionMUS

Represents: Artists/Bands

Genres: Contemporary; Indie; Pop; Rock; Singer-Songwriter; Alternative; Jazz; Punk; R&B; Rap; Hip-Hop

Send query and links to music online via submission form on website.

Feeling Productions, Inc.

1131A Leslie St
North York, ON, M3C 2J6
Website: https://www.celinedion.com

Represents: Artists/Bands

Genres: Pop

Management company based in Ontario.

Macklam Feldman Management

#200 – 1505 West 2nd Avenue
Vancouver, BC
V6H 3Y4
Email: info@mfmgt.com
Website: http://www.mfmgt.com
Website: https://twitter.com/MFMGT

Represents: Artists/Bands; Producers

Genres: Pop; Rock; Jazz; World; Alternative; Indie

Contact: Sam Feldman; Steve Macklam

Management company based in Vancouver, Canada. Send demos by email with links to music online (soundcloud, spotify, etc.).

Nettwerk Management

1675 West 2nd Ave, 2nd Floor
Vancouver, BC. V6J 1H3
Email: info@nettwerk.com
Website: http://www.nettwerk.com

Represents: Artists/Bands; Film / TV Composers; Producers; Songwriters; Sound Engineers; Studio Technicians

Genres: Contemporary; Christian; Electronic; Folk; Indie; Latin; Pop; Punk; Rap; Rock; Hip-Hop; Dance; Singer-Songwriter

Music company based in Vancouver, Canada (head office), with other offices in the US and Europe. Includes label, management, and publishing arms.

Talk's Cheap Management

Website: https://talks-cheap.com/contact
Website: https://www.facebook.com/Voivod

Represents: Artists/Bands

Genres: Metal; Punk; Hardcore; Rock; Roots

Management company based in Canada.

Managers Index

This section lists managers by their genres, with directions to the section of the book where the full listing can be found.

You can create your own customised lists of managers using different combinations of these subject areas, plus over a dozen other criteria, instantly online at https://www.musicsocket.com.

*To claim your **free** access to the site, please see the back of this book.*

All types of music
!K7 (*UK*)
360 Artist Development (*UK*)
4 Tunes Ltd (*UK*)
7pm Management (*UK*)
A&R Factory (*UK*)
ACA Music & Entertainment (*US*)
Aesthetic V (*US*)
Amber Artists (*UK*)
American Artiste (UK) (*UK*)
Amour:Music (*UK*)
AMW Group Inc. (*US*)
Anger Management (*UK*)
The Animal Farm (*UK*)
APA (Agency for the Performing Arts) (*US*)
Artistes International Representation (AIR) Ltd (*UK*)
ASM Talent (*UK*)
ATC Management (*UK*)
Autonomy Music Group (*UK*)
Avenoir Records (*UK*)
AWA Entertainments (*UK*)
Backer Entertainment (*US*)
Backstage Entertainment (*US*)
Bedlam Music Management (*Can*)
Big Hug Management (*UK*)
Big Life Management (*UK*)
Big Noise (*US*)
BiGiAM Promotions & Management (*UK*)
Bill Silva Management (*US*)
Black Fox Management (*UK*)
BLOCS (*UK*)
Blue Raincoat Music (*UK*)
Brian Yeates Associates Ltd (*UK*)
Bruce Allen Talent (*Can*)
Bsquared MGMT (*US*)
Bulldozer Media Ltd (*UK*)
C Management (*US*)
Catalyst Management (*UK*)
Celebrity Enterprises (CE) Inc. (*US*)
Century Artists Management Agency, LLC (*US*)
Closer Artists Management & Publishing (*UK*)
CMP Entertainment (*UK*)
Conchord (*UK*)
Covert Talent Management (*UK*)
Creative Artists Agency (CAA) (*US*)
Creative Sounds UK (*UK*)
Creeme Entertainments (*UK*)
Crockford Management (*UK*)
Crush Music Media Management (*US*)
Culler Talent Management (*US*)
Cumberland Music Collective (*US*)
Danny Brittain Band Management (DBBM) (*UK*)
Darkspin Music Management (*UK*)
Deltasonic Records (*UK*)
Deluxxe Management (*UK*)

Deuce Management & Promotion (*UK*)
Dog & Pony Industries (*US*)
Duroc Media (*UK*)
East Coast Entertainment (ECE) (*US*)
Elevation Group Inc. (*US*)
Empire Artist Management (*UK*)
End of the Trail Creative (*UK*)
Everybody's Management Ltd (*UK*)
Fave Sounds (*UK*)
Feraltone (*UK*)
Ferocious Talent (*UK*)
Flat Cap Music (*UK*)
Friends Vs Music Ltd (*UK*)
Funzalo Music / Mike's Artist Management (*US*)
Gary Stamler Management (*US*)
Gayle Enterprises, Inc. (*US*)
The Gorfaine/Schwartz Agency, Inc. (*US*)
Grizzly Management (*UK*)
Hal Carter Organisation (*UK*)
Hannah Management (*UK*)
Happy House Management & Marketing Services (*UK*)
Heard and Seen (*UK*)
Hoffman Entertainment (*US*)
Hot House Music Ltd (*UK*)
Hot Vox (*UK*)
Howard Rosen Promotion, Inc. (*US*)
ie:music (*UK*)
Impact Artist Management (*UK*)
In Touch Entertainment (*US*)
Indevine (*UK*)
Innate – Music Ltd (*UK*)
International Creative Management (ICM) Partners (*US*)
Intune Addicts (*UK*)
Invasion Group, Ltd (*US*)
JA Artist Management (*UK*)
James Joseph Music Management (*UK*)
James Joseph Music Management LA (*US*)
Jampol Artist Management (*US*)
Jay Anthony's Next Level Booking and Entertainment Agency, LLC (*US*)
Kaleidoscope (*UK*)
Karma Artists Music LLP (*UK*)
KBH Entertainment (*US*)
KRMB Management & Consultancy (*UK*)
LA Personal Development (*US*)
Laissez Faire Club (*UK*)
Lake Transfer Artist & Tour Management (*US*)
Larro Media (*US*)
Legacy Records (*UK*)
Leonard Business Management (*US*)
Liquid Management (*UK*)
MaDa Music Entertainment (*UK*)
Madison House Inc. (*US*)
Major Labl (*UK*)
Manners McDade Artist Management (*UK*)
MBM (Music Business Management Ltd) (*UK*)
The MGMT Company (*US*)
Million Dollar Artists (*US*)
MJM Agency (*UK*)
Monotone, Inc. (*US*)
Mother Artist Management (*UK*)
MSH Management (*US*)
Murphy to Manteo (MTM) Music Management (*US*)
Music by Design (*UK*)
Music City Artists (*US*)
Music Group Entertainment Worldwide, LLC (*US*)
MusicBizMentors (*US*)
Nettwerk Management UK (*UK*)
New Heights Entertainment (*US*)
New Level Music Management (*UK*)
NewLevel Management (*UK*)
Nightside Entertainment, Inc. (*US*)
No Half Measures Ltd (*UK*)
One Fifteen (*UK*)
141a Management (*UK*)
140dB Management Limited (*UK*)
Open All Nite Entertainment (*US*)
Pacific Talent (*US*)
Paradigm Talent Agency (*US*)
Persistent Management (*US*)
Petty Music Management (*UK*)
Pieces of 8 Music (*UK*)
Platinum Star Management (*US*)
PMS Music Management (*UK*)
Pretty Lights (*US*)
Primary Wave (*US*)
Program Music, Ltd (*UK*)
Prolifica Management (*UK*)
Psycho Management Company (*UK*)
Push Music Management (*UK*)
Quest Management (*UK*)
Radius Music Ltd (*UK*)
Real Media Music (*UK*)
Red Afternoon Music (*UK*)
Regime Seventy-Two (*US*)
Rock Hippie Management & Music (*UK*)
Rockstar Management (*UK*)
Rollover Productions (*UK*)
Rollover (*UK*)
Roundface Music Management (*UK*)
S&B Creative (*UK*)

SB Management (*UK*)
Scope Music Management (*UK*)
Second Sun Management (*UK*)
Selak Entertainment, Inc. (*US*)
Self Group (*US*)
September Management (UK) (*UK*)
September Management (US) (*US*)
74 Promotions (*UK*)
SGO Ltd (*UK*)
Sherrod Artist Management (*US*)
Sidewinder Management Ltd (*UK*)
SKH Music (*US*)
SMC Artists (*US*)
Solar Management (*UK*)
Solid Music Company (*US*)
Sound Consultancy (*UK*)
The Soundcheck Group (*UK*)
Steve Allen Entertainments (*UK*)
Stiletto Entertainment (*US*)
Storm5 Management (*UK*)
Take Out Management (*US*)
Talent Source (*US*)
Tap Music (*UK*)
Tape (*UK*)
Tenth Street Entertainment (*US*)
That's Entertainment International Inc. (TEI Entertainment) (*US*)
Third Bar Artist Development (*UK*)
Threee (*US*)
Tom Callahan & Associates (TCA) (*US*)
A Train Entertainment (*US*)
Transgressive (*UK*)
Trinifold Management (*UK*)
Tsunami Entertainment (*US*)
UAC Management (*UK*)
Uncle Booking (*US*)
Underplay (*UK*)
United Talent Agency (*US*)
Universal Attractions Agency (*US*)
Various Artists Management (*UK*)
Velvet Hammer Music & Management Group (*US*)
Verdigris Management (*UK*)
Walker Entertainment Group (*US*)
We Like Oliver (*UK*)
Whiplash PR and Management (*US*)
William Morris Endeavor (WME) (*US*)
Wolfson Entertainment, Inc. (*US*)
XIX Entertainment Ltd (*UK*)
XVII Music Group (*UK*)
Yellow Couch Management (*US*)
Yellowbrick Music (*UK*)
Z Management (*UK*)

Acoustic

A2E – Artists 2 Events (*UK*)
ADSRecords (*UK*)
Aspire Music Management (*UK*)
Bandzmedia (*UK*)
Dawson Breed Music (*UK*)
Fat City Artists (*US*)
HardKnockLife Entertainment (*US*)
Heist or Hit (*UK*)
Hello! Booking, Inc. (*US*)
Jelli Records (*UK*)
Kari Estrin Management & Consulting (*US*)
Music Media Events (*UK*)
Nashville Records, LLC (*US*)
Opre Roma (*UK*)
Outrider Music, LLC (*US*)
Park Promotions (*UK*)
Pillar Artists (*UK*)
Reckless Yes (*UK*)
Red Grape Music (*UK*)
TAC Music Management (*US*)
Toonteen Industries: Management & Promotions (*UK*)

Alternative

ADSRecords (*UK*)
Advanced Alternative Media (AAM) (*US*)
Allure Media Entertainment Group (*US*)
Associated London Management (*UK*)
Bad Apple Music Group (*UK*)
Big Hassle Management (*US*)
Bitchin' Entertainment (*US*)
Burgess World Co. (*US*)
BUT! Management (*UK*)
Coalition Music (*Can*)
Craft Management (*UK*)
DDB Productions (*US*)
Deep South Artist Management (*US*)
Dissention Records + Artist Management (*UK*)
Don't Try (*UK*)
Down For Life (*UK*)
East City Management (*UK*)
Elephant Management (*UK*)
F&G Management (*UK*)
Feed Your Head (*UK*)
5B Artist Management (*US*)
Flow State Music (*UK*)
FP / Fantastic Plastic Music (*UK*)
Freaks R Us (*UK*)
Ganbei Records (*UK*)
Golden Arm (*UK*)
Goo Music Management Ltd (*UK*)
Hardin Entertainment (*US*)
Heist or Hit (*UK*)
Holier than Thou (HTT) Music (*UK*)
Hope Management (*UK*)

Hornblow Group USA, Inc. (*US*)
Ignition Management (*UK*)
Impact Artist Management (*US*)
JBLS Management (*UK*)
Jude Street Management (*UK*)
Key Music Management (*UK*)
Kuper Personal Management (*US*)
Listen to This Management (*UK*)
Loggins Promotion (*US*)
Lonewolf Talent Management (*UK*)
Macklam Feldman Management (*Can*)
Metal Music Bookings (*UK*)
MOB Agency (*US*)
Moksha Management (*UK*)
Monqui Presents (*US*)
Music Gallery International (*US*)
Music Media Events (*UK*)
Orean Music Ltd (*UK*)
Outrider Music, LLC (*US*)
Pillar Artists (*UK*)
Position Music (*US*)
Prodigal Son Entertainment (*US*)
Q Prime Management, Inc. (*US*)
Raw Power Management (*UK*)
Reaction Management (*UK*)
Rebel Rebel Artists (*UK*)
Reckless Yes (*UK*)
Russell Carter Artist Management (*US*)
Saviour Management (*UK*)
Semaphore Mgmt & Consulting (*US*)
Silva Artist Management (SAM) (*US*)
Siren Artist Management (UK) (*UK*)
Steven Scharf Entertainment (SSE) (*US*)
Stormcraft Music (*UK*)
Sweet! Music Management (*US*)
TAC Music Management (*US*)
Toonteen Industries: Management & Promotions (*UK*)
Travelled Music (*UK*)
Trunk Bass Entertainment (*US*)
Union Entertainment Group (*US*)
Vector Management (*US*)
YMU Group (*UK*)
Youthquake (*UK*)
Zero Myth (*UK*)

Ambient

Bitchin' Entertainment (*US*)
Hot Gem (*UK*)
Lonewolf Talent Management (*UK*)
Outrider Music, LLC (*US*)
Toonteen Industries: Management & Promotions (*UK*)
Tuscan Sun Music (*US*)

Americana

Aguia Music (*UK*)
Bitchin' Entertainment (*US*)
Brighthelmstone Promotions (*UK*)
Brilliant Productions (*US*)
Dawson Breed Music (*UK*)
Deep South Artist Management (*US*)
Grassy Hill Entertainment (*US*)
Hard Head Management (*US*)
Hardin Entertainment (*US*)
Kari Estrin Management & Consulting (*US*)
Kuper Personal Management (*US*)
Loggins Promotion (*US*)
Mike's Artist Management (*US*)
Music Gallery International (*US*)
Myriad Artists (*US*)
Nashville Records, LLC (*US*)
Opre Roma (*UK*)
Rosier Artist Management (RAM) (*UK*)
Russell Carter Artist Management (*US*)
SAS Entertainment (*UK*)
Steven Scharf Entertainment (SSE) (*US*)
Sweet! Music Management (*US*)
TAC Music Management (*US*)
Vector Management (*US*)

Atmospheric

Outrider Music, LLC (*US*)
Semaphore Mgmt & Consulting (*US*)

Avant-Garde

Semaphore Mgmt & Consulting (*US*)

Blues

A2E – Artists 2 Events (*UK*)
Act 1 Entertainment (*US*)
Artist Representation and Management (ARM) Entertainment (*US*)
Big Bear Music (*UK*)
Bitchin' Entertainment (*US*)
Blind Ambition Management, Ltd (*US*)
Brilliant Productions (*US*)
Burgess World Co. (*US*)
Cantaloupe Music Productions, Inc. (*US*)
Collin Artists (*US*)
Concerted Efforts (*US*)
Emcee Artist Management (*US*)
Fat City Artists (*US*)
Fleming Artists (*US*)
Gold Mountain Entertainment (*US*)
Hardin Entertainment (*US*)
Harmony Artists (*US*)
Impact Artist Management (*US*)
The Kurland Agency (*US*)
Max Bernard Management (*US*)
Myriad Artists (*US*)
Q Prime Management, Inc. (*US*)
Red Light Management (RLM) (*US*)
Rock People Management (RPM) (*UK*)

Ron Rainey Management Inc. (*US*)
Russell Carter Artist Management (*US*)
Sterling Artist Management (*US*)
Steven Scharf Entertainment (SSE) (*US*)
Sweet! Music Management (*US*)
TAC Music Management (*US*)
Union Entertainment Group (*US*)
Universal Tone Management (*US*)
Val's Artist Management (VAM) (*US*)
Westwood Music Group (*US*)

Break Beat
Finger Lickin' Management (*UK*)
Nexus Artist Management (*US*)

Celtic
A2E – Artists 2 Events (*UK*)
Fat City Artists (*US*)
Worldsound, LLC (*US*)

Chill
Involved Management (*UK*)

Christian
25 Artist Agency (*US*)
The Brokaw Company (*US*)
Deep South Artist Management (*US*)
Hardin Entertainment (*US*)
Jeff Roberts & Associates (*US*)
MTS Management (*US*)
Nashville Records, LLC (*US*)
Nettwerk Management (*US*)
Nettwerk Management (*Can*)
Prodigal Son Entertainment (*US*)
Proper Management (*US*)
Red Light Management (RLM) (*US*)

Classic
Act 1 Entertainment (*US*)
Arslanian & Associates, Inc. (*US*)
Artist Representation and Management (ARM) Entertainment (*US*)
Big Beat Productions, Inc. (*US*)
Entertainment Services International (*US*)
IMG Artists (*US*)
Michael Anthony's Electric Events (*US*)
Suncoast Music Management (*US*)
TAC Music Management (*US*)

Classical
American International Artists, Inc. (*US*)
Askonas Holt Ltd (*UK*)
BBA Management & Booking (*US*)
Bitchin' Entertainment (*US*)
Columbia Artists Music LLC (CAMI Music) (*US*)
Crossfire (*UK*)
Dawn Elder Management (*US*)
Domo Music Group Management (*US*)
Intertalent Rights Group (*UK*)
Jude Street Management (*UK*)
Opus 3 Artists (*US*)
Silverword Music Group (*UK*)
Val's Artist Management (VAM) (*US*)
Young Guns (*UK*)

Commercial
Create Management (*UK*)
Crown Talent & Media Group (*UK*)
Freedom Management (*UK*)
Handshake Ltd. (*UK*)
Insomnia Music UK (*UK*)
MTS Management (*US*)
Run the Sound (*UK*)
TAC Music Management (*US*)
Viral Music (*UK*)

Contemporary
Amour:Music (*UK*)
Big Beat Productions, Inc. (*US*)
Black Dot Management (*US*)
Booking Entertainment (*US*)
Chapman & Co. Management (*US*)
Coalition Music (*Can*)
Collin Artists (*US*)
David Belenzon Management, Inc. (*US*)
Domo Music Group Management (*US*)
Fleming Artists (*US*)
Gold Mountain Entertainment (*US*)
Hardin Entertainment (*US*)
Impact Artist Management (*US*)
Magus Entertainment Inc. (*US*)
MBK Entertainment (*US*)
Michael Hausman Artist Management Inc. (*US*)
MM Music Agency (*US*)
Moksha Management (*UK*)
Nettwerk Management (*US*)
Nettwerk Management (*Can*)
Riot Artists (*US*)
Ron Rainey Management Inc. (*US*)
Russell Carter Artist Management (*US*)
Serious (*UK*)
Stiefel Entertainment (*US*)
Val's Artist Management (VAM) (*US*)
Vector Management (*US*)

Country
Act 1 Entertainment (*US*)
Aguia Music (*UK*)
American Artists Entertainment Group (*US*)
Artist Representation and Management (ARM) Entertainment (*US*)
Big Beat Productions, Inc. (*US*)
Bitchin' Entertainment (*US*)
Brick Wall Management (*US*)
The Brokaw Company (*US*)
Bulletproof Artist Management (*US*)

Case Entertainment Group Inc. (*US*)
Deep South Artist Management (*US*)
Fat City Artists (*US*)
Hardin Entertainment (*US*)
Hello! Booking, Inc. (*US*)
Impact Artist Management (*US*)
Listen to This Management (*UK*)
Loggins Promotion (*US*)
Lupo Entertainment (*US*)
Maine Road Management (*US*)
Major Bob Music, Inc. (*US*)
Mascioli Entertainment (*US*)
McGhee Entertainment (*US*)
Michael Anthony's Electric Events (*US*)
Modern Management (*US*)
Monqui Presents (*US*)
Morris Higham Management (*US*)
MTS Management (*US*)
Nashville Records, LLC (*US*)
Prodigal Son Entertainment (*US*)
Red Light Management (RLM) (*US*)
Ron Rainey Management Inc. (*US*)
Silverword Music Group (*UK*)
Spinning Plates (*US*)
Sweet! Music Management (*US*)
TAC Music Management (*US*)
Third Coast Talent (*US*)
TKO Artist Management (*US*)
Union Entertainment Group (*US*)
Val's Artist Management (VAM) (*US*)
Vector Management (*US*)
Westwood Music Group (*US*)

Dance

2-Tone Entertainment (2TE) (*UK*)
AuthorityMGMT (*UK*)
Celebrity Talent Agency Inc. (*US*)
Crossfire (*UK*)
DEF (Deutsch Englische Freundschaft) (*UK*)
Defenders Ent (*UK*)
East City Management (*UK*)
F&G Management (*UK*)
Feed Your Head (*UK*)
Finger Lickin' Management (*UK*)
Flow State Music (*UK*)
Fruition Music (*UK*)
Graphite Media (*UK*)
Hardin Entertainment (*US*)
Hope Management (*UK*)
Hot Gem (*UK*)
House of Us (*UK*)
Loggins Promotion (*US*)
Michael Anthony's Electric Events (*US*)
Moksha Management (*UK*)
Nettwerk Management (*US*)
Nettwerk Management (*Can*)
Orean Music Ltd (*UK*)
Ornadel Management (*UK*)
Perfect Havoc Ltd (*UK*)
Phono Sounds UK (*UK*)
Position Music (*US*)
Red Light Management (RLM) (*US*)
Rhythmic Records Management and Production (*UK*)
SAS Entertainment (*UK*)
Silverword Music Group (*UK*)
Spectrum Talent Agency (*US*)
Stiefel Entertainment (*US*)
Upside Management Ltd (*UK*)
Val's Artist Management (VAM) (*US*)
Viral Music (*UK*)
YMU Group (*UK*)

Deep Funk

Sweet! Music Management (*US*)

Disco

Big Beat Productions, Inc. (*US*)
Perfect Havoc Ltd (*UK*)
Suncoast Music Management (*US*)

Drum and Bass

OnDaBeat Talent Management (*UK*)

Dubstep

Nexus Artist Management (*US*)

Electronic

AJM (*UK*)
AprilSeven Music (*UK*)
Bitchin' Entertainment (*US*)
DEF (Deutsch Englische Freundschaft) (*UK*)
F&G Management (*UK*)
Feed Your Head (*UK*)
Finger Lickin' Management (*UK*)
Flow State Music (*UK*)
Freaks R Us (*UK*)
From the Whitehouse (*UK*)
Graphite Media (*UK*)
Hard Head Management (*US*)
Hardin Entertainment (*US*)
Holier than Thou (HTT) Music (*UK*)
Hot Gem (*UK*)
HQ Familia (*UK*)
Humans & Other Animals (*UK*)
Involved Management (*UK*)
JBLS Management (*UK*)
Lucky Number Music Limited (*UK*)
Magus Entertainment Inc. (*US*)
Moksha Management (*UK*)
Music + Art Management (*US*)
Nettwerk Management (*US*)
Nettwerk Management (*Can*)
New Champion Management (*UK*)

Nexus Artist Management (*US*)
OnDaBeat Talent Management (*UK*)
Orean Music Ltd (*UK*)
Outrider Music, LLC (*US*)
Phono Sounds UK (*UK*)
Position Music (*US*)
Rebel Rebel Artists (*UK*)
Red Light Management (RLM) (*US*)
Saga Entertainment (*UK*)
Salvation Records (*UK*)
Semaphore Mgmt & Consulting (*US*)
This Is Music Ltd (*UK*)
Travelled Music (*UK*)
Up On Mars (*UK*)
Waxploitation (*US*)
The Weird and the Wonderful (*UK*)
YMU Group (*UK*)

Emo

Music Gallery International (*US*)
Outrider Music, LLC (*US*)
Revolt Artist Management (*UK*)
Toonteen Industries: Management & Promotions (*UK*)

Ethnic

Domo Music Group Management (*US*)

Experimental

Bitchin' Entertainment (*US*)
F&G Management (*UK*)
Freaks R Us (*UK*)
Hot Gem (*UK*)
Incendia Music (*UK*)
Music + Art Management (*US*)
Semaphore Mgmt & Consulting (*US*)

Folk

21st Century Artists, Inc. (*US*)
Aguia Music (*UK*)
Bitchin' Entertainment (*US*)
Blind Ambition Management, Ltd (*US*)
Brighthelmstone Promotions (*UK*)
Bulletproof Artist Management (*US*)
Case Entertainment Group Inc. (*US*)
Concerted Efforts (*US*)
Dawson Breed Music (*UK*)
DCA Productions (*US*)
DMF Music Ltd (*UK*)
Domo Music Group Management (*US*)
Fat City Artists (*US*)
Fleming Artists (*US*)
From the Whitehouse (*UK*)
Front Room Songs (*UK*)
Ganbei Records (*UK*)
Gold Mountain Entertainment (*US*)
Grassy Hill Entertainment (*US*)
Hardin Entertainment (*US*)
Hello! Booking, Inc. (*US*)
Humans & Other Animals (*UK*)
IMG Artists (*US*)
Impact Artist Management (*US*)
Jelli Records (*UK*)
Kari Estrin Management & Consulting (*US*)
Kuper Personal Management (*US*)
Maine Road Management (*US*)
Mike's Artist Management (*US*)
Music Media Events (*UK*)
Myriad Artists (*US*)
Nettwerk Management (*US*)
Nettwerk Management (*Can*)
New Champion Management (*UK*)
NSI Management (*US*)
Off the Chart Promotions (*UK*)
Opre Roma (*UK*)
Park Promotions (*UK*)
Q Prime Management, Inc. (*US*)
Red Grape Music (*UK*)
Russell Carter Artist Management (*US*)
Steven Scharf Entertainment (SSE) (*US*)
Sweet! Music Management (*US*)
TAC Music Management (*US*)
Val's Artist Management (VAM) (*US*)
Variety Artists International (*US*)
Vector Management (*US*)
The Weird and the Wonderful (*UK*)
Worldsound, LLC (*US*)

Funk

Bitchin' Entertainment (*US*)
Fat City Artists (*US*)
Nexus Artist Management (*US*)
Plus Music (*UK*)
Pyramid Entertainment Group (*US*)
Red Entertainment Agency (*US*)
Sweet! Music Management (*US*)
TAC Music Management (*US*)

Funky

Sweet! Music Management (*US*)
TAC Music Management (*US*)

Fusion

Moksha Management (*UK*)
Sweet! Music Management (*US*)
TAC Music Management (*US*)
Young Guns (*UK*)

Garage

Music Gallery International (*US*)
Revolt Artist Management (*UK*)
Salvation Records (*UK*)

Glam

MTS Management (*US*)
Semaphore Mgmt & Consulting (*US*)

Gospel

Blind Ambition Management, Ltd (*US*)

Celebrity Talent Agency Inc. (*US*)
Concerted Efforts (*US*)
Enlight Entertainment, Inc. (*US*)
Fat City Artists (*US*)
Fresh Flava Entertainment (*US*)
IMG Artists (*US*)
Len Weisman Personal Management (*US*)
MBK Entertainment (*US*)
Nashville Records, LLC (*US*)
Pyramid Entertainment Group (*US*)
RAM Talent Group (*US*)
Red Entertainment Agency (*US*)
Silverword Music Group (*UK*)
Vector Management (*US*)
Westwood Music Group (*US*)

Gothic

Bitchin' Entertainment (*US*)
Holier than Thou (HTT) Music (*UK*)
Music Gallery International (*US*)

Grime

Lucky House Management (*UK*)

Guitar based

MTS Management (*US*)
Opre Roma (*UK*)
Pillar Artists (*UK*)
Reaction Management (*UK*)
Reckless Yes (*UK*)
Revolt Artist Management (*UK*)
Stormcraft Music (*UK*)
TAC Music Management (*US*)
Youthquake (*UK*)

Hard

MTS Management (*US*)
Music Gallery International (*US*)
Outrider Music, LLC (*US*)
Prodigal Son Entertainment (*US*)
Semaphore Mgmt & Consulting (*US*)
Sweet! Music Management (*US*)
TAC Music Management (*US*)

Hardcore

Down For Life (*UK*)
Hardin Entertainment (*US*)
Music Gallery International (*US*)
Outrider Music, LLC (*US*)
Position Music (*US*)
Red Light Management (RLM) (*US*)
Revolt Artist Management (*UK*)
Singerman Entertainment (*US*)
Talk's Cheap Management (*Can*)
Tone Management (*UK*)
Toonteen Industries: Management & Promotions (*UK*)

Heavy

Incendia Music (*UK*)
Music Gallery International (*US*)
Outrider Music, LLC (*US*)
Semaphore Mgmt & Consulting (*US*)
Singerman Entertainment (*US*)
TAC Music Management (*US*)
Toonteen Industries: Management & Promotions (*UK*)

Hip-Hop

Aguia Music (*UK*)
Allure Media Entertainment Group (*US*)
Bitchin' Entertainment (*US*)
The Brokaw Company (*US*)
Celebrity Talent Agency Inc. (*US*)
Coalition Music (*Can*)
DAS Communications Ltd (*US*)
Def Ro Inc. (*US*)
Finger Lickin' Management (*UK*)
First Access Entertainment (*US*)
Fresh Flava Entertainment (*US*)
HardKnockLife Entertainment (*US*)
Hello! Booking, Inc. (*US*)
Len Weisman Personal Management (*US*)
Lippman Entertainment (*US*)
Loggins Promotion (*US*)
The Lost Atlantis Records (*UK*)
Lucky House Management (*UK*)
Lupo Entertainment (*US*)
Magus Entertainment Inc. (*US*)
Mauldin Brand Agency (*US*)
MBK Entertainment (*US*)
Nettwerk Management (*US*)
Nettwerk Management (*Can*)
Nexus Artist Management (*US*)
OnDaBeat Talent Management (*UK*)
Position Music (*US*)
Pyramid Entertainment Group (*US*)
Red Entertainment Agency (*US*)
Red Light Management (RLM) (*US*)
Rhythmic Records Management and Production (*UK*)
Run the Sound (*UK*)
Spectrum Talent Agency (*US*)
Steven Scharf Entertainment (SSE) (*US*)
Trunk Bass Entertainment (*US*)
Union Entertainment Group (*US*)
Val's Artist Management (VAM) (*US*)
Waxploitation (*US*)
Wright Entertainment Group (WEG) (*US*)

House

Bitchin' Entertainment (*US*)
Crossfire (*UK*)
F&G Management (*UK*)
House of Us (*UK*)
Involved Management (*UK*)
The Lost Atlantis Records (*UK*)
M24 Management (*UK*)

Waxploitation (*US*)
Wildlife Entertainment Ltd (*UK*)

Industrial
Music Gallery International (*US*)
Semaphore Mgmt & Consulting (*US*)

Instrumental
Bitchin' Entertainment (*US*)
Collin Artists (*US*)
Columbia Artists Music LLC (CAMI Music) (*US*)
Outrider Music, LLC (*US*)
Prodigal Son Entertainment (*US*)
Westwood Music Group (*US*)

Jazz
Act 1 Entertainment (*US*)
American International Artists, Inc. (*US*)
AprilSeven Music (*UK*)
B.H. Hopper Management Ltd. (*UK*)
BBA Management & Booking (*US*)
Big Bear Music (*UK*)
Big Beat Productions, Inc. (*US*)
Bitchin' Entertainment (*US*)
Black Dot Management (*US*)
Booking Entertainment (*US*)
Burgess World Co. (*US*)
Cantaloupe Music Productions, Inc. (*US*)
Celebrity Talent Agency Inc. (*US*)
Chaney Gig Affairs (CGA) (*US*)
Chapman & Co. Management (*US*)
Coalition Music (*Can*)
Collin Artists (*US*)
Columbia Artists Music LLC (CAMI Music) (*US*)
Concerted Efforts (*US*)
Dawn Elder Management (*US*)
DDB Productions (*US*)
DFJ Artists (*UK*)
DMF Music Ltd (*UK*)
Emcee Artist Management (*US*)
Entourage Talent Associates, Ltd (*US*)
Fat City Artists (*US*)
Fresh Flava Entertainment (*US*)
Harmony Artists (*US*)
Hello! Booking, Inc. (*US*)
IMG Artists (*US*)
Impact Artist Management (*US*)
Ina Dittke & Associates (*US*)
The Kurland Agency (*US*)
Loggins Promotion (*US*)
LSH Management (*UK*)
Macklam Feldman Management (*Can*)
Maine Road Management (*US*)
The Major Group (*US*)
The Management Ark, Inc. (*US*)
Mars Jazz Booking (*US*)
Mascioli Entertainment (*US*)
Max Bernard Management (*US*)
MM Music Agency (*US*)
Music + Art Management (*US*)
Myriad Artists (*US*)
Opus 3 Artists (*US*)
PRA [Patrick Rains & Associates] (*US*)
Pyramid Entertainment Group (*US*)
Red Entertainment Agency (*US*)
RPM Music Productions (*US*)
Russell Carter Artist Management (*US*)
Serious (*UK*)
Silverword Music Group (*UK*)
Sterling Artist Management (*US*)
Steven Scharf Entertainment (SSE) (*US*)
TAC Music Management (*US*)
Val's Artist Management (VAM) (*US*)
Variety Artists International (*US*)
Westwood Music Group (*US*)
Young Guns (*UK*)

Kraut
Semaphore Mgmt & Consulting (*US*)

Latin
BBA Management & Booking (*US*)
Cantaloupe Music Productions, Inc. (*US*)
Celebrity Talent Agency Inc. (*US*)
Collin Artists (*US*)
Hardin Entertainment (*US*)
Harmony Artists (*US*)
IMG Artists (*US*)
Impact Artist Management (*US*)
Ina Dittke & Associates (*US*)
Magus Entertainment Inc. (*US*)
Nettwerk Management (*US*)
Nettwerk Management (*Can*)
Once 11 Entertainment (*US*)
RAM Talent Group (*US*)
Red Entertainment Agency (*US*)
Red Light Management (RLM) (*US*)
Universal Tone Management (*US*)
Val's Artist Management (VAM) (*US*)
Westwood Music Group (*US*)

Leftfield
Semaphore Mgmt & Consulting (*US*)

Mainstream
Max Bernard Management (*US*)
Music Gallery International (*US*)
Sweet! Music Management (*US*)

Melodic
Aspire Music Management (*UK*)
Holier than Thou (HTT) Music (*UK*)
MTS Management (*US*)
Outrider Music, LLC (*US*)

Metal
Artist Representation and Management (ARM) Entertainment (*US*)
Bitchin' Entertainment (*US*)
Ciulla Management, Inc. (*US*)
Creative International Artist Management (*UK*)
Deathless MGMT (*UK*)
Down For Life (*UK*)
Enso Music Management (*UK*)
5B Artist Management (*US*)
Holier than Thou (HTT) Music (*UK*)
In De Goot Entertainment (*US*)
Incendia Music (*UK*)
McGhee Entertainment (*US*)
Metal Music Bookings (*UK*)
MTS Management (*US*)
Music Gallery International (*US*)
Northern Music Co. Ltd (*UK*)
Outrider Music, LLC (*US*)
Position Music (*US*)
Q Prime Management, Inc. (*US*)
Raw Power Management (*UK*)
Reaction Management (*UK*)
Red Light Management (RLM) (*US*)
Revolt Artist Management (*UK*)
Saviour Management (*UK*)
Silva Artist Management (SAM) (*US*)
Singerman Entertainment (*US*)
Steven Scharf Entertainment (SSE) (*US*)
Street Smart Management (*US*)
TAC Music Management (*US*)
Talk's Cheap Management (*Can*)
Tone Management (*UK*)
Toonteen Industries: Management & Promotions (*UK*)
Vector Management (*US*)

Modern
Sweet! Music Management (*US*)

New Age
Domo Music Group Management (*US*)
Tuscan Sun Music (*US*)

New Wave
Semaphore Mgmt & Consulting (*US*)
Sugar House Music (*UK*)

Non-Commercial
Semaphore Mgmt & Consulting (*US*)

Nostalgia
Revolt Artist Management (*UK*)

Pop
2-Tone Entertainment (2TE) (*UK*)
ADSRecords (*UK*)
Advanced Alternative Media (AAM) (*US*)
AJM (*UK*)
Allure Media Entertainment Group (*US*)
American Artists Entertainment Group (*US*)
Aspire Music Management (*UK*)
AuthorityMGMT (*UK*)
Bandzmedia (*UK*)
Bear Music Management (*UK*)
Big Dipper Productions Ltd (*UK*)
Big Hassle Management (*US*)
Bitchin' Entertainment (*US*)
Bold Management (*UK*)
Booking Entertainment (*US*)
Brick Wall Management (*US*)
The Brokaw Company (*US*)
Bulletproof Artist Management (*US*)
BUT! Management (*UK*)
Case Entertainment Group Inc. (*US*)
Coalition Music (*Can*)
Consolidated Artists (*UK*)
Create Management (*UK*)
Creative International Artist Management (*UK*)
Crossfire (*UK*)
Crown Talent & Media Group (*UK*)
D. Bailey Management, Inc. (*US*)
DAS Communications Ltd (*US*)
David Belenzon Management, Inc. (*US*)
Dawn Elder Management (*US*)
Dawson Breed Music (*UK*)
DCA Productions (*US*)
Deep South Artist Management (*US*)
Def Ro Inc. (*US*)
Direct Management Group (DMG) (*US*)
Domo Music Group Management (*US*)
Entourage Talent Associates, Ltd (*US*)
Equator Music (*UK*)
Fat City Artists (*US*)
Feeling Productions, Inc. (*Can*)
Fire Tower Entertainment (*US*)
First Access Entertainment (*US*)
Flat50 (*UK*)
Fleming Artists (*US*)
Freedom Management (*UK*)
Front Room Songs (*UK*)
Future Songs (*UK*)
Gold Mountain Entertainment (*US*)
Golden Arm (*UK*)
Good Guy Entertainment (*US*)
Guvnor Management (*UK*)
Hand in Hive Independent Records & Management (*UK*)
Handshake Ltd. (*UK*)
Hardin Entertainment (*US*)
HardKnockLife Entertainment (*US*)
Hello! Booking, Inc. (*US*)
Hornblow Group USA, Inc. (*US*)

Hot Gem (*UK*)
House of Us (*UK*)
Ignition Management (*UK*)
IMC Entertainment Group (*US*)
In De Goot Entertainment (*US*)
Insomnia Music UK (*UK*)
Intertalent Rights Group (*UK*)
Intrigue Music (*US*)
JBLS Management (*UK*)
Jude Street Management (*UK*)
KMY (Keep Me Young) (*UK*)
Laffitte Management Group (*US*)
Lippman Entertainment (*US*)
Loggins Promotion (*US*)
LSH Management (*UK*)
Lucky Number Music Limited (*UK*)
Lupo Entertainment (*US*)
Macklam Feldman Management (*Can*)
Magus Entertainment Inc. (*US*)
Major Bob Music, Inc. (*US*)
The Major Group (*US*)
Mauldin Brand Agency (*US*)
MBK Entertainment (*US*)
Michael Anthony's Electric Events (*US*)
Michael Hausman Artist Management Inc. (*US*)
Mike's Artist Management (*US*)
Moksha Entertainment and Music Management (US) (*US*)
Monqui Presents (*US*)
MTS Management (*US*)
Music Media Events (*UK*)
N.O.W. Music Management (*UK*)
Nashville Records, LLC (*US*)
Nettwerk Management (*US*)
Nettwerk Management (*Can*)
New Champion Management (*UK*)
Off the Chart Promotions (*UK*)
Orean Music Ltd (*UK*)
Outrider Music, LLC (*US*)
Paradise Artists (*US*)
Phono Sounds UK (*UK*)
Pierce Entertainment (*UK*)
Plus Music (*UK*)
Position Music (*US*)
PRA [Patrick Rains & Associates] (*US*)
Progressive Global Agency (PGA) (*US*)
Q Prime Management, Inc. (*US*)
Rainmaker Artists (*US*)
Reaction Management (*UK*)
Rebel Rebel Artists (*UK*)
Red Entertainment Agency (*US*)
Red Grape Music (*UK*)
Red Light Management (RLM) (*US*)
Revolt Artist Management (*UK*)
Rhythmic Records Management and Production (*UK*)
Ron Rainey Management Inc. (*US*)
RPM Music Productions (*US*)
Run the Sound (*UK*)
Russell Carter Artist Management (*US*)
Saga Entertainment (*UK*)
SAS Entertainment (*UK*)
Saviour Management (*UK*)
SGM Music Group Ltd (*UK*)
Shaw Thing Management (*UK*)
Silva Artist Management (SAM) (*US*)
Silverword Music Group (*UK*)
Sound Management, Inc. (*US*)
Spectrum Talent Agency (*US*)
Starkravin' Management (*US*)
Steven Scharf Entertainment (SSE) (*US*)
Stiefel Entertainment (*US*)
Stormcraft Music (*UK*)
Street Smart Management (*US*)
Sugar House Music (*UK*)
Sweet! Music Management (*US*)
This Day And Age Management (*US*)
This Is Music Ltd (*UK*)
Tone Management (*UK*)
Toonteen Industries: Management & Promotions (*UK*)
Trunk Bass Entertainment (*US*)
Tuscan Sun Music (*US*)
Union Entertainment Group (*US*)
Universal Tone Management (*US*)
Up On Mars (*UK*)
Upside Management Ltd (*UK*)
Val's Artist Management (VAM) (*US*)
Variety Artists International (*US*)
Vector Management (*US*)
Westwood Music Group (*US*)
Worldsound, LLC (*US*)
Wright Entertainment Group (WEG) (*US*)
YMU Group (*UK*)
Young Guns (*UK*)
Zero Myth (*UK*)

Post

Freaks R Us (*UK*)
Ganbei Records (*UK*)
Lonewolf Talent Management (*UK*)
Outrider Music, LLC (*US*)
Semaphore Mgmt & Consulting (*US*)
Tone Management (*UK*)

Power

MTS Management (*US*)
Music Gallery International (*US*)

Progressive

Holier than Thou (HTT) Music (*UK*)
Incendia Music (*UK*)

Involved Management (*UK*)
MTS Management (*US*)
Nexus Artist Management (*US*)
Outrider Music, LLC (*US*)
Toonteen Industries: Management & Promotions (*UK*)

Psychedelic

Elephant Management (*UK*)
Ganbei Records (*UK*)
Moksha Entertainment and Music Management (US) (*US*)
Salvation Records (*UK*)
Semaphore Mgmt & Consulting (*US*)

Punk

Bitchin' Entertainment (*US*)
Coalition Music (*Can*)
Dissention Records + Artist Management (*UK*)
Freaks R Us (*UK*)
Ganbei Records (*UK*)
Gold Mountain Entertainment (*US*)
Lonewolf Talent Management (*UK*)
Magus Entertainment Inc. (*US*)
Media Five Entertainment (*US*)
Moksha Entertainment and Music Management (US) (*US*)
Music Gallery International (*US*)
Nettwerk Management (*US*)
Nettwerk Management (*Can*)
New Champion Management (*UK*)
Outrider Music, LLC (*US*)
Raw Power Management (*UK*)
Reaction Management (*UK*)
Revolt Artist Management (*UK*)
Salvation Records (*UK*)
Saviour Management (*UK*)
Silva Artist Management (SAM) (*US*)
Sweet! Music Management (*US*)
Talk's Cheap Management (*Can*)
Tone Management (*UK*)
Toonteen Industries: Management & Promotions (*UK*)
Val's Artist Management (VAM) (*US*)

R&B

Act 1 Entertainment (*US*)
Aguia Music (*UK*)
Allure Media Entertainment Group (*US*)
American Artists Entertainment Group (*US*)
Bandzmedia (*UK*)
Big Beat Productions, Inc. (*US*)
Bitchin' Entertainment (*US*)
Black Dot Management (*US*)
Booking Entertainment (*US*)
Case Entertainment Group Inc. (*US*)
Celebrity Talent Agency Inc. (*US*)
Chaney Gig Affairs (CGA) (*US*)
Coalition Music (*Can*)
Collin Artists (*US*)
D. Bailey Management, Inc. (*US*)
David Belenzon Management, Inc. (*US*)
Def Ro Inc. (*US*)
Defenders Ent (*UK*)
Enlight Entertainment, Inc. (*US*)
Fat City Artists (*US*)
First Access Entertainment (*US*)
Fresh Flava Entertainment (*US*)
Future Songs (*UK*)
HardKnockLife Entertainment (*US*)
IMC Entertainment Group (*US*)
Impact Artist Management (*US*)
Laffitte Management Group (*US*)
Len Weisman Personal Management (*US*)
Lippman Entertainment (*US*)
Loggins Promotion (*US*)
Lupo Entertainment (*US*)
Magus Entertainment Inc. (*US*)
Major Bob Music, Inc. (*US*)
The Major Group (*US*)
Mascioli Entertainment (*US*)
Mauldin Brand Agency (*US*)
Max Bernard Management (*US*)
MBK Entertainment (*US*)
Pierce Entertainment (*UK*)
Plus Music (*UK*)
Position Music (*US*)
Pyramid Entertainment Group (*US*)
Red Entertainment Agency (*US*)
Silverword Music Group (*UK*)
Spectrum Talent Agency (*US*)
Starkravin' Management (*US*)
TAC Music Management (*US*)
This Day And Age Management (*US*)
True Talent Entertainment (*US*)
Trunk Bass Entertainment (*US*)
Val's Artist Management (VAM) (*US*)
Westwood Music Group (*US*)
Wildlife Entertainment Ltd (*UK*)
Wright Entertainment Group (WEG) (*US*)

Rap

Aguia Music (*UK*)
Bitchin' Entertainment (*US*)
Case Entertainment Group Inc. (*US*)
Coalition Music (*Can*)
Defenders Ent (*UK*)
Enlight Entertainment, Inc. (*US*)
First Access Entertainment (*US*)
Flat50 (*UK*)
HardKnockLife Entertainment (*US*)
Lippman Entertainment (*US*)

Loggins Promotion (*US*)
The Lost Atlantis Records (*UK*)
Lucky House Management (*UK*)
Magus Entertainment Inc. (*US*)
The Major Group (*US*)
Mauldin Brand Agency (*US*)
MBK Entertainment (*US*)
Nettwerk Management (*US*)
Nettwerk Management (*Can*)
OnDaBeat Talent Management (*UK*)
Position Music (*US*)
Red Light Management (RLM) (*US*)
Run the Sound (*UK*)
Steven Scharf Entertainment (SSE) (*US*)
This Day And Age Management (*US*)
Union Entertainment Group (*US*)
Val's Artist Management (VAM) (*US*)
Variety Artists International (*US*)
Waxploitation (*US*)
Wright Entertainment Group (WEG) (*US*)

Reggae

Act 1 Entertainment (*US*)
Celebrity Talent Agency Inc. (*US*)
Defenders Ent (*UK*)
DMF Music Ltd (*UK*)
Fat City Artists (*US*)
Gold Mountain Entertainment (*US*)
MBK Entertainment (*US*)
Nexus Artist Management (*US*)
Waxploitation (*US*)

Regional

Big Beat Productions, Inc. (*US*)
Brilliant Productions (*US*)
Cantaloupe Music Productions, Inc. (*US*)
MM Music Agency (*US*)
TAC Music Management (*US*)

Rhythm and Blues

TAC Music Management (*US*)

Rock and Roll

Fat City Artists (*US*)
Handshake Ltd. (*UK*)
Lazy Daze (*UK*)
Paradise Artists (*US*)
Revolt Artist Management (*UK*)
Singerman Entertainment (*US*)
Sweet! Music Management (*US*)
TAC Music Management (*US*)
Worldsound, LLC (*US*)

Rock

21st Century Artists, Inc. (*US*)
Act 1 Entertainment (*US*)
Advanced Alternative Media (AAM) (*US*)
Allure Media Entertainment Group (*US*)
American Artists Entertainment Group (*US*)
Arslanian & Associates, Inc. (*US*)
Artist Representation and Management (ARM) Entertainment (*US*)
Aspire Music Management (*UK*)
Bad Apple Music Group (*UK*)
Bandzmedia (*UK*)
BBA Management & Booking (*US*)
Bear Music Management (*UK*)
Big Beat Productions, Inc. (*US*)
Big Dipper Productions Ltd (*UK*)
Big Hassle Management (*US*)
Bitchin' Entertainment (*US*)
Bold Management (*UK*)
Booking Entertainment (*US*)
Brick Wall Management (*US*)
Brilliant Corners Artist Management (*US*)
The Brokaw Company (*US*)
Bulletproof Artist Management (*US*)
Burgess World Co. (*US*)
BUT! Management (*UK*)
Case Entertainment Group Inc. (*US*)
Chaos & Bedlam Management (*UK*)
Ciulla Management, Inc. (*US*)
Coalition Music (*Can*)
Concerted Efforts (*US*)
Consolidated Artists (*UK*)
Creative International Artist Management (*UK*)
D. Bailey Management, Inc. (*US*)
dandomanagement (*UK*)
DAS Communications Ltd (*US*)
Dave Kaplan Management (*US*)
David Belenzon Management, Inc. (*US*)
Dawn Elder Management (*US*)
DCA Productions (*US*)
Deathless MGMT (*UK*)
Deep South Artist Management (*US*)
Domo Music Group Management (*US*)
Don't Try (*UK*)
Down For Life (*UK*)
Elephant Management (*UK*)
Emcee Artist Management (*US*)
Entertainment Services International (*US*)
Entourage Talent Associates, Ltd (*US*)
Epic Venom (*UK*)
Equator Music (*UK*)
5B Artist Management (*US*)
Flat50 (*UK*)
Fleming Artists (*US*)
Fresh Flava Entertainment (*US*)
Ganbei Records (*UK*)
Gold Mountain Entertainment (*US*)
Golden Arm (*UK*)
Goo Music Management Ltd (*UK*)
Guvnor Management (*UK*)

Hand in Hive Independent Records & Management (*UK*)
Hard Head Management (*US*)
Hardin Entertainment (*US*)
Hello! Booking, Inc. (*US*)
Holier than Thou (HTT) Music (*UK*)
Hornblow Group USA, Inc. (*US*)
Humans & Other Animals (*UK*)
Ignition Management (*UK*)
Impact Artist Management (*US*)
In De Goot Entertainment (*US*)
Incendia Music (*UK*)
Intrigue Music (*US*)
Kuper Personal Management (*US*)
Laffitte Management Group (*US*)
Lazy Daze (*UK*)
Lippman Entertainment (*US*)
Listen to This Management (*UK*)
Loggins Promotion (*US*)
Lonewolf Talent Management (*UK*)
Lupo Entertainment (*US*)
Macklam Feldman Management (*Can*)
Magus Entertainment Inc. (*US*)
Maine Road Management (*US*)
The Major Group (*US*)
Mascioli Entertainment (*US*)
McDonough Management LLC (*US*)
McGhee Entertainment (*US*)
Media Five Entertainment (*US*)
Memphia Music Management (*UK*)
Metal Music Bookings (*UK*)
Michael Anthony's Electric Events (*US*)
Michael Hausman Artist Management Inc. (*US*)
Mike's Artist Management (*US*)
Miller Music Management (*UK*)
MOB Agency (*US*)
Moksha Entertainment and Music Management (US) (*US*)
Monqui Presents (*US*)
Morningstar (*UK*)
MTS Management (*US*)
Music + Art Management (*US*)
Music Gallery International (*US*)
N.O.W. Music Management (*UK*)
Nettwerk Management (*US*)
Nettwerk Management (*Can*)
Nice Management (*US*)
Northern Music Co. Ltd (*UK*)
NSI Management (*US*)
Off the Chart Promotions (*UK*)
Outrider Music, LLC (*US*)
Paradise Artists (*US*)
Park Promotions (*UK*)
Position Music (*US*)
PRA [Patrick Rains & Associates] (*US*)
Prodigal Son Entertainment (*US*)
Progressive Global Agency (PGA) (*US*)
Q Management (*US*)
Q Prime Management, Inc. (*US*)
Rainmaker Artists (*US*)
Raw Power Management (*UK*)
Reaction Management (*UK*)
Red Entertainment Agency (*US*)
Red Light Management (RLM) (*US*)
Revolt Artist Management (*UK*)
Rock People Management (RPM) (*UK*)
Ron Rainey Management Inc. (*US*)
Rosier Artist Management (RAM) (*UK*)
Russell Carter Artist Management (*US*)
Saga Entertainment (*UK*)
Salvation Records (*UK*)
SAS Entertainment (*UK*)
SGM Music Group Ltd (*UK*)
Silva Artist Management (SAM) (*US*)
Silverword Music Group (*UK*)
Singerman Entertainment (*US*)
Siren Artist Management (UK) (*UK*)
Sound Management, Inc. (*US*)
Spinning Plates (*US*)
Starkravin' Management (*US*)
Steven Scharf Entertainment (SSE) (*US*)
Stiefel Entertainment (*US*)
Street Smart Management (*US*)
Sugar House Music (*UK*)
Suncoast Music Management (*US*)
Sweet! Music Management (*US*)
TAC Music Management (*US*)
Talk's Cheap Management (*Can*)
Thirty Tigers (*US*)
Tone Management (*UK*)
Toonteen Industries: Management & Promotions (*UK*)
Travelled Music (*UK*)
Union Entertainment Group (*US*)
Universal Tone Management (*US*)
Val's Artist Management (VAM) (*US*)
Variety Artists International (*US*)
Vector Management (*US*)
Waxploitation (*US*)
Westwood Music Group (*US*)
Wildlife Entertainment Ltd (*UK*)
Worldsound, LLC (*US*)
Wright Entertainment Group (WEG) (*US*)
YMU Group (*UK*)
Zero Myth (*UK*)

Rockabilly

Act 1 Entertainment (*US*)
Fat City Artists (*US*)
Hello! Booking, Inc. (*US*)

TAC Music Management (*US*)
Roots
21st Century Artists, Inc. (*US*)
Act 1 Entertainment (*US*)
Blind Ambition Management, Ltd (*US*)
Brilliant Productions (*US*)
Dawn Elder Management (*US*)
Fleming Artists (*US*)
Front Room Songs (*UK*)
Grassy Hill Entertainment (*US*)
Hardin Entertainment (*US*)
Impact Artist Management (*US*)
Jelli Records (*UK*)
Kari Estrin Management & Consulting (*US*)
Kuper Personal Management (*US*)
Park Promotions (*UK*)
Steven Scharf Entertainment (SSE) (*US*)
TAC Music Management (*US*)
Talk's Cheap Management (*Can*)
Val's Artist Management (VAM) (*US*)
Shoegaze
Elephant Management (*UK*)
Singer-Songwriter
ADSRecords (*UK*)
Amour:Music (*UK*)
AuthorityMGMT (*UK*)
Bitchin' Entertainment (*US*)
Blind Ambition Management, Ltd (*US*)
Brick Wall Management (*US*)
Brilliant Corners Artist Management (*US*)
Burgess World Co. (*US*)
BUT! Management (*UK*)
Coalition Music (*Can*)
Concerted Efforts (*US*)
Create Management (*UK*)
dandomanagement (*UK*)
Domo Music Group Management (*US*)
Entourage Talent Associates, Ltd (*US*)
Fire Tower Entertainment (*US*)
From the Whitehouse (*UK*)
Future Songs (*UK*)
Gold Mountain Entertainment (*US*)
Grassy Hill Entertainment (*US*)
Hardin Entertainment (*US*)
Hornblow Group USA, Inc. (*US*)
IMG Artists (*US*)
Impact Artist Management (*US*)
JBLS Management (*UK*)
Lippman Entertainment (*US*)
Lyricom (*UK*)
Magus Entertainment Inc. (*US*)
Max Bernard Management (*US*)
McGhee Entertainment (*US*)
Michael Hausman Artist Management Inc. (*US*)
Miller Music Management (*UK*)
Nettwerk Management (*US*)
Nettwerk Management (*Can*)
NSI Management (*US*)
Off the Chart Promotions (*UK*)
Park Promotions (*UK*)
Position Music (*US*)
Q Prime Management, Inc. (*US*)
Reaction Management (*UK*)
Red Grape Music (*UK*)
Red Light Management (RLM) (*US*)
Revolt Artist Management (*UK*)
Running Media Group Ltd (*UK*)
Russell Carter Artist Management (*US*)
Sterling Artist Management (*US*)
Steven Scharf Entertainment (SSE) (*US*)
Stiefel Entertainment (*US*)
Stormcraft Music (*UK*)
Sweet! Music Management (*US*)
TAC Music Management (*US*)
Vector Management (*US*)
Wright Entertainment Group (WEG) (*US*)
Ska
DMF Music Ltd (*UK*)
Fat City Artists (*US*)
Soul
Act 1 Entertainment (*US*)
AprilSeven Music (*UK*)
Bandzmedia (*UK*)
Chaney Gig Affairs (CGA) (*US*)
Concerted Efforts (*US*)
The Lost Atlantis Records (*UK*)
Lucky House Management (*UK*)
Major Bob Music, Inc. (*US*)
Max Bernard Management (*US*)
Plus Music (*UK*)
Silverword Music Group (*UK*)
Sweet! Music Management (*US*)
Soulful
Max Bernard Management (*US*)
TAC Music Management (*US*)
Soundtracks
First Artists Management (*US*)
Kraft-Engel Management (*US*)
Max Bernard Management (*US*)
Soundtrack Music Associates (SMA) (*US*)
Steven Scharf Entertainment (SSE) (*US*)
Spoken Word
Bitchin' Entertainment (*US*)
Surf
Revolt Artist Management (*UK*)
Swing
Act 1 Entertainment (*US*)

Big Bear Music (*UK*)
Cantaloupe Music Productions, Inc. (*US*)
Collin Artists (*US*)
Fat City Artists (*US*)
Harmony Artists (*US*)
Mascioli Entertainment (*US*)

Techno

Bitchin' Entertainment (*US*)
F&G Management (*UK*)
The Lost Atlantis Records (*UK*)
The Major Group (*US*)
Nexus Artist Management (*US*)
OnDaBeat Talent Management (*UK*)
The Weird and the Wonderful (*UK*)

Thrash

Holier than Thou (HTT) Music (*UK*)
Semaphore Mgmt & Consulting (*US*)
Singerman Entertainment (*US*)

Traditional

Dawn Elder Management (*US*)
Riot Artists (*US*)
TAC Music Management (*US*)

Trance

Bitchin' Entertainment (*US*)
Involved Management (*UK*)
Phono Sounds UK (*UK*)

Underground

In De Goot Entertainment (*US*)
Semaphore Mgmt & Consulting (*US*)
This Is Music Ltd (*UK*)

Urban

2-Tone Entertainment (2TE) (*UK*)
Bitchin' Entertainment (*US*)
Black Dot Management (*US*)
Good Guy Entertainment (*US*)
HQ Familia (*UK*)
Lippman Entertainment (*US*)
Loggins Promotion (*US*)
The Lost Atlantis Records (*UK*)
Lucky House Management (*UK*)
Lyricom (*UK*)
Magus Entertainment Inc. (*US*)
Max Bernard Management (*US*)
MBK Entertainment (*US*)
Position Music (*US*)
Pyramid Entertainment Group (*US*)
RAM Talent Group (*US*)
Red Entertainment Agency (*US*)
Silverword Music Group (*UK*)
Thirty Tigers (*US*)
Val's Artist Management (VAM) (*US*)
The Weird and the Wonderful (*UK*)

World

Bitchin' Entertainment (*US*)
Cantaloupe Music Productions, Inc. (*US*)
Collin Artists (*US*)
Columbia Artists Music LLC (CAMI Music) (*US*)
Concerted Efforts (*US*)
Dawn Elder Management (*US*)
DDB Productions (*US*)
DMF Music Ltd (*UK*)
Domo Music Group Management (*US*)
Fat City Artists (*US*)
From the Whitehouse (*UK*)
Front Room Songs (*UK*)
Gold Mountain Entertainment (*US*)
Hardin Entertainment (*US*)
IMG Artists (*US*)
Impact Artist Management (*US*)
Ina Dittke & Associates (*US*)
Line-Up pmc (*UK*)
Macklam Feldman Management (*Can*)
McGhee Entertainment (*US*)
Music + Art Management (*US*)
Nettwerk Management (*US*)
Once 11 Entertainment (*US*)
Position Music (*US*)
Progressive Global Agency (PGA) (*US*)
Red Light Management (RLM) (*US*)
Riot Artists (*US*)
Serious (*UK*)
Steven Scharf Entertainment (SSE) (*US*)
Val's Artist Management (VAM) (*US*)
Worldsound, LLC (*US*)

Get Free Access to the MusicSocket Website

To claim your free access to the **MusicSocket** website simply go to https://www.musicsocket.com/subscribe and begin the subscription process as normal. When you are given the opportunity to enter a voucher / coupon enter the following code:

- MSC-AZP-173

You should then be able to take out a subscription for free, or a longer term subscription at a reduced price.

Please note that this code will only remain valid until the release of the next edition, and is only permitted for use in the creation of one account for the owner of this book.

If you need any assistance please email support@musicsocket.com.

If you have found this book useful, please consider leaving a review on the website where you bought it!

What you get

Once you have set up access to the site you will be able to benefit from all the following features:

Databases

All our databases are updated almost every day and include powerful search facilities to help you find exactly what you need. Searches that used to take you hours or even days in print books or on search engines can now be done in seconds and produce more accurate and up-to-date information. You can try out any of our databases before you subscribe:

- Search **over 1,200 record labels**
- Search **over 500 managers**

PLUS advanced features to help you with your search:

- Save searches and save time – set up to 15 search parameters specific to your work, save them, and then access the search results with a single click whenever you log in. You can even save multiple different searches if you have different types of work you are looking to place.
- Add personal notes to listings, visible only to you and fully searchable – helping you to organise your actions.

- Set reminders on listings to notify you when to submit your work, when to follow up, when to expect a reply, or any other custom action.
- Track which listings you've viewed and when, to help you organise your search – any listings which have changed since you last viewed them will be highlighted for your attention!

Daily email updates

As a subscriber you will be able to take advantage of our email alert service, meaning you can specify your particular interests and we'll send you automatic email updates when we change or add a listing that matches them. So if you're interested in labels dealing in hard rock in the United States you can have us send you emails with the latest updates about them – keeping you up to date without even having to log in.

User feedback

Our databases all include a user feedback feature that allows our subscribers to leave feedback on each listing – giving you not only the chance to have your say about the markets you contact but giving a unique artist's perspective on the listings.

Save on copyright protection fees

If you're sending your work away to record labels or managers, you should consider first protecting your copyright. As a subscriber to **MusicSocket** you can do this through our site and save 10% on the copyright registration fees normally payable for protecting your work internationally through the Intellectual Property Rights Office.

Terms and conditions

The promotional code contained in this publication may be used by the owner of the book only to create one subscription to MusicSocket at a reduced cost, or for free. It may not be used by or disseminated to third parties. Should the code be misused then the owner of the book will be liable for any costs incurred, including but not limited to payment in full at the standard rate for the subscription in question. The code may be used at any time until the end of the calendar year named in the title of the publication, after which time it will become invalid. The code may be redeemed against the creation of a new account only – it cannot be redeemed against the ongoing costs of keeping a subscription open. In order to create a subscription a method of payment must be provided, but there is no obligation to make any payment. Subscriptions may be cancelled at any time, and if an account is cancelled before any payment becomes due then no payment will be made. Once a subscription has been created, the normal schedule of payments will begin on a monthly, quarterly, or annual basis, unless a life Subscription is selected, or the subscription is cancelled prior to the first payment becoming due. Subscriptions may be cancelled at any time, but if they are left open beyond the date at which the first payment becomes due and is processed then payments will not be refundable.